A Wilder Way

BLOOMSBURY PUBLISHING
Bloomsbury Publishing Plc
50 Bedford Square, London, WC1B 3DP, UK
Bloomsbury Publishing Ireland Limited,
29 Earlsfort Terrace, Dublin 2, D02 AY28, Ireland

BLOOMSBURY, BLOOMSBURY PUBLISHING and the Diana logo are trademarks of
Bloomsbury Publishing Plc

First published in Great Britain 2025

Copyright © Poppy Okotcha, 2025
Illustrations © Frances Whitfield, 2025

Poppy Okotcha and Frances Whitfield are identified as the author and illustrator of
this work in accordance with the Copyright, Designs and Patents Act 1988.

All rights reserved. No part of this publication may be: i) reproduced or transmitted
in any form, electronic or mechanical, including photocopying, recording or by means
of any information storage or retrieval system without prior permission in writing
from the publishers; or ii) used or reproduced in any way for the training, development or operation of artificial intelligence (AI) technologies, including generative AI
technologies. The rights holders expressly reserve this publication from the text and
data mining exception as per Article 4(3) of the Digital Single Market Directive (EU)
2019/790

Bloomsbury Publishing Plc does not have any control over, or responsibility for, any
third-party websites referred to in this book. All internet addresses given in this book
were correct at the time of going to press. The author and publisher regret any inconvenience caused if addresses have changed or sites have ceased to exist, but can accept
no responsibility for any such changes

A catalogue record for this book is available from the British Library

ISBN: HB: 978-1-5266-6651-2; eBook: 978-1-5266-6649-9; ePDF: 978-1-5266-6652-9

2 4 6 8 10 9 7 5 3 1

Designed and typeset by Olivia Bush
Illustrated by Frances Whitfield

Printed and bound in Great Britain by Clays Ltd, Elcograf S.p.A.

MIX
Paper | Supporting
responsible forestry
FSC   FSC® C018072
www.fsc.org

To find out more about our authors and books visit www.bloomsbury.com and sign
up for our newsletters
For product-safety-related questions contact productsafety@bloomsbury.com

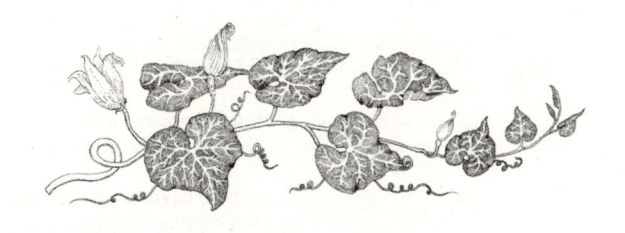

A Wilder Way

how gardens grow us

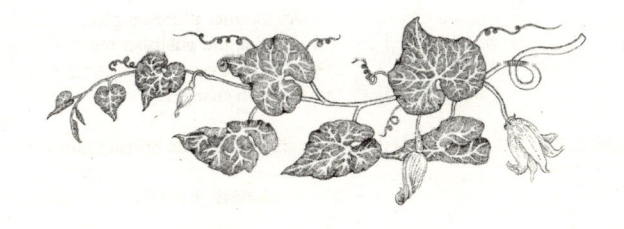

Poppy Okotcha

Illustrated by Frances Whitfield

INTRODUCTION

Late Autumn

OCTOBER:	Endings as Beginnings	25
	Rest as Radical – *Nettle and Meadowsweet Tea*	28
	Samhain – *Poor Man's Capers* & *How to Prepare a No-Dig Bed*	36
	Water – *How to Make a Pond*	45
	Apple Rot – *Cider Vinegar*	53
NOVEMBER:	The Garden Gut	59
	Lessons from the Heap (or Heaplore) – *Compost Three Ways*	63
	Short Days, Patience and the Dark Magic of Garlic – *How to Plant Garlic*	80
	Rose Hips – *Rose Hip Syrup* & *One-Pot Food Forest*	84

Winter

DECEMBER:	Hibernating Insects – *Sunshine Tea*	97
	First Frost – *Birdfeed Fat-brick*	102
	Evergreens – *Sage and Parsnip Nut Roast*	109
JANUARY:	We Lose Our Broad Beans – *Zero Waste Veg Stock*	119
	Hens in Winter Don't Lay	124
	Earthly Delights	130
FEBRUARY:	Bare Root Planting – *How to Plant a Bare Root Perennial*	137
	Imbolc	142
	Winter's Edge – *Sowing Chillies*	145

Spring

MARCH:	Time to Sow – *Sowing Timetable*	153
	Uninvited Guests	164
	Spring Equinox – *Easter Biscuits* & *Easter Branch*	175
APRIL:	The Hungry Gap: An Ode to Weeds – *Foraged plant feed*	183
	Knowing a Place – *Wild Garlic Salt*	187
	Itadori – *Itadori and Apple Compote*	193

MAY:	May Day – *Cleavers Water*	199
	The Magical Whimsy of it All	205
	Direct Sowing – *How to Direct Sow*	210
	Biodiversity – *Cultivating Diversity*	214

Summer

JUNE:	Gut Health and Soil Health	227
	Elderflower – *Elderflower Vinegar*	231
	Summer Solstice – *Midsummer Tea*	236
	Garlic Comes Back Up – *Honey-infused Garlic*	238

JULY:	The Plants Will Grow Themselves – *Garden Iced Tea*	243
	Married to My Garden – *Smashed Courgettes*	250
	Companion Planting	257
	Sharing Time, Labour and Harvests – *Celery Salt*	264
	Land of Plenty– *Lemon Verbena Syrup* & *Lemon Verbena and Elderflower Nectar*	272

AUGUST:	Lifting Potatoes	277
	Lammas – *Broad Bean Dip*	282
	Tomatoes – *Devon-dried Tomatoes*	284
	Elderberries – *Elderberry Syrup Three Ways*	290

Early Autumn

SEPTEMBER:	Root of the Word – *Calendula Healing Balm*	299
	Autumn Equinox	302
	We Harvest the Winter Squash – *Squash Soup*	305
	Bumblebees at Michaelmas – *Nearly Raw Tomato Sauce*	308

OCTOBER:	Saving Seed – *How to Save Tomato Seeds*	313

EPILOGUE
Endings as Beginnings

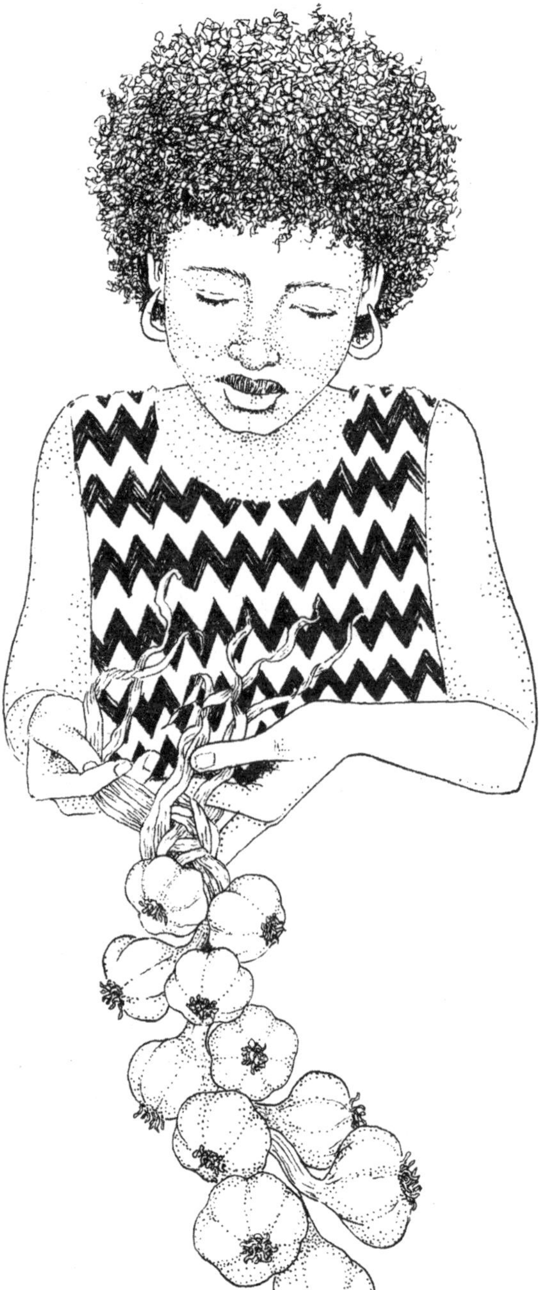

Introduction

In May 1996, I was born in a hospital in Hampstead, to my Nigerian father and white British mother.

At first I was raised in North London, where strangely, although I was so small in such a large urban sprawl, my earliest memories are of the natural world. The non-human world has always played a significant role in my life. In the park down the road from where we lived, I discovered what to mini-me was a giant hedge. I'd crawl inside it and play house, clearing out separate pockets for a bedroom, bathroom and kitchen. I'd invite my mum to visit, and she'd shuffle into my new hedge-home on hands and knees and have a cup of tea like a good house guest. We had a buddleia or butterfly bush at the end of our modest urban garden, coated in peacock butterflies, and I would go hunting for slugs, snails and spiders; I loved to inspect their tiny bodies, so different to mine, through which *they* experienced the world.

I remember my maternal grandmother's garden. I've called her 'Grandma With The Nice Garden' for as long as I can recall. Her magic-filled plot was out in the countryside, in a market town a couple hours' drive down the motorway from our home in the city. She still lives with and tends that garden today, nearly thirty years later.

My mum made the outdoors feel safe, exciting. Even her clothing brought the outside in. When she was pregnant with my younger sister, she would wear a billowing red dress, scattered with white blossoms, that hung over her huge bump like a tent. While she was cooking, I'd crawl under her dress to be immersed in a world of pink-red light dotted with flowers, the comforting touch and smell of my mother's skin, and the sound of sizzling pots on the stove.

Just before I turned six, my little sister, pregnant mum, dad and I relocated to Johannesburg, South Africa where I attended a Waldorf Steiner school. There, I learned about compost and played in the dust. We designed and built cob structures made from mud bricks, the result of squashing up wet earth and straw with our feet, the cool, moist mixture oozing out between our toes while the hot sun baked our skin. One term, our teacher sent us off to wander the sprawling school grounds alone, tasked with choosing a plant that was preparing to flower and drawing it. Every few days, we went back to document the bud blooming, the flower flourishing and then dying back and turning to seed. Those solitary hours, when I was still small enough to swear my life on the existence of fairies, examining that flower – a glorious purple and yellow iris – and watching its cycles, still live vividly in my mind. That was the first time I recall being struck with awe at nature.

During our nearly six years in South Africa, we lived in five different houses, each I remember most distinctly by its garden; I don't recall spending much time indoors. The first had a shady stepping-stone path that wound through dense shrubbery. I had to dare myself to run down there; it felt too hidden, spooky. The veranda which framed the back of the house was wrapped in Cape leadwort, its soft green foliage a backdrop to piles of pale blue blooms. They were sticky to touch, smelt unknown, looked excitingly unfamiliar and were covered with equally alien insects. The second house had a neglected swimming pool that remained a vibrant green for the months we lived there, only ever used by mosquito larvae. A mulberry tree rose up out of the grassy back garden and when its fruit was ripe my siblings and I would tumble into the house on a sugar high, crazed by the thrill of infinite sweeties growing on its branches, and looking like we'd returned from war, covered in the staining red juice of the berries. Mum tried to grow carrots with

INTRODUCTION

us at the third house. In the foreign soil and climate the carrots were small – but we were thrilled. We stayed the longest in our fourth home, where an enormous jacaranda tree presided over the garden, so it is known to us as 'Jacaranda House'. In springtime the tree erupted into brilliant lilac blossoms, their colour so saturated they could have been a hallucination or vivid dream. The canopy hummed with bees. When summer arrived and the flowers fell the bees came down with them, continuing to flit in and out of the bell-shaped blooms. We would hop and skip down the garden on our tiptoes, picking out the few gaps in the buzzing sea of purple. A wrong step and you'd be stung! When Jacaranda House's plum tree had fruit, we'd gorge until we had tummy aches. As the fruit ripened, the tree would drop plums down on our trampoline. There they would settle, turning to fermented jam unless we came and bounced and ate. Now plums and trampolines will forever hold hands in my mind. There was a lemon tree too, but I always preferred the sweet honey scent of its tiny white blossoms to the actual fruit itself. When it rained, my sister and I would pick the giant leaves of the Elephant Ear plant that fanned out of the front garden and use them as umbrellas. Mostly, though, we lived off sweet fruits and sunshine.

Our final home had a garden full of boulders that reached nearly the height of the house, a pond filled with fish and so many trees that in summer, you felt wrapped in a bubble of green. In the rainy season we'd watch lighting cracking down amongst the boulders and trees.

When I was eleven, my parents separated and my little brother, sister, Mum and I returned to the UK. This time to Wiltshire. This was the quintessential English countryside. Thatched cottages, deciduous woodlands and being close to my grandma's garden were novel marvels of this time... as was mud. One winter, us three siblings went on a walk and found a wide, wet squelchy path down the edge of a field... we ran, slid, fell, rolled and wriggled in that mud, hysterical with the delightful texture, the messiness and the wonderfully freeing feeling of slip-sliding down the hill on our backs, mud spraying out, engulfing our feet. I don't remember my mum's response when we returned home, caked head to toe in muck, but knowing her, she probably laughed and congratulated us.

The transition back to England, coupled with the divorce, was messy. In a strange, cold country with no money and social workers sprinkled in the mix, it was hard for our family, especially Mum who was trying to hold us all in her arms, but they couldn't quite stretch far enough to wrap around her too. Relying on family and renting, we continued to move in and out of places all the time; in the first two years, we lived in four different houses.

For me, the most healing occurred in a mouldy old bungalow surrounded by a simple, empty lawned garden with a couple of tumble-down sheds which the spiders had claimed as their own. We stayed there the longest, long enough to watch that garden grow and we grew too. A hedge reached up tall and wild; honeysuckle embraced the twisted, dying plum tree that had stopped giving blossoms or fruit; my mum didn't mow the lawn, so it turned into a meadow; and my siblings and I dug out a pond which a frog swiftly made its home. Mum grew giant poppy flowers, sweet peas and fennel in front of the sunny old porch, built a compost heap and some raised veggie beds. She would walk around taking photos of the flowers, close-ups of their sacred geometry.

I was now in mainstream British education, which, it's safe to say, was a culture shock. No more days learning about compost, drawing flowers or making cob buildings. But when we got home from school, I'd go into our garden and pick lettuce to have in cheese sandwiches.

Since there was no money, this garden was made from old bits and bobs, our sweat and joy and a couple of packets of seeds. Witnessing how that effort breathed life back into my mum was one of the defining moments of my life. Seeing her love for the flowers and how they loved her in return, seeing her attempt to feed us from that veg patch made of a square of lawn... She demonstrated and offered to us what I now see as the most precious gift: solace and trust in nature. In that garden, we rested for a while. It was the first to teach me that when we tend the land well it tends us in turn. As the garden came to life, so did we.

Despite living in the countryside, our little home and my mum's

INTRODUCTION

untamed garden were not surrounded by very much wild nature at all. We lived amongst miles of monoculture farms, with the odd woodland or semi-wild stretch spotted along the river or canal. As I grew into my teens and our dad visited, he'd explain how the majority of this bucolic British landscape surrounding us, the rolling fields of wheat, the sprawling acid-yellow rapeseed fields where we played hide and seek, were really deserts, likely drenched in chemicals, divorced from nature, devoid of life. He reminded us of the expanses of eroded soil we had driven through in South Africa, explaining that if large-scale, industrial, monoculture farming continued, that was likely to become the fate of those patches of English land too.

As we loped through the fields on our long chatty ambles, Dad would laugh and laugh, and catching his breath he'd exclaim, 'Look at this massive farm, but where are all the farmers? Who is farming all this land? Where are the people!?' My father had grown up in Nigeria and had seen the people work the land, so he was not blind to the hilarity in this paradox: 'So much farm, so little farmer.' Nor to the fact that most of the crops were not even destined to feed humans at all...

Now that I'm older and understand the severity of what we are facing as people divorced from the land, I respect his knowing bemusement. He managed to find dark humour in a tragic situation, a human touch. In that laugh I have found hope.

Even at that young age, I understood that it didn't have to be that way. I saw sprawling industrial farms, but I also saw thriving pockets of wild ecosystems, and I saw my grandma's garden. I saw how my mum transformed her garden and how her garden changed her. I recalled the biodynamic farms I had visited with school in South Africa, and I saw the picture Dad painted in my mind of people thriving with the land.

As is typical, in my late teens I drifted away from all this in the search of independence and adventure. I ended up working as a model, travelling the world, which sounds more glamorous than it was. I was lucky, it gave me the financial security I had craved and experiences that led me to where I am today. For most of that time I lived in London with my boyfriend Toby, who is now my husband, on a canal boat. Our floating home became my retreat from an unpredictable job that I found increasingly challenging.

As I became more invested in the climate movement, I started to see the hypocrisy in how I was living. I was attending demonstrations and ranting about green futures. I ate vegan to reduce my carbon footprint and harm to life, I was trying to consume more 'consciously'. I felt and thought about my impact all the time. Meanwhile, I was working as a model in the fashion industry, helping to sell clothes to people who often didn't need them. As my career progressed, more and more of those clothes were coming out of sweat factories that cause all sorts unimaginable harm: from the vulnerable humans working inside them who are mistreated, exploited and poisoned, to the life in the waters, whose habitat is destroyed by the factories' pumped-out pollution. So much destruction. I couldn't help but begin to see the connections between the global fashion complex I was engaged with now and the industrial farming I had come to understand as a teenager. I was flying around the world to participate in this business. So much air travel was making me sick, and it was making the planet sick too. I discovered that just one flight could easily wipe the carbon saved from a whole year of me living as a vegan.

As the bigger picture gradually came into focus, I began to grasp the utter insanity of it all. I had no option but to make a change, because what I was doing was not only self-harm, it was ecocide. As a fashion model, I was more than complicit in the systems of harm the industry was fuelled by – I was actively helping it to grow, validating it by being its face. A young Brown woman with my natural afro hair, I was applauded for increasing 'visibility'; for showing young Black and Brown girls that they too could be part of this industry, that the clothes are made for *them* to wear. I had become a symbol of progress. 'Look, see how we support Black women now? Look at her smile and her afro. We are good. We have *all* of your best interests at heart,' the campaigns would say.

My face hid the truth that a Brown woman had been exploited to make those clothes I posed in. But, to begin with, I never suspected it. I had no clue. I had believed the lie that I was promoting.

The final straw, I think, was when I listened to a professor speak about the danger of people of colour being invited into the world of exploitative capitalism, which we know all too well is harmful. He questioned the value in having a seat at that table. And he explained that, as a Black man, he'd prefer to help build a new world instead. I felt sick at the thought that my face was being used as bait, a disguise, to lure a whole new demographic of newly 'empowered' Black and Brown spenders to the market to participate in overconsumption. And that, unbeknownst to them, they were helping to fund the mistreatment of fellow humans, the new exploited class.

Growing up in South Africa, I was keenly aware of the injustices of the freshly dismantled apartheid and had promised myself I would do good in this world. It was a rude awakening when I finally accepted I was not. I felt trapped, hoodwinked. I felt compelled to see, with my own eyes, where *everything* I participated in and consumed began. It was overwhelming. I didn't have the time or the resources to investigate it all. But one way or another, I came to understand that the common denominator was the land. Everything – all the 'resources' required to make the aeroplanes, clothes, laptops, shops, food – came from the earth.

Searching for a new path, I rediscovered the power in growing food. This became a way to participate in a culture of care, to nourish my body and my mind, reconnect with community, the seasons and the living world. It was a means of contributing to building healthy soils and ecosystems, rather than destroying them. I could explore the possibilities of shifting to a more local, equitable food system and way of life. This was my first step on the path of detangling myself from a culture I could see was harming so many lives on Earth. I realised that while our gardens can feed us, they also tell us valuable tales of connection – we may *think* that *we* tend and grow *them*, while really *gardens grow and change far more in us*. I wanted to share what I was learning and to leave the industrial fashion industry far behind. This change in direction brought with it a desire to move, to find somewhere to really root into and call home. Somewhere I could grow gardens.

After two long years of searching, we eventually decided home would be Devon, where Toby grew up, in an area where a progressive culture meant I felt at ease (which, with my brown skin, is not always the case in the British countryside). The strong network of agro-ecological food growing projects here made my tummy tickle with excitement. The day we decided on Devon, a small house with a modest but magical garden came on the market. It was perfect, and so we moved.

A couple of years later, I joined the community garden that I now work in, a fifteen-minute bike ride from home along winding lanes wrapped in overgrown hedgerows. The roughly 600 square metres of market garden sits within four acres of wider land which is managed for wildlife. I go there at least once a week; both it and my fellow gardeners there have taught me as much, if not more, than my own garden.

*

There is now an urgent need for us humans to consider ourselves as responsible and empowered citizens who are *part* of the Earth's living systems. Not in a metaphorical, figurative or symbolic sense, but in real terms, since the Earth and its ecosystems quite literally

INTRODUCTION

give us life, yet we are systematically destroying them.

To rekindle that connection, we need access to information and spaces that allow us to engage with landscapes in ways that bring us both health.

As far as I'm concerned, remembering that we are nature is not a passive act, looking out on a pretty view and thinking 'Ahh, nature looks nice' and then carrying on with our lives. To reconnect with nature is to create a radical shift both in how we see the world and in our behaviour. This comes about from repeated, active practice of skills and activities that tie us to our wider landscapes and to one another, and an understanding of a generous and equitable economy of care. Living landscapes teach us reciprocity and circularity and this is best learnt through doing and being in and with them. Understanding where our food comes from and participating in its creation, however we can, offers a well-trodden route into grasping a truly convivial relationship with life on Earth. We can then carry these lessons with us as a blueprint for a way of living that is ultimately healthier for our bodies, minds, souls, the Earth and all the life Earth carries. Gardens can teach us care, kindness and connection.

Gardens in Britain cover an estimated 10 million acres, an area currently greater than all our nature reserves combined. Collectively they offer vast opportunities for growing the health of the land, wildlife, people and communities.

I want to help grow a world that I would be proud to pass on to my children, grandchildren and great-great-grandchildren. A world filled with the life that makes it possible for us to thrive. My contribution to that world so far has been grassroots, it's been in the garden.

This book tells the story of me and my garden, but it also tells the story of us as Earth's gardeners. I hope it offers inspiration and information for this transformative process of reconnecting and remembering that we are part of the living world.

*

As I engaged more closely with the seasons through growing food, I began to crave some kind of map that could help to explain the rhythms that I was now taking part in. Understanding the routine that governs the living world is important for growing plants, but I was noticing that it was important for me too. As a member of the living world, I am no less impacted by our Earth spinning on its axis around the sun.

Hunting at first for a cosmology from England, the land I grew on, I came across *The Wheel of the Year*, a neo-pagan calendar of seasonal festivals. Initially, I romantically believed this was a genuine and original Celtic relic, preserved over thousands of years, despite all odds. I now know, however, that it was patched together in the nineteenth and twentieth centuries as neo-paganism boomed in popularity in Northern Europe. People like me were searching for stories that celebrated the beautiful mystery of the world, stories that had their roots in the old spirituality of the lands the people called home.

A mishmash of rituals, rumours, myths and legends gleaned from ancient peoples of Northern Europe, the calendar was an attempt to construct a framework of seasonal allegories, through which people could learn from the rhythms of the year and so connect more meaningfully with themselves, one another, the land and Earth we call home.

The tales and festivals gathered in *The Wheel of the Year* are mainly drawn from the Celts and their druids (the mystical and powerful class of priests, doctors, judges and scholars who lived between 750 BCE and 43 CE), and from the Anglo-Saxons, from about 410 CE until 1066. There is little authenticated written history of these cultures, but we do know that the practice of celebrating significant moments through the seasons – the height of summer and winter, the end of summer and the harvest, the return of life in spring – was (and in many cultures still is) widespread. In that respect, *The Wheel of the Year* is very much inspired by 'reality'. We still experience the same seasons, more or less, that unfolded on this land in 750 BCE, and they can still offer an opportunity to meaningfully root ourselves in a time and place and to connect with all life that is governed by the seasons too.

The Wheel of the Year describes eight festivals, or 'sabbats': on the two solstices (the longest and the shortest days of the year), the two equinoxes (the two days a year when day and night are of equal length), and four further festivals, landing roughly between each solstice and equinox. These are opportunities to invoke gratitude, to celebrate life and engage in whatever rituals make sense for us. The wheel leads us around and around, year on year, acting as a sort of liveable teaching on the circularity of life and our ultimate interdependence.

A ritual is a sequence of formalised, repeated symbolic actions. We have a tendency to crave them in our lives. All around the world and through all time humans have created and performed a great variety of rituals, the commonality between them being that, despite the sequence of actions seeming fairly nonsensical or random, they produce an outcome.

Rituals can serve as a force for good. When performed in groups they can increase the sense of connection and bonding between participants, even those who do not know one another. When we are grieving, or particularly in uncertain times when we feel out of control, the structure of ritual can bring us humans together, help to make us feel safe, reduce anxiety, ease our suffering.

These days, however, many of us lack opportunities to engage meaningfully with rituals that bring positive social and personal outcomes. As our society and lives have shifted with industrialisation, the boom in urban living and rise in secularity, we have lost our physical relationship with land and our food. Two aspects of life often rich in beneficial ritual practice.

Growing involves engaging with forces beyond our control. So it makes sense to me then that gardens can become places of ritual, both sacred and mundane, that draw out the best in humanity: nurturing and connecting; gratitude, sharing and savouring; letting go and ceding control.

Working in the garden has helped create a structure for my own small rituals to emerge. I welcome this. It enriches my life. If collective rituals can help connect us humans, perhaps they can help us to connect with the non-human world too. Given the choice, I would opt to live in a world filled with soothing magical ritual over one without, every time.

I've come to map my own route through the year, charting both my life and the life of the garden by the seasons. The map guides practical tasks which also offer opportunity for meaningful and seasonal personal rituals to emerge. Their rhythm has formed a more general map of life, from birth to death, including all the smaller lives and deaths we experience along the way.

My map starts with the theme of *return* – the period in autumn when leaves finally drift to the ground, plant life returning what it took from the soil and thereby feeding future life with its *decay*.

Winter's cold is *restorative*: a time of peaceful rest. The garden is quieter, nights are longer.

Late winter and early spring bring *preparation*: I sow seeds, ready beds and get the garden prepared for the nascent horde of new life. The garden becomes a tightly wound coil, ready to explode into life.

Renewal follows in spring proper: the sap rises once again, bursting into the first fresh buds, blossoms and leaves. Then comes the period of *growth*, when the whole world seems suddenly swathed in emerald green.

I think of the height of summer as a time of *actualisation*: everything seems at its most extravagant; fertilised blooms turn to fruits.

As the year tips into late summer, we enter the period of *ripening*: fruits now take their time to become rosy in the sun, while I turn a deep earthy brown. To me, this time is like the moment of soaring through the air after a run-up to a jump.

The flying leap eventually lands back to the ground as *return*, once again.

*

While writing this book, I also reconnected with the cosmology of my Nigerian ancestors. I have unearthed myths from the complex, cultural belief system called 'Odinala'. I have sometimes seen Odinala translated to literally mean 'as it is on the land' or 'existence on the Earth'.

Ultimately that is what this book is, a year of living on the Earth with all its beauties, tragedies, joy and hope.

MY DEVON GARDEN

On 2 January 2020, we went to view our potential new home. It was small and run-down, but the garden was a fantasy.

The cottage is dug down into the ground so that the windows of the lowest floor look out onto an alleyway that runs along an old stone wall holding back the earth. It feels like a burrow or den down there. Above the wall are terraces that step up and away from the house. A little concrete footbridge lined with rusty old railings flies from the living room, on the second floor, over the wall and terraces and into the garden. The terraces once overcome with brambles are now planted with culinary herbs. I've trained honeysuckles, which flower at different moments throughout the year, and a rambling rose along the railings of that bridge. At the right time of year it smells sweet to cross it.

Stepping off the bridge the garden stretches out ahead towards the south, five metres wide but nearly thirty metres long. The trees and shrubs along its edges blur the garden into the hilly landscape that holds it. Despite its narrowness it feels expansive. On that first viewing it was bare, the vegetation having been cut all the way back for the house to go on the market. Out of the ground, though, some telltale signs of the garden's green inhabitants were just starting to emerge. The greenery glistened, moist on that cool bright day. I stooped to check the soil, scooping some up into my hand. It was beautifully dark and soft.

At the end of the garden is a collection of old apple trees; no one had gathered their fruit that autumn, so a thick squishy layer of pulp lay underfoot. A hint to us of their abundance. Beyond them squat a pair of ancient stone sheds. Perhaps once used as piggeries, someone had given them glass roofs, stuffed them with junk and then let brambles scramble in on top. The plot was magical and felt forgotten and ancient.

We now know that our garden was once part of a 'burgage plot' – a medieval term for a long narrow plot behind a home with street frontage, that was typically used for subsistence. This garden would have fed many people over the centuries.

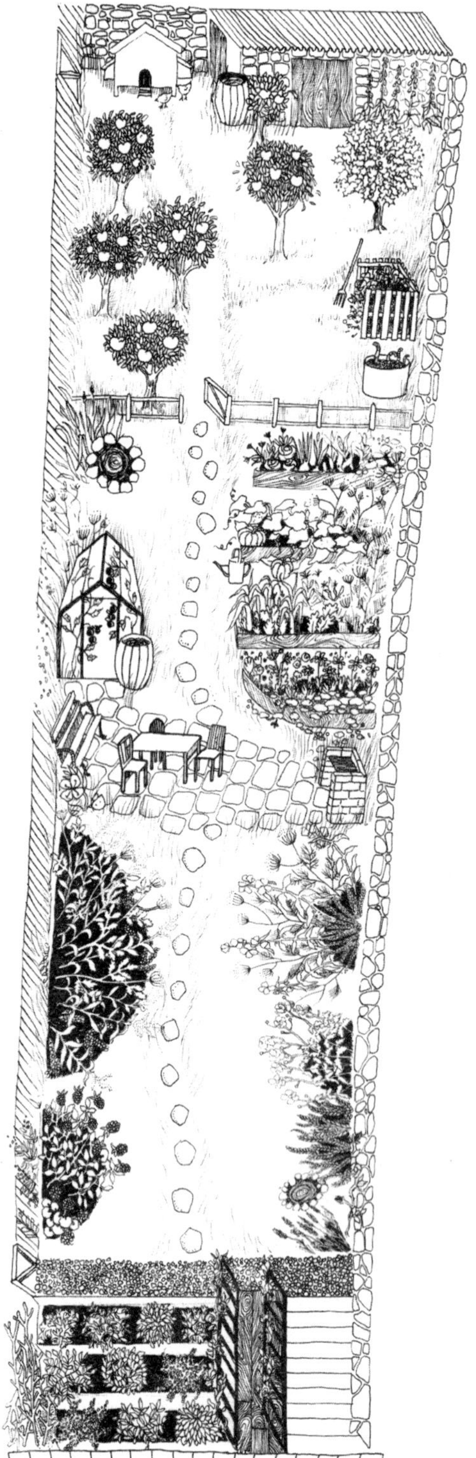

INTRODUCTION

A high stone wall runs the western length of our house, garden and then beyond, dividing our neighbours' gardens too. I like to think that this wall is an original medieval relic, from the burgage plot times. It was (and still is) bursting with plant life; out of it grows red valerian, St John's wort, creeping bellflower, sweet blackberries, ivy and its Jurassic-looking parasitic partner ivy broomrape. Pyracanthas grow from its top, their blossoms humming with bees throughout spring and summer, and come autumn their berries feeding many birds.

Despite first meeting the garden in its sleepy winter state, we were enchanted. It was whispering to us of its potential. Plus the soil and aspect were good. We made an offer right away. Then the Covid-19 pandemic swept through the world, and life in the UK was put on hold. It was six months later, in June, before we finally saw the garden again on the day we moved in.

Left to its own devices through that hot early summer, the garden had exploded into life; a tapestry of bramble patches, nettle patches, creamy yellow evening primrose flowers which glowed in the low evening light, fennel forests towered high. Scarlet poppies, alpine strawberries, pretty forget-me-nots, spikes of purple toadflax, glowing golden ragwort and fruit laden raspberry canes all muddled in together. There were several huge mounds of wild marjoram which were plastered in insects when they flowered. I found a couple of old lavender bushes being choked by purple and pink flowering cranesbill; an unruly myrtle shrub which reminded me of trips around Corsica in our campervan; and the brambles in the warmth of the old glass-roofed stone sheds were fruiting. I gathered those berries to have with our first lunch here. Clover, crow garlic and greater quaking grass grew out of the tall flowering meadow that was once a lawn, chirping with brown grasshoppers. In the first year in this garden, I largely let everything grow so I could see what was already established here. There was no path remaining through the space, so I would pick my way through the garden, noting every plant I found. As I brushed through, the plants rustled in the dry heat and insects went flying. There was and still is a particular abundance of hoverflies; their striped bodies hang steady in the air, humming, and then zip off sharply to do battle with another or alight on a fennel umbel. That first summer and the following spring, I listed over fifty different plants growing all together in a one hundred and fifty square metre plot.

The garden had a brilliant collection of all sorts of plants supporting a variety of life, many of which are generally considered weeds or, at best, undesirable wild things, but which I really love. So when I did begin work, I left the pockets that seemed to be the most alive and, to my eyes, the most beautiful, just as they were, only pulling up bindweed and chopping back any overly ambitious brambles that threatened to take over.

I found several sacks of rubbish which had been engulfed by angry nettles and still more bags of green waste (presumably from when the garden had been chopped to the ground). The bags full of plant matter had rotted down into a wonderfully dark compost, crawling with woodlice and their hunters, the orange woodlice spiders. These bin bags full of waste had excluded light in the areas where they lay, killing off the plants beneath. I made these the sites for my greenhouse and annual veg beds. I used the composted green waste in those bags as the first layer. It took me days to sift it. Removing any large woody bits and depositing them in the compost bays so they'd continue to decay.

Through the middle of the garden, I dug in a stepping-stone path, made from Cornish slate I collected for free from someone in a neighbouring town who was renovating their patio (one woman's loss was another woman's gain!). I made a clearing in front of the greenhouse to create room for a garden table and had a patio of sorts laid with the remaining slates loosely jigsawed on top of sand so plants can pop up through the cracks and water can drain away. That 'patio' is now dotted with little lemon balms and more marjoram, both of which have self-seeded and are kept short by our constant walking over them. Some wild carrots have come up too, with their lacy leaves and delicate white flowers.

I've introduced a couple of ponds. One, beside the apple trees and annual veg beds, was dug out by Toby and his son one spring. The other, close by the house, is made from an old enamel shower tray

INTRODUCTION

with its hole blocked up. It's not uncommon for frogs, sometimes two or three, to be found bathing in both on hot summer days.

The patch below the apple trees is now home to our little flock of chickens. As for the sheds, the brambles have been evicted and one is now filled with cobwebs and gardening tools, the other I've dusted, swept and claimed as my 'office'. It has a desk, some shelves holding my most referenced gardening books and many packets of seeds. The chickens like to squeeze under the door to peck about in there on wet winter days. A Virginia creeper battles an ivy for wall space on the outside. Sometimes they send inquisitive tendrils inside too. Parts of this book were written there.

Some years later the garden is a mixture of wild and semi-tamed – some plants brought in by me and accepted by the garden, others offered up by the garden and accepted by me. It still looks and feels very wild, it is still a very full tapestry of many plants, and the grasshoppers still chirp in summer. If a bare patch emerges, either I fill it, or if I leave it too long the garden does it for me, covering the empty ground with welcome weeds. I hoped that this garden would feed us and be a place for me to experiment and learn. It's done that and more. I am very lucky indeed to tend this space.

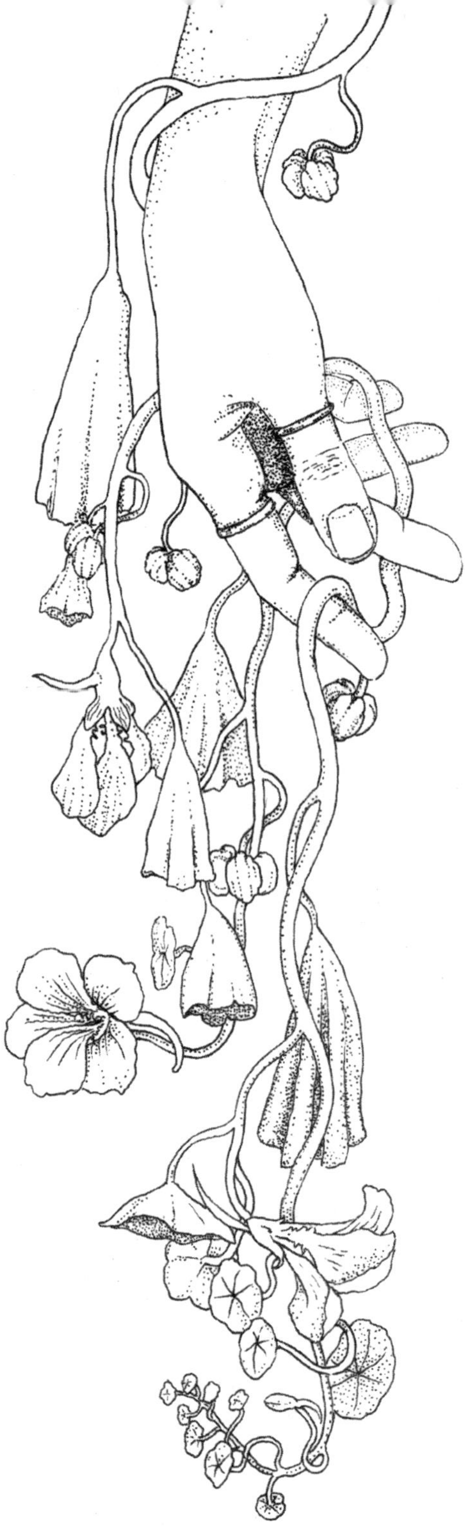

October — *Late Autumn*

ENDINGS AS BEGINNINGS

In a placeless point in no space or time, everything existed all at once, while nothing existed at all. This was the epoch of oneness. The infinite void was a being known as 'Oma'. Gradually this monolith drifted apart and separated into two: the masculine counterpart 'Chi'; and the feminine 'Eke'. Together they make up 'Chineke'. They are the two parts of the original energy that moves all things, 'Chukwu'.

One day Chi begins to build a house known as 'Obi Kwu Uto' – in English, 'The Upright House'. It is architecturally and geometrically perfect, with four corners and a central pillar. On its completion, Chi drifts into a cosmic dance, weaving in and out of this house, always entering backwards and exiting forwards and therefore never gazing directly at the contents of the home. Each time Chi moves through the privacy of the house he takes some time inside to work on a secret project.

Eke watches Chi's elegant and purposeful dance, feeling the loss of their previous oneness. To content herself, she begins to weave a cloth. But with a mind so full of curiosity, Eke's craft does not hold her attention for long. One evening Eke hatches a plan to sneak into the Upright House while Chi is dancing elsewhere.

Time passes in this state of post-oneness. Eventually Chi's dance takes him away from the perfect house. Darkness falls and Eke climbs the steps up to its door; as dawn breaks she finally pushes it open. The moment Eke's eyes fall on what is held within, an almighty flash and expansive explosion rip out of the doorway and through all that is, radiating out the sound 'uuwwwwaaaaaa!' 'Uwa' – the sound babies make when they are born and the sound of the universe scattering and rolling out into itself. This sound was the birth of the universe and our epoch of duality. Through Eke's observation, Chi's creation had come into being. But the blast throws Eke back down the steps, tearing life from her.

On his return, Chi finds Eke's dead body. He holds her, cloaking her in salty tears. His tears are the 'oshimmiri', the original source-water that never runs dry and that one day forms the great oceans. In his grief, Chi climbs up the steps to find the door to his house wide open, he steps inside and closes it behind him, committing himself to eternal isolation. But as he does, Eke begins to stir. Shrouded in Chi's tears, she rises as Ala, the Earth mother, Goddess of the Earth and the Earth herself.

*

This creation story, as told by my Igbo ancestors who come from a place now known as South East Nigeria, is not one I was raised on, but one I searched out more recently. It is part of Odinala, the traditional pantheistic cultural belief system of the Igbo people. Odinala venerates nature, which is seen as the great teacher. When I first heard this story, I cried quietly, my round brown cheeks glowing wet with my very own oshimmiri. A water that flowed from the grief that this story had not been carefully passed down to me by my family. I cried because the fabric of this newly learnt tale feels familiar; it feels of me; I know it so well and yet not at all. Perhaps I cried from the surprise of being reunited in my late twenties with something I didn't know I had lost. I felt the mortality of cultures and cosmologies that hold deep intangible wisdom gathered through time. Just like soil, without care these things may erode.

I have been feeling out stories like these for years now, attempting to piece together a new but old cosmology that would jive better with the worldview grown in me by the gardens I have tended. The garden worldview feels so at odds with the dominant culture I find all around me today.

As I tried to learn how to grow food that is good for the land and for us, my garden spaces have been whispering unexpected lessons to me, lessons about the interconnected and cyclical nature of all life. I now hear these same lessons in this origin myth, which invites us to reassess the notion of time as linear and abstract, and to see the entire living world as eternally in motion, in a constant process of unfolding. It teaches me that when we sow seeds and water them with love, they will grow. It also tells of the anguish that so often accompanies change, of a co-creation that takes place in the stillness of the void. I had turned to the garden for physical sustenance, only to find spiritual sustenance there too.

My very distant ancestors on my British mother's line told similar tales of life starting in stillness, dark and discomfort. Contraction creating expansion. From what we know, for the ancient pre-Christian Celts, days did not start at dawn but at dusk, and they did not perceive the new year to begin on the first of January; rather it began with the summer's end. These ancient people saw beginnings in autumn's falling leaves and seeds, in the sun drifting away and in the cold darkness drawing near. It was the start of a necessary period of preparation before the sun's return and the bright abundance of spring and summer.

For me, gardening in a culture besotted with the abundance, growth and beauty of spring and summer had influenced the emphasis I placed on certain moments or seasons. I thought I had been participating in the cycle of birth, growth, senescence, death and decay. When I read about my ancient Celt ancestors, however, I realised that in fact I had been engaging with death and decay *followed* by birth and growth. Through the death of old life, new growth can arise.

I had experienced that the fertility – and so, ultimate sustainability – of any garden depends on the process of decay, a process so important that I see it as foundational. But it took the faint whispers of a culture now so distant in time to plainly point out what I had been staring at all along – endings as beginnings.

Understanding the endings of autumn instead as *returnings*, I rewrote the story of my garden and, in many ways, the story of *me*.

REST AS RADICAL

Overripe fruits fall and rot, seeds drift and settle. Deciduous trees lose their leaves and turn to skeletons, the death phase, their dormancy. Annual plants are dying back having set their seed; the seed falls to the soil, lies dormant, resting in the underworld until it is ready to return to life again in spring. As plant life dies back, leaves fall to the ground, their decay feeds the very soil that, with water, sunlight and air, made them. The soil made them. Now they make the soil.

This is the time in the garden I refer to as 'return', the season which has, perhaps, the most to teach us today.

*

My hands are damp from the cool earth. One palm holds the chunky seeds of the broad bean (*Vicia faba*). Dull, khaki-brown, large as my thumbnail, they could be smooth clods of clay. Together, the beans and I are wrapped in a grey day. The cold air is heavy with a rain that's shy to come, but I'm warm after clearing a bed overcome by a tangle of squash plants and nasturtiums. I wrestled their soggy old limbs from the ground, stretched my arms around the bundled-up jumble of theirs and put them to rest on the compost heap. Compost from that same heap had grown them – a return.

Putting these bean seeds into the soil feels like a return too. The seeds had swelled on the stems of strong tall plants in the summer sun, before I plucked them once their pods were dry. This soil grew these little brown nuggets and now it is taking them back again. I find something meaningful and magical in tucking them into the autumn earth. It feels almost sacrificial, yet buried in the soil, despite the cold, they will send down roots, sprouting to stand squat and stoic through winter, then come spring burst back into growth, branching out before flowering and producing more beans still.

*

On Halloween's eve, Meg, my mother-in-law and great friend, passed away suddenly after a minor surgery that went wrong. In the weeks that followed, my garden felt far away. Meg had so often guided me in the garden, and when I finally went out to it, it looked how I felt – missing so much life, confused, tired and ready to rest. The garden robin I know so well watched me as I cleared the bed for the beans. 'Where have *you* been?' he asked. 'Grieving,' I'd say. 'Watching others grieve and grieving for their grief too.'

I hadn't really wanted to go outside to plant the beans. I didn't want to clear that bed, to be watched by my robin. It was confronting that the world carried on, that the garden continued to need my attention. In its confusion and exhaustion, it was still beautiful, cool and bright. The soft blue of the sky, gently stroked by faint lines of white clouds, wrapped itself around the deep greens, golden yellows and ochre browns of the leaves, the perfect apples still hanging on the trees, and the sharp crimson rose hips. There were even some stubborn flowers, pretty pink geraniums, deep orange nasturtiums. It made the greatness of Meg's loss surreal. I wanted the garden to stop like she had, so that, just for a while, I could stop too. But the garden only laughed and told me, 'The dance goes on.'

So, I stepped into line and prepared to put my beans in the ground, knowing that their next twirl would be to sprout green in about a month's time. Come late spring, bumblebees would bustle in their blooms, and then in summer there'd be pods to shell. She would have wanted all that to carry on for us. I planted the beans for Meg as much as for Toby, her son, my husband, for whom I wanted to grow the world back into softness and green. That year, sowing in sorrow, I saw the symbol of resurrection more keenly than ever before. I knew time would transform them, they would metamorphose, and us too... but the path forwards was less certain for us. The beans would act as our guide – proof that dull sorrow sown can become something beautiful, something even to sustain, to share.

Some autumns on, I don't know how many more bean sowings will pass before this act no longer feels so tightly wrapped up in memories of Meg and the strangeness and sorrow of death. I don't know if that connection can really ever go away and I don't know if I want it to. I don't think I do. Planting broad beans will be my own form of prayer to the turning of time and its transformative powers.

I have learnt that to achieve circularity in a garden, or any sustainably designed system, one must close the loop – there must be a return, a giving of rest, whether to soil, plants or people. My mother-in-law's death was only the first in a series of events that proved this point over and over again. Shortly after Meg passed, my partner and I conceived. Arriving in my belly just as Meg left us, that baby was so wrapped up in her death. But just before Valentine's Day, when I usually begin sowing seeds for spring, and the week we were due to see the baby at our first scan, I miscarried. By then the bean seedlings were standing firm in their garden bed, and I dissolved.

*

To germinate, the bean seed goes through dramatic change. Once in the soil, moisture causes the seed to swell and, soon, the tough outer casing holding in all that potential life splits open, allowing the radicle (the plant's first immature root) to thrust down into the dark earth in search of anchoring support. The first leaves, folded neatly inside the seed, begin to push up and out from the earth, then on breaking the surface, they begin to photosynthesise. With the root now pumping water and nutrients into the plant, the broad bean seedling begins to grow, and before long nothing is left of what once was the small, dull, khaki-brown seed.

After my miscarriage, I too needed tucking away, to bury myself somewhere quiet and peaceful where I could absorb and process and slowly begin to swell back into myself. All living things need nourishing rest, and yet this universal prerequisite runs in the face of a modern Western culture built for efficient, mechanised extraction. Rest is not valued. It felt bold, therefore – and I felt like the luckiest woman in the world to have the luxury to choose – to turn inwards for a while. To be able to say, 'This has broken me', and then

OCTOBER

take time to learn and grow through that damage. That time of rest was a form of resistance. I wanted to wake up from the deep sadness of loss, but in order to wake restored, I had to stop thrashing about and really, *deeply*, sleep.

I now know that deep rest isn't just for when the going gets tough, or something that takes place in the living world only once a year, in the stern face of autumn and winter. Rest takes place daily; even in the vibrant height of summer, the moon rises and plants pause their photosynthesis for a while. The culture I grow my garden in may not value rest, but the culture the garden has grown in me *worships* it. Rest is radical because it allows life to regenerate.

The garden has shown me a kind of rest that allows us to dream, welcoming a pause and a light wandering of the mind; one that does not require an expensive spa, fancy soap, smelly candles, or very much at all. When Meg departed, despite my wanting to turn away, sowing those broad beans was *my* form of rest. Likewise, turning the compost, watching the chickens, weeding or just sitting amongst the life in the garden and looking, smelling – simply being present and connected – is all a type of rest. It feeds me, buoys me up and soothes. The garden doesn't busy itself trying to comfort or fix me, it just looks back at me. Sometimes it mirrors me; it points at death and weird melancholy struggles and says bluntly: 'Look, it happens to us all, being part of this is life.' The common ground is peaceful and strengthening, it's restful.

The kind of rest the garden teaches is unrushed, but it is far from idle. It allows us, like Chi, to first create in a realm we can't right away touch or see – our imagination. Just as the return of autumn builds fertility for spring, we need that pause to build visions of beauty into our world.

Perhaps deep down we have known all along that being present and connected in certain wild and living landscapes can offer us a balm. Now that hypothesis has been backed up by reams of research, from soil sciences through to psychology. Over thirty years ago, professors of psychology Rachel and Stephen Kaplan devoted their studies to Attention Restoration Theory, carrying out research into how our mood and health is affected by nature. They proposed that modern work and life requires the mind to focus for extended periods on complex problem-solving, leading to fatigue, irritability and burnout. Immersion in the living world, or 'nature', they concluded, could offer restorative benefits. By allowing the mind to drift and wander, taking in the broad experience of nature's sights, sounds and smells, the brain can recover from the stress of direct attention.

Similarly, in the 1980s, the American professor of architecture and healthcare design researcher Robert Ulrich carried out an experiment involving a group of patients recovering from gall bladder surgery. Half had rooms enjoying a view of trees; the others looked onto a wall. Those looking out onto the trees reported better pain tolerance, appeared to have fewer negative side effects, and spent less time in hospital than the patients who saw only the wall. Green, growing life, it would appear, both teaches the necessity of restorative rest and is a rest in itself.

But regrowth cannot happen in isolation – the radical rest of nature requires collaboration. The tangled limbs of the squashes and nasturtium return to the soil as nourishment for new growth only with the support of bacteria, fungi and invertebrates, which allow the material to decay. And as the bean seed stirs in its earthy bed, it sends out a root that will support the bean as it grows, reaching out to receive gifts of water and nutrients from the soil.

The garden teaches us to connect with and understand the plants, creatures and other people around us; to unhurriedly explore what it is to be alive amongst other life; to build communities of support in which we can all share both abundance and labour, so that we all have a chance to rest.

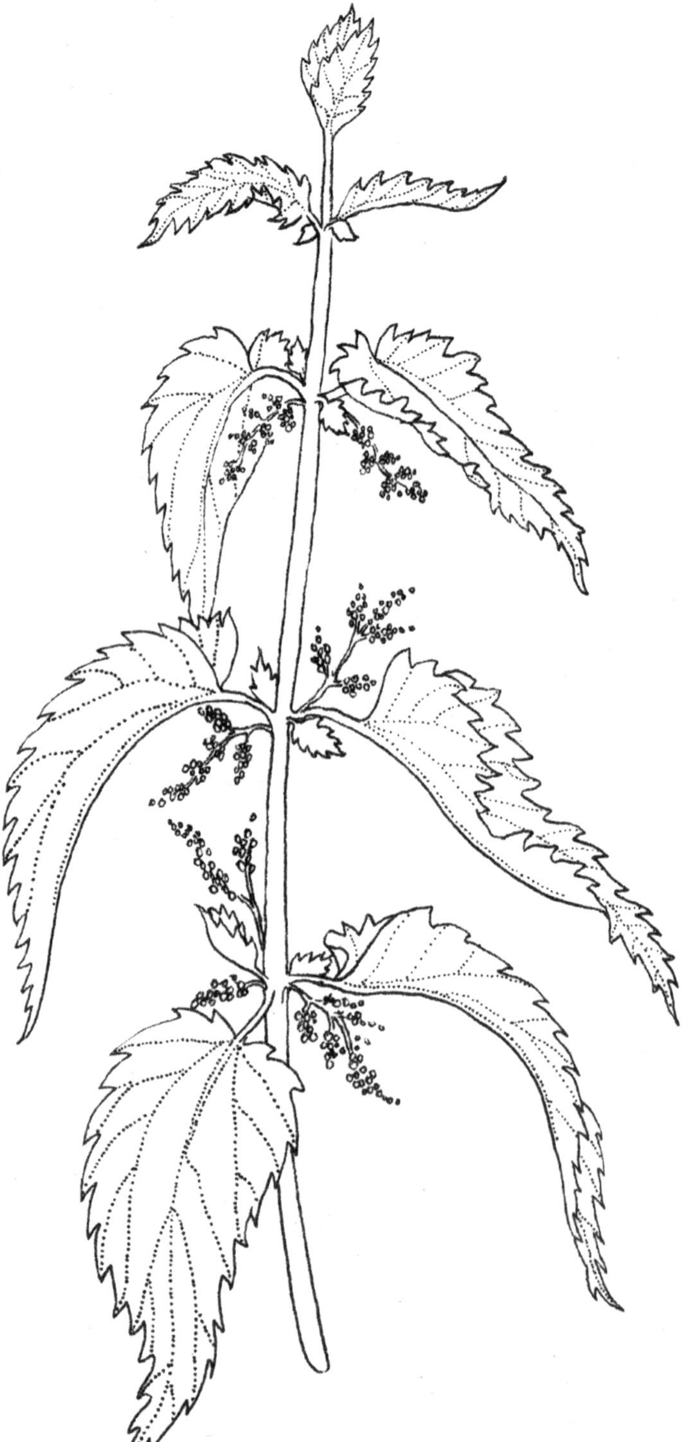

OCTOBER

NETTLE AND MEADOWSWEET TEA

- Handful of dried or fresh grown or foraged nettle tops
- Handful of dried or fresh grown or foraged meadowsweet leaves and/or flowers
- Milk of choice (I like nut milk)
- Sweetener of choice (I like honey)

Often regarded as a weed, the nettle (*Urtica dioica*) is one of my favourite plants. Nettles grow abundantly almost all year round, nearly everywhere, and are an excellent community member. In the garden, they provide habitat and are a useful cut-and-come-again ingredient for compost and homemade plant feed. In the kitchen, cooked much like spinach or brewed into an earthy-tasting, iron-rich tea, the leaves are delicious and nutritious. Most prolific in spring and summer, they often also have a fresh flush of growth in mild autumns and winters.

Meadowsweet (*Filipendula ulmaria*) is common across the British Isles, growing in damp meadows, woodland and along hedgerows. Her creamy white flowers can be gathered in midsummer and her leaves from spring to autumn. The flowers and the leaves are aromatic, with an incredible, almondy, hay-mixed-with-vanilla-and-honey scent, but I find the flowers sweeter. Meadowsweet leaves and blooms contain salicylic acid, a traditional painkiller. In the late 1800s, a chemist used meadowsweet to synthesise acetylsalicylic acid, or aspirin, which takes its name from the plant's old botanical one, *Spiraea ulmaria*. I enjoy meadowsweet flowers and leaves in teas, to soothe physical or emotional tension and pain.

Together nettle and meadowsweet combine to make a tea that tastes sweet and earthy while being nourishing, calming and grounding, especially good when resting up in the winter months.

- Place the nettles and meadowsweet in a small saucepan and add enough milk to cover them.
- Place on a medium heat and bring to a gentle simmer.
- Once at a simmer, remove from the heat and steep for about five minutes.
- Strain the infused liquid into a mug, add your sweetener of choice and stir.
- Enjoy, ideally buried in blankets on the sofa or in bed.

SAMHAIN

Our world has turned to muted ashy greys. It is the night of the Gaelic festival of Samhain, the origin of our modern Halloween. Walking in the woods in the early darkness, no colour and near no sound, it is easy to imagine I am entering the spirit realm.

For the ancient Celts, this cross-quarter festival between the autumn equinox and the winter solstice was a celebration of all things ending and marked the 'start' of a new year.

Samhain sits at the close of the light part of the year – the period of fertility, growth, abundance and production is ended. The harvest is brought in, new crops have been planted, and now we move into the darker, stiller months, a time of decay, perhaps a quiet kind of sorrow, of peace, learning and processing.

In the ancient folklore of Northern Europeans, we find tales of the Sun King who is sacrificed at this time of year. He returns to the earth where he travels through the underworld, gathering knowledge which he brings back on his return with the sun in the spring. The tales also tell of a goddess who during the dark half of the year enters her crone phase. It's easy to imagine how alive these stories would have felt in a time when surviving winter in Northern Europe was nearly as harsh as travelling the underworld. But they can still teach us a great deal today.

Once, this period of late October was a time to commune with and honour the dead, and to accept the other losses that winter would likely bring. But in our modern culture, death has become such a taboo. Rather than Halloween being a day to really contemplate the reality of death in life, we distract ourselves, playing with humorous symbols of mortality, never stopping to ponder too deeply.

When Meg passed away, one of her oldest friends, Toby and I spent much of the day with her body, watching it laying still, with her but without her. Eventually her friend told the beautiful nurse who looked after us all that she was ready to lay Meg out. Apparently, no one had asked to do this before and the nurse disappeared into the ICU to find out if it was allowed. She came back confirming that yes, Meg's friend could lay her out, if she was sure. She was, she said, and explained she had done it before.

The nurse removed the cables and tubes from Meg's empty body, and we were left to gently wash her and smooth frankincense, rose and myrrh oils onto her skin. Then we said goodbye and left. I never saw her again.

The next day was Halloween, Samhain. In her diaries we found a note 'Shallow grave = compost. Good.'

Meg wanted to be buried high up on a hill in an ecological burial ground which provides much shallower graves than the average graveyard would, allowing the body to decay quickly into the soil. So, the next time I was near her body was in a beautiful and wild meadow on a piercingly bright, still day, the sky crystal blue. A wide river weaves its way around the hill and moves far off between distant valleys, making its way towards the sea. High up there, where storms blow hard, we left her body to the Earth. I imagine all those ghosts dancing in the wind.

After being so close to real death, watching Halloween unfold around us felt abstract and peculiar. Glowing plastic skeletons hung in windows, children in zombie masks wandered the streets, and masqueraded as living ghosts. It all seemed to miss the point. It didn't capture the wild intensity of a death, its peace and power, impossible pain and relief.

I hankered for something more substantial, something that would move me and help me process the grief of loss. For my British ancestors, I imagine Samhain may have functioned as a preparatory ritual for the community on the edge of the dying time of year. For now, my ritual of piling dead matter, compost, on top of the soil around Samhain each year just about scratches that itch, giving me proximity to living lifelessness. The broad beans help too.

In Odinala there is a vibrant tradition of regular communion with the dead, gifts and offerings are left at altars to loved ones who have passed. My Igbo ancestors did not perceive death as the final ending. They would have told me that Ala, Goddess of the Earth and the Earth herself, presides over the cycle of birth, death and rebirth. On death our body is be returned to her, buried in her womb, in the soil. Our spirit would then move on to another plane. There Chukwu would give it a destiny and other elements that make up a life, including our Chi, the God in all of us, through whom we can access divinity; the part of us that sings when we are on the right path or cringes when we undermine ourselves or our gut instinct. The spirit then travels back to Ala where it receives further gifts, including a personal identity, before returning to the mortal plane, embodied once more. They would have told me the *mmuo* is part of the human soul that holds memories and is most the 'self'. It is believed that this part of a person can linger on Earth, perhaps drifting among us on Halloween. They would say we help to carry out the will of the dead, that they visit us, help and support us through the tests of life. Keeping the memory of a loved one alive is important, a form of immortality.

I wonder how we could think, feel and behave if, as a society, our day for the dead made more time for actually contemplating death and truly remembering our passed loved ones. Might we feel somehow reinvigorated, rested, put at ease and renewed by stopping to acknowledge the only certainty in this life – the ending and the beginning of all? So much of the terror of death is the friction that arises from futile resistance. In the garden, at least, I have found real comfort in both accepting and celebrating death. It has altered my perception of any sense of 'endings' or even 'failure'. As a result, I am less fearful. After all, any failures can return to the soil as precious compost. Embracing circularity has given me grace. As the Igbo saying goes 'echi di ime' – 'tomorrow is pregnant'.

*

Pea-sized seeds pop off their trailing stems into my fingers. Each one is like a small, smooth, green brain. They are still young and crisp, their cells turgid with water, and if I were to bite down on one, it would burst open with a sharp, peppery crunch. Had the seeds formed earlier, they would have eventually dried in the summer sun, becoming hard, brown, papery balls. But they were too late; the summer is long gone. The plants' final velvety red and orange flowers are wide open, in hopeful wait for insects that never come. I haven't seen a bumblebee in weeks.

I'm gathering the last few seeds from the nasturtium plants which trail along the edges of the vegetable patch and over the low, chestnut-stave fence into the chickens' orchard. Frost will soon be here and when it comes, the nasturtiums will turn to a sludgy mess as their cells rupture in the cold. Today, I will take the firm small green brains to the kitchen and pickle them to make 'poor man's capers'. These seeds are one of this garden's last summer harvests. From now on, it's just the remaining apples and hardy winter veg.

Seeds gathered, the nasturtiums come out, chopped at the base to leave their roots to rot into the earth. I take their trailing foliage and flowers to the compost heap and leave with a barrow full of compost. A good trade. For me, the months between summer and winter, or winter and summer, are times of transition and preparation, they are good moments to start new beds or give some extra care to the ones already here. As winter draws in, I dress the annual veg beds and perennial areas in a coat of compost to shield the soil from the pummelling erosion of winter rains. The repeated freezing and thawing of winter will gradually work the compost down into the soil, as will the creatures who call it their home. This is known as the 'no-dig method'.

In conventional horticulture, veg beds are prepared with double digging, a technique that disturbs and mixes up the soil down to two spades depth. Compost or manure is also muddled in by digging or forking. But in a wild landscape, organic matter falls to the soil surface where it rots away and is incorporated into the earth by life, mostly earthworms, rather than digging. In my garden, I prepare the veg beds following this logic.

To create a new bed, first I chop back the vegetation, then, as best I can, remove the blackberry, bindweed and nettle roots – plants considered weeds since they would happily swamp any veg if I attempted to grow in amongst them. Next, I cover the area in sheets of old cardboard, followed by a layer of compost about 10 cm deep. The cardboard excludes light, suppressing weed growth and seed germination, while also breaking down and decaying back into the soil. The compost holds the card in place, mulches any weeds and feeds the soil. These fresh beds are ready to plant into right away. Then each year I simply top them up with more compost, if they need it.

I do dig when necessary, but avoid unnecessary soil disturbance as much as possible. I like to say that I 'grow' soil in this garden. Following this wilder approach helps to protect the soil's structural integrity and preserve the lives who call it home. Where I do dig or disturb the earth, I make sure to give it time to heal and regenerate (more on soil health on page 229).

Now when I pour the rich compost onto the soil, I think of the Odinala belief that the buried rise again in new life. I think of the creation myth that saw the birth of the Earth through the watery burial of Eke, and her rebirth as Ala, the original Earth mother goddess. Within that cosmology, and according to the lore of the garden, this practice of cloaking makes sense. Ultimately, it will give life.

As temperatures gently fall and days draw shorter, I prepare for the arrival of the real cold by making ferments and pickles, drying and freezing, preserving the energy of the summer sun to enjoy in the months when it has drifted far away.

POOR MAN'S CAPERS

- 1 cup juicy green nasturtium seeds
- 1 cup vinegar– I find white wine or cider vinegar is best
- 1 tbsp salt (you want it quite salty)

OCTOBER

- ½ tsp of sugar
- 2 or 3 sprigs your herb of choice – dill, bay leaves, fennel fronds all work well

---

This is a very rough cottage recipe, as I find myself using different measures of fresh green nasturtium seeds and cider vinegar every time, but it always works. Use it as a point of inspiration to experiment yourself, making the pickle your own. Mixed with the garden's homemade cider vinegar, some sugar and salt, the gathered nasturtium seeds slowly lose some of their pepper heat and turn a dull greenish brown. Add these 'capers' to pasta sauces or boiled potatoes, sprinkle them on pizzas and salads, or any dish that needs a salty, peppery pop!

- Rinse nasturtium seeds well in cold water and drain. Place in a sterilised glass jam jar.
- To make the pickling brine, add the vinegar, salt and sugar to a small saucepan and warm to dissolve sugar and salt. Take off the heat and leave to cool.
- Once cool, add the vinegar to the jar, covering the nasturtium seeds, and a sprig or two of any herbs you fancy.
- Loosely cover the jar with a lid and leave at room temperature for a week or two before securing the lid and transferring to the fridge.

NOTES:
- *You can also simply add the miniature green brains to a jar of leftover shop-bought caper brine.*
- *Pre-soak the seeds in salty water for twenty-four hours to reduce their fieriness, if preferred.*

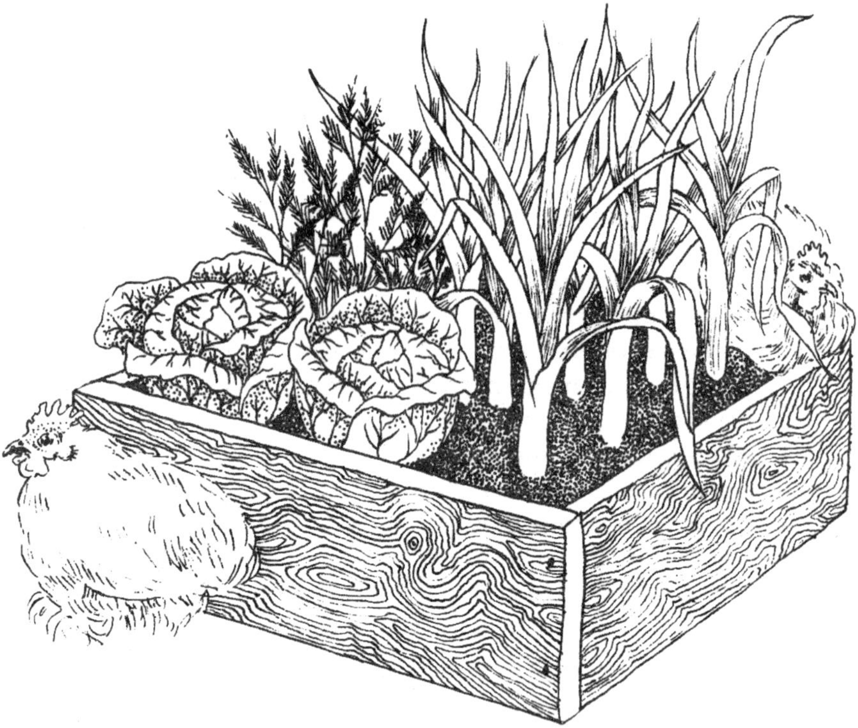

HOW TO PREPARE A NO-DIG BED

1. Mark out the area for your new bed and thoroughly clear it of perennial weeds.
2. If you are regenerating fairly degraded soil (or if you have the time and patience!), start by sowing a cover crop to act as a 'green manure'. Cover crops are plants which are grown to protect and condition the soil while suppressing weeds. Select the crop depending on your site's needs. If working with poor, nutrient-depleted soil, try hairy vetch (*Vicia villosa*) – also called fodder vetch or winter vetch – which fixes nitrogen in its root nodes through summer. If your soil is compacted, go for the robust winter annual fiddleneck (*Phacelia tanacetifolia*), whose vigorous root network helps break up the soil.
3. Before your chosen cover crop sets seed, chop the plants down at the base, leaving the roots to rot into the earth. You can also leave the cut foliage in situ, or add it to the compost heap, to create magic to spread on your plot at a later date. Either option will feed soil life and contribute to that all-important organic matter.
4. Cover the entire bed (and any green manure foliage left to rot) with non-laminated cardboard. (I find shops tend to have loads of cardboard boxes they are more than happy to give away.) Failing card you can use any biodegradable, light-excluding material such as old pieces of wool carpet or heavy linen or cotton remnants. They will likely just take longer to break down.
5. Spread a 7–10 cm layer of compost on top of the card or whatever material you choose to use. Accessible options include homemade, municipal or 'spent' mushroom compost, i.e., rotted horse manure or straw that has been used for farming mushrooms. I've had the best success with no-dig beds started in autumn and not planted up until spring the following year. This gives any weeds time to die back, and the card and compost will have broken down a

little and been drawn down into the soil below. That said, I have also had success with planting straight into a no-dig bed started in spring or summer.

NOTE:
To make sure I can reach all parts of the bed, I keep my no-dig beds roughly 1 m wide. If only one length is accessible, I go for around 80 cm width. I find 3 m is the maximum practical length for a no-dig bed – any longer and I find myself hopping or walking over it to get to the other side. Measure your arm span to figure out the best arm-reach, and thus bed width for you.

NOTE:
Following the no-dig method can really grow a garden's hunger for resources, in the form of compost. It can increase the cost of growing and the 'ghost acres' supporting the space. I find the best way to address this is by either producing my own compost in and from the garden (with the help of year-round food scraps and chicken manure) or by sourcing compost that would otherwise be considered 'waste'. At the community garden, as well as making our own compost, we also have a 12-tonne truck load of municipal compost delivered (at the moment, every two years) made from the food scraps and garden waste collected locally by the council.

NO-DIG CONTAINER GARDENING

While growing a container garden for many years, I brought some of the practices of no-dig to my planters. Each year, I'd add a layer of organic matter to them. When my annual plants died back, I'd chop them at the base and leave the roots in the pot to rot down. I also protected exposed soil with mulches of card, compost or chopped and dropped leaves. Although planters will not benefit from the same soil life as a garden plot, I was overjoyed to find that lots and lots of worms began to call my larger plant pots home. And because all this mulching limited evaporation from the soil surface, I didn't need to water the planters so often.

WATER

As I climb up the slopes near our town, water tumbles down, babbling over stones and around fallen amber leaves. It fell out of the sky only an hour or so ago, and now it wriggles down the edge of the path in a stream, then widens to a thin film, quietly engulfing the entire flat tarmacked surface. The water is clear, any sediment is caught up in the piles of leaves it navigates past and through as it gushes around my feet, then twists back into a furrow, leaping down as the eroded tarmac drops into a small ravine. This little rain stream has so much to say as it races, chattering to me in a low varied tone as I walk.

It was still pattering when I left home, but now the sky has cleared. I'm wrapped in yellow waterproof dungarees and a coat which keep water out but tend to keep it in too, so I'm wet with sweat as I push myself up the steep incline. The cool sun is sparkling on the last few golden wet leaves, playing with the water droplets that cling then plop from the ferns that line the track. When the wind blows, it seems that it has started raining again, as crystal-bright droplets fling themselves from the branches they were balancing on, flying through the air to land on me and my waterproofs. They shimmer and roll off my smooth, rubber clothes, dripping finally to the ground. Some join the rippling stream that accompanies me on my walk.

I reach the top of the hill and turn to the view. There's a rainbow. It seems too perfect, silly, a beautiful cliche, so I start to laugh. I wonder if the burbling of the stream is the sound of water laughing too. I turn for home.

Many more rain streams come and go, accompanying me for a while as I walk. They rush and gush, dashing fiercely across roads, out of farm gates and under hedges, all in a hurry to get where they're going. As I near home, the water no longer runs clear, but red, tinged with the clay earth that surrounds this town. These streams are carrying topsoil away with them.

Topsoil is the uppermost layer of soil that covers the earth, about 6 inches; above it should be a layer of organic matter such as decaying plants; below it lies the subsoil. Topsoil is the most productive part of the soil, from which many plants grow. It's rich in nutrition and in soil life. Thus, this layer of the earth is incredibly valuable, but it is also vulnerable. All around the red road rivulets are bare ploughed fields, their precious topsoil exposed to the elements. When it rains, there is no carpet of foliage and organic matter providing a high surface area to slowly filter the water, allowing it to gradually trickle down into the earth, to be safely held in the soil. So instead, when the rain pummels the bare ground, some of it impatiently rushes off before having time to sink into the earth. As it slides away it takes some of the topsoil with it, running red down the hill. Precious nutrients are washed away too, ending up in our waterways where they can wreak havoc on ecosystems, like eutrophication.

Loss of topsoil and nutrients makes the land less fertile and can ultimately lead to desertification. Erosion of vast swathes of precious topsoil is one of the major issues that accompanies industrial agriculture. Ironically, a growing system designed in an attempt to extract maximum value from land corrodes the very thing which produces that value. We humans are dependent on topsoil for food, fibre and all manner of other materials. Healthy soils quite literally give us life.

When I see the water running clay red, my heart tightens.

*

At home my garden is swelling with wetness. This is no accident – I've carefully designed it this way. The topsoil, rich in organic matter and blanketed with all manner of mulch, has been able to soak up much of the rainfall like a sponge. The plants that remain, despite summer's departure, glisten in their sogginess. The water butts are filling up, and the collection of buckets I've set out around the garden to catch more rain are overflowing. In spring and summer, I use the buckets for light watering. Last summer they ran dry more than once. The ponds, which also fell low then, are now full too.

In Odinala, the water goddess Oshimmiri originated in Chi's tears, and in the first great gift of life from water rose the Earthly Ala from her death. Water and soil. The two original sustainers. A garden can't be grown without these precious resources. So, I care for Soil and invite Water in wherever I can, making it as comfortable as possible for her to stay. Be that in the ponds, in the ground, in the mulch that covers the soil and reduces surface level evaporation, in the plants themselves, or in the buckets and water butts that dot the garden, it is a simple way to create resources rather than deplete them. Clean tap water, which has undergone a significantly energy-expending process to make it drinkable, is a precious resource which I don't like to pour onto a garden that, in any case, prefers the rain-harvested variety.

Climate change has already brought with it ever more extreme weather patterns, from flooding to drought, both of which put pressure on our municipal water and drainage systems. Gardens that are paved over or concreted into drives become smooth surfaces off which water simply slides away, in heavy rains potentially contributing to flooding. But a garden full of healthy soil that is able to hold water, plants that slow its flow, and other receptacles for capture, can do the opposite.

By harvesting water, our gardens can become an asset in flood mitigation. When welcomed and captured in our gardens, the same water that, if forced to run can cause damage and destruction, instead grows life. Establishing even a tiny pond – really any water source – in a growing space is one of the best things we can do to support native wildlife, from creatures big to the smallest of insects.

After the rain, I go to the end of the garden and check on the water barrel that is fed from the shed roof. This old barrel once held alcohol and, years later, still has a slight sweet boozy whiff to it; when I open the tap, the water that comes out does too. I peer down into its gloomy darkness. It's already nearly full and winter hasn't even arrived. I wonder if I should trade some more of the garden for another water butt. The limiting factor for water harvesting in this garden is space, how much of it I am willing to give over to store the water, rather than a lack of the water itself.

I find real satisfaction in gathering up this free but valuable offering from the sky. Water harvesting in this garden contributes to my ideal of the closed-loop system, a key part of ecological growing. The part of me that laughs at rainbows is also thrilled by the simplicity of this relationship with rainwater.

HOW TO MAKE A POND:

The subject of wildlife pond creation and maintenance could and does fill many books – have a look around for information and examples that suit you and your space's needs. What follows is a general guide.

YOU WILL NEED
🌢 Watertight container. The container does not have to be big,

OCTOBER

as long as it's at least 15–20 cm deep. Half an old barrel, a salvaged bathtub, or butler sink could all work well. I have a shower-tray pond in my garden: the frogs love it in the summertime.
- Bricks, rocks, pebbles, gravel
- Log(s)
- Pond plants

NOTE:
While visiting her magical wild garden, I learned from the talented gardener and garden designer Jo McKerr that there is huge ecological value in creating a pond and then, rather than planting it up, leaving it for life to colonise of its own accord. It was incredible to see how her ponds, large rainwater-filled bowls dug into the ground, were spontaneously bursting with life. The arrival of life is a gradual process that I imagine would be enchanting to observe and offer a cheaper route too.

METHOD
1. Dig a hole for your container, or simply place it on the ground.
2. Arrange the bricks, gravel, pebbles and rocks in the container, creating varied levels.
3. Position the log so that it will be partly submerged in the water, creating an exit point for wildlife. If you have simply placed your container on the soil surface, use more bricks etc. to create an entry and exit point for the pond.
4. Allow your pond to fill up with rainwater (tap water contains chemicals).
5. Add your pond plants.
6. Certain plants prefer different depths of water. Below is a list of native plants (making them extra excellent for wildlife) for each zone.

NOTE:
Whatever the depth of your pond, you will also need to add floating oxygenator plants so that life can survive in it. Native oxygenators include hornwort, water crowfoot and willow moss.

ZONE ONE

Moisture-loving bog plants for planting along the outer edge and shallowest areas of the pond.

MARSH MARIGOLD *(Caltha palustris):* One of my favourite bog plants, the large sunny yellow flower cups sit amongst shiny dark green rounded leaves. A great source of pollen for insects, they also make a beautiful sight gathered en masse around a pond.

LESSER WATER PLANTAIN *(Baldellia ranunculoides):* Perfect for small ponds, this creeping plant has little lilac flowers with yellow centres. As it spreads, lesser water plantain will cover pond edges as well.

WATER FORGET-ME-NOT *(Myosotis scorpioides):* Another favourite of mine. With its clusters of little sky blue flowers dotted between butter yellow cups, the water forget-me-not looks beautiful alongside marsh marigold. Newts like to lay their eggs on the leaves of this plant, which can also enjoy a marginal position in Zone Two.

BROOKLIME *(Veronica beccabunga):* This plant is good for small ponds. Similar to water-forget-me-not, constellations of dark blue flowers bloom all through the summer. The foliage offers shelter for tadpoles.

PILLWORT *(Pilularia globulifera):* This grassy looking fern can develop into a creeping mat around the pond edge. It is sadly in decline across the UK and is protected under the Wildlife and Countryside Act.

ZONE TWO

Marginal plants growing at 15 cm depth in the water.

OCTOBER

WATER FORGET-ME-NOT *(Myosotis scorpioides):* see above, Zone One.

WATER MINT *(Mentha aquatica):* There are many varieties of water mint, and like garden mint, it spreads enthusiastically. Water mint (which will also do well in Zone One) has clusters of lilac flowers atop long stems which appear between July and October and are great for pollinators. Water mint can be used just like other mints in food and drinks.

YELLOW FLAG IRIS *(Iris pseudacorus):* This tall iris (reaching 40–100 cm in height) can take over a small pond, so keep it in its pot. It is crowned with yellow flowers, offers great protection in its rhizome (root system) for pond dwellers, and is great for emerging damsons and dragonflies. Also suitable for Zone Three.

FLOWERING RUSH *(Butomus umbellatus):* Much loved by dragonflies, this beautiful rush produces umbels of pinkish-red flowers. It's best in larger ponds, where it can be planted directly into the ground, but can also be grown in large pond baskets. It can reach 1m in height. Also suitable for Zone Three.

BOGBEAN *(Menyanthes trifoliata):* With clusters of feathery white star-like flowers atop spikes, this plant gets its name from its foliage, which resembles that of a broad bean. Best for larger ponds, it's also suitable for Zone One.

ZONE THREE
Deep marginal plants growing at 40 cm depth.

WATER LILY *(Nymphaeceae alba):* The UK's only native water lily, this archetypal pond plant offers plenty of habitat for wildlife, both in and out of the water. It is best suited to larger ponds and can also occupy Zone Four.

MARES TAIL *(Hippuris vulgaris):* This prehistoric-looking oxygenator has whorls of blueish green needle-like leaves, arranged on stems that emerge from the water. It provides great cover for aquatic life. Though it has a similar name, this is not the same as the prehistoric plant horsetail (*Equisetum arvense*), which is impossible to get rid of.

ZONE FOUR

These plants like to be in deep water, planted at more than 40 cm depth or floating.

SPIKED WATER MILFOIL *(Myriophyllum spicatum):* This plant grows almost entirely submerged in the pond, with only their small reddish flowers visible above the water's surface.

WATER VIOLET *(Hottonia palustris):* The feathery leaves of the water violet, which remain submerged, create a real underwater-world feeling in a pond. The plant also has elegant stems holding little lilac and white flowers. The flowers only appear between June and July, but the underwater foliage offers great cover for wildlife.

ZONE FIVE

Floating plants, which thrive on the surface of the pond.

FROGBIT *(Hydrocharis morus-ranae):* This plant looks a little bit like a water lily but floats freely on the pond's surface.

WATER SOLDIER *(Stratiotes aloides):* This plant is classified as 'near threatened'. As the name evokes, sword-like leaves pierce through water like an army of soldiers' arms. With foliage sometimes described as resembling a pineapple top, this plant looks lovely growing alongside water lilies.

APPLE ROT

At the end of our long thin garden, the apple trees' arms are now bare of fruits. I've already gathered and stored some of the crop from the late-season trees (which produce apples that ripen later in the year) to enjoy over winter. I copy my grandma's technique for storing apples. I pick perfectly unblemished specimens from the tree, wrap each one in newspaper, then place them in a single layer in a cardboard box, which I keep in a cool, dry spot in the shed. Every time I raid my store, I pick over each one, removing any that look or smell keen on rotting. We have four different apple varieties in the garden, although I don't know any of their names beyond 'apple'.

Today the autumn garden forces me to stare death in the face; I can either battle its advances or smile at this familiar friend.

'I suppose the party's over? I knew you'd come, welcome,' I murmur as I prod a rotting apple. The chickens explode into nervous, cackling laughter, perhaps not expecting me to strike up conversation with a fruit.

I pull my hand away from the apple when its skin suddenly gives way, leaving my finger sticky and cold with its sweet decaying insides. As morbid as it sounds, I can't get enough of poking and prodding at mouldering things in the garden. They fascinate me. The perishing autumn garden is just as magical to me as the garden alive. It's certainly in the quiet months that I've learned most from her. I suppose, in a funny way, this is when she is sleepy. And when her guard is down, she's more likely to let slip little secrets than when she's wide awake, all dolled up and putting on a show. And what a spectacular show... but I do love secrets...

I poke at a few more apples, any that don't collapse I deposit in my pockets. I turn to go back inside. Mervin, the young cockerel, dashes over to peck my foot, trying to claim my retreat as his brave feat. The last few days he's been starting to think he's a big man, so I coo at him, remind him who feeds him and that he best not get any big ideas about doing away with me. I vaguely wonder if one day he might become violently aggressive like my friend's cockerel did. In the end, they had to 'give him away'. In an attempt to befriend him and ward off such a day's arrival, I try to pet him again. I like Mervin.

CIDER VINEGAR

You will need
- Large ceramic crock or glass jar
- Clean piece of fabric – an old, washed T-shirt or dishcloth will do
- Piece of string or elastic

Ingredients
- 1 l water
- 6–12 organic apples, unwashed (to preserve beneficial yeasts and bacteria). Organic homegrown or wild gathered apples are best, preferably windfalls. Leftover apple cores and peels can work well too. You can also experiment with crab apples.
- 100 g organic Fairtrade sugar

This is a handy recipe to use up any bruised windfall apples which may have been nibbled at by fellow garden creatures.

Fermentation is a clever sort of controlled decay, in which yeasts and bacteria preserve and transform foodstuff that might otherwise go to rot, in this case my apples. The yeasts feast on sugars turning the apple juice into cider, then friendly bacteria ferment the alcohol into acetic acid, or vinegar. Once the apple solids are strained and the vinegar is bottled, it won't go off and can be used to stop other foods from going off too.

Before the advent of refrigeration or access to huge quantities of sugar for preserving, fermentation (along with smoking and salt brining) was a vital means to extend the 'shelf life' of the harvest. An added benefit of this process is that consuming fermented foods regularly is really very good for us, as is making them. Both expose us to a host of beneficial bacteria that, in our highly sanitised lives, we wouldn't necessarily come into contact with otherwise.

It is possible to make cider vinegar without the addition of cane sugar by simply relying on the sweetness of the fruits, but I am yet to have success that way, so I stick to this dependable method.

- Pre-heat the oven to 160°C.
- Bring the water to boil and leave to simmer on a medium heat for 20 minutes. This dechlorinates the water, giving the fermentation the best chance of success.
- Take the water off the heat, add the sugar and stir until fully dissolved. Leave aside to cool.
- To sterilise the fermentation crock or jar, wash it thoroughly, rinse well and place the wet receptacle in the pre-heated oven for 10 minutes.
- Meanwhile, roughly chop the apples, discarding any really bruised or rotten bits.
- Add the chopped apples to the sterilised jar and cover with the cooled sugar water. To keep the apples submerged, I use a ceramic weight.
- Cover the top of the container with the clean cloth and secure with string or elastic (this allows air to get out but stops insects from getting in).
- Leave somewhere warm and dark to ferment for 7–10 days. Check and stir the contents from time to time. After a day or two, bubbles will begin to form and the mixture will start to smell like cider.
- After 7–10 days, strain the liquid into a clean bowl (the apple mush can be eaten – it's good in dal – fed to chickens or added to compost.)
- Return the strained liquid to the container, loosely cover and leave to ferment for a further week or two, tasting from time to time.

— Once it tastes sharply of vinegar, transfer to sterilised airtight jars or bottles and store in a cool cupboard.

NOTE:
This is a live fermentation, so be mindful of pressure build-up once bottled! Carefully open the jars/bottles and burp regularly to avoid explosions.

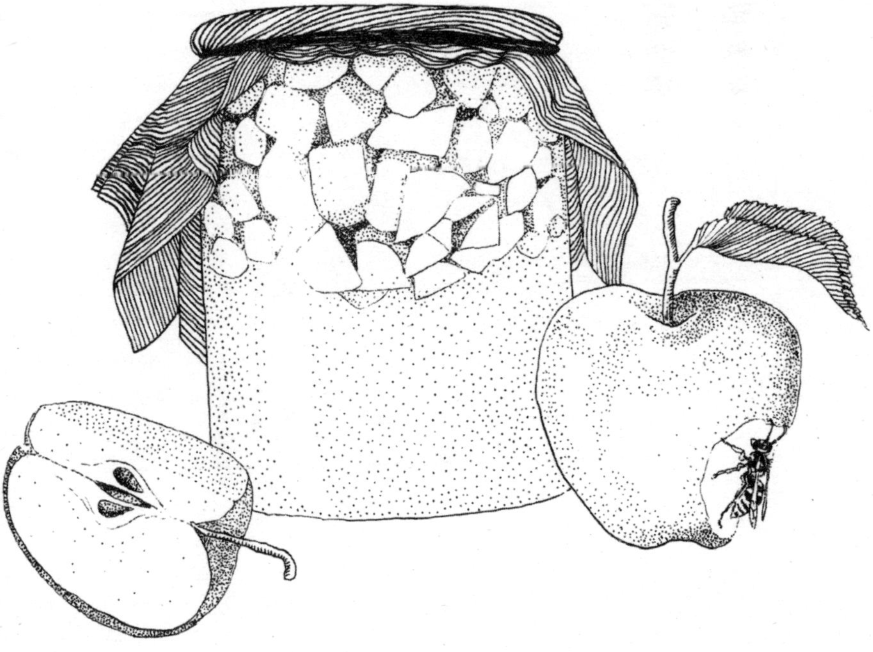

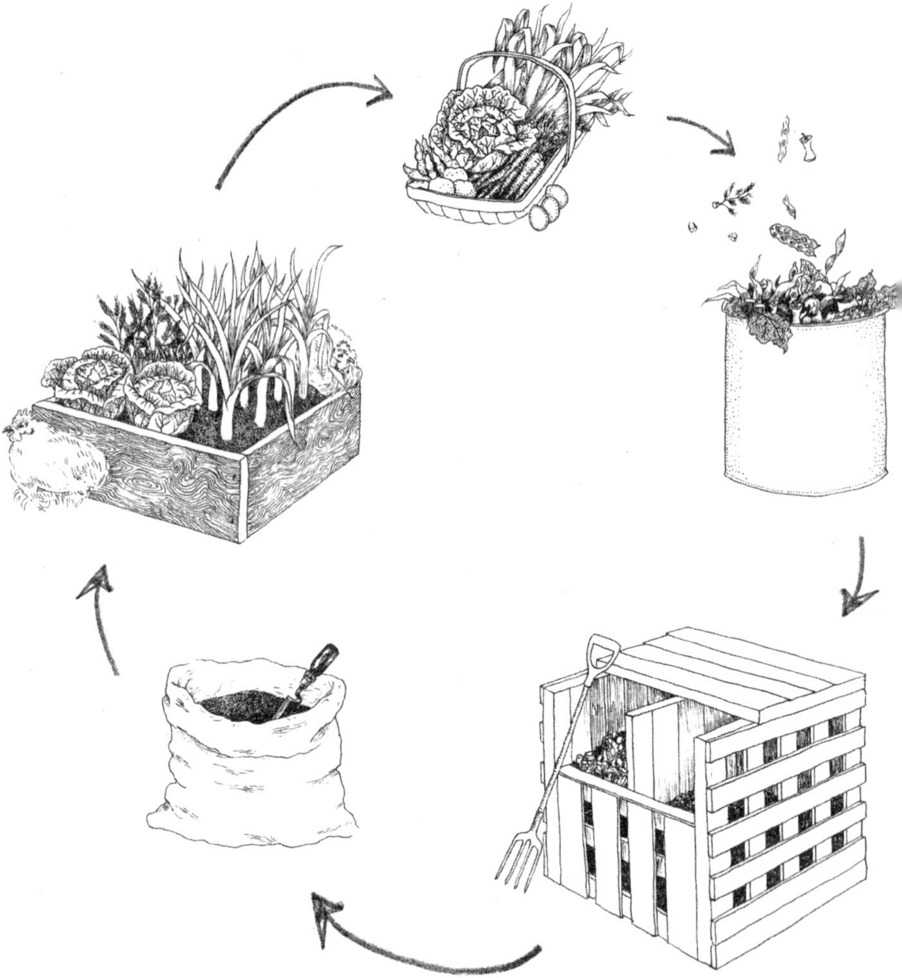

November

THE GARDEN GUT

Below the apple trees, the compost and I are twisting and turning. Or I'm twisting and the compost is turning, as I fork over one of the heaps. I think of my compost area as the heart of the garden, though perhaps more accurately it's the all-digesting gut. I have two bays made of pallets, topped with a shingled wooden roof. The bays take it in turns to either be gradually filled with organic matter or, once full, to wait for that organic matter to turn to compost. The dark pile I am turning seems to glow in the cold bright sun, a great steaming stomach. The compost itself looks to be alive, seething with squirming worms, scurrying insects and great clumps tumbling as I work. If I leave it for several weeks it will have morphed itself, changed completely. But this heap of decomposing organic matter does not live, its animation is lent to it by the unimaginable number of life forms that dwell within, contributing to a process of dramatic metamorphosis. Hard as I work with my fork, I am merely their humble and dutiful assistant, aiding the many millions of bacteria, fungi and insects as they break carbon-based life forms down into compost. These creatures big and small chomp, nibble and churn the organic matter, some even secreting enzymes to assist in the process.

I rhythmically bend, skewer, pull, then twist my torso to flip and dump my fork full of writhing matter on the piece of old tarp laid on the ground below. Nearby the chickens linger, their beady eyes on the lookout for worms, but they stay back, not brave enough to scrabble into the bay, for fear of being turned into the compost themselves! Now I proudly cart the prized fresh compost about the garden, spreading it here and there on the vegetable garden, my offering to the soil.

The next mission for me and my fork is to shift the second, only half-ready pile into the now-empty bay next door. This churns up the organic matter, incorporates air and allows me to have a good look at it. The matter is already becoming dark and crumbly, but is still very much in the slow process of breaking down. I assess my concoction of decay with eyes, nose and even ears. Does it need more carbon, more nitrogen, more water, less water? Hearing too much slopping, slurping and splatting is not a good sign: it tells me the heap is too wet. As would a foul scent. If the heap is hardly decayed it may need more moist nitrogen-rich material.

Watching the decaying pile's dark glowing and squirming distracts me from my labour, and I interrupt my flow to squat down close and see who's scurrying out of the light, to grab, squeeze and smell moist handfuls of the stuff.

I pick out half-vanished bits of matter – some squash peel housing a tangle of worms; an elastic waistband (all that remains of some old cotton knickers left in spring to end their days on the heap); a metal zip hanging onto the wispy cobwebs of a tattered linen duffel bag. I probably could have mended it for the hundredth time, but I'd been itching to watch it decay. It has taken its time; after the zip, the stubborn, sturdy handle is slowest to disintegrate. Added to a compost heap, near anything can be turned into food for the soil: clothes, wood ash, paper and card, leather and wood. I find it fascinating to unearth and identify a long-forgotten item, now so changed. It reminds me where all this stuff originally came from – the soil. This garden is a site of alchemy, turning waste to riches. The compost heap is a site of intense transformation, a huge mound of processes.

A garden compost heap is a wildly diverse ecosystem, its vibrancy often compared to that of a reef. If we were to dive into a compost heap with goggles and snorkels and swim about, it would likely feel warm, heated by the activity of all the organisms who call it home. In fact, a compost pile can break matter down so rapidly that it may sometimes become hot enough to heat water, warm a greenhouse and, in some cases, even bake a potato. As well as warm, the world would be dark, so many of the creatures living there adapted to a dim realm without sunlight. These creatures would be busy feasting on their home itself, consuming one another's faeces, and sometimes each other. As the inhabitants gradually erode the firm structures of the matter that arrives on their pile, they turn it into a spongy carbon-rich material which over time becomes harder to decompose; we call this stuff compost. So much of this compost heap world would feel soft to touch and moist too, as water is released when organic matter decomposes.

As we swim through this warm, dark, soft, moist universe, we may meet fungal hyphae, arms that reach out in search of fresh food matter. A dense patch of these colonises a chip of old apple-tree wood, spreading through it, engulfing it. The chip seems to be coated in a pale network of white veins; in this dense spot, as a collective, these hyphae are known as 'mycelium'. This is the less visible part of a mushroom, sometimes compared with the hidden roots of a tree, hard at work retrieving valuable nutrients from an old rotten bit of wood. Given the right conditions, one day this fungus might bloom and mushrooms appear on or around the compost heap.

All around are bacteria-secreting enzymes which degrade the matter they are attempting to consume. Like the fungi, bacteria do not ingest their food (i.e., digest it internally), instead they break it down externally to themselves and then absorb the nutrients they have made available. These microorganisms are assisted by larger creatures living in this edible home – familiar garden characters like slugs, snails, woodlice, millipedes, mites, burying beetles, worms and many more, all of which spend most of their life scavenging dead plant matter. Thus, they are called 'detritivores', from the Latin 'to rub away' – their life's work is processing the earth's detritus.

As we swim in the heap, we'll encounter worms that delight both in inhabiting and feasting on the wet, warm dark of decaying matter. But these are *not* the common earthworms we find in soil. Typically compost-dwelling worms are *Eisenia fetida*, known as brandling or tiger worms due to the fetching stripes that ring their wriggling reddish-brown bodies. Like us, tiger worms ingest their food, and also like us, they digest it through a combination of their own enzymes and the actions of the microbes that dwell in their gut. What the worms poop out is called worm castings or vermicompost. Vermicompost is teeming with micronutrients and microbes, both of which support healthy and strong plant growth. Tiger worms have a ferocious appetite – in the right conditions, they can get through half their body weight in organic matter each day.

Next, we may happen upon a family of woodlice dining alongside a millipede. The millipede might be enjoying an old leaf – already softened by the decaying action of the microbes – with a side of decomposing insect carcass. The woodlice, meanwhile, probably chomp through a bit of woody kale stalk. Woodlice faeces will later be colonised by more microbes, breaking it down yet further as they consume any last trace of nutrients. Nothing in this compost heap goes to waste. The nibbling of these larger creatures helps to increase the surface area of the matter, making it more accessible for microorganisms to do their work. As they chew through the waxy outer layers of tougher leaves, they create an opening for the microbes to enter and feast. Finally, we'll likely meet characters like spiders, beetles, centipedes, even predatory mites – the hunters who prey on the detritivores.

Meanwhile mice, hedgehogs, toads, birds and frogs come and go from the pile which provides an endless menu of tasty morsels and a warm, safe place in which to enjoy them. Essentially, composting – or decomposition – supports life.

*

This army of decomposers gets to work outside of the compost heap too but generally with less intensity. A deciduous forest floor is a fecund site of decay, with annual leaf fall and any other dead plant or animal life slowly decomposing, eventually turning to humus. Humus – that dark spongy material we find cloaking old forest floors, often protected by a decaying layer of leaves, soft, loose and crumbly to touch, nutty and rich smelling – is the final stage of organic matter after undergoing the long transformative process of decomposition. It is a very stable mixture of substances that is hard for life to break down further. Even the best compost we make in our gardens is often a little way off from the humus that coats the forest floor – to arrive at that state of fluffy dark softness would really require several more years of decay.

I always assumed the garden would be a place of creativity and productivity. In my mind's eye I imagined plenty of flowers, fruits, leaves, eggs and roots to feed me and those I love. But when growing as a practice to heal the earth and the human, composting takes centre stage. Unassuming, dull, seemingly inanimate compost is a gift to the earth's soil. Along with humus, compost acts as both a home and food source to a multitude of underworld life forms. They are vital to the health of the soil, increasing its ability to absorb and hold water, its resilience to drought, as well as its aeration and its ability to store nutrients. All of this grows healthy plants, on which life above ground depends.

LESSONS FROM THE HEAP (OR HEAPLORE)

Life can exist in ongoing loops, or cycles – it always has. But it requires living things to both not take too much and to ultimately, and in a timely manner, return what is given. In any healthy ecosystem, be it a wild one, a man-made garden or farm, this fine balance is maintained. Composting allows us to grasp and participate in this genuine circularity in more ways than one. Composting introduces us to the carbon cycle: the way carbon moves between the earth, oceans, plants and animals and the atmosphere in a closed cycle (the total carbon does not increase or decrease, so if there is more carbon in one reservoir there will be less in another). In a time when so much carbon is being misused, dug out of the ground and released into the atmosphere as we burn it to fuel our lifestyles, compost shows us that it can also be returned to the land and that the return can be generative. Compost and humus are carbon, first soaked up by the plants in a very stable form which can be kept safely locked in the earth's soil for many years.

Extracting fossil fuels is not the only way we humans release carbon into the atmosphere from its earthy stores. On most industrial farms regular deep ploughing of fields is the norm; it is a fast and simple means to break up the earth and dig in weeds in preparation for sowing. It also releases significant amounts of carbon into the atmosphere. But that is not the only damage it causes.

Like my compost heap, soil is teeming with life. In fact, vibrant soils are now believed to be the most species-rich habitats on Earth, and the altitude of the British Isles gives us some of the most lively, biodiverse soils on our planet. Again, as in the compost heap, living organisms in soil break down organic matter, but they also form complex relationships with the plants that coexist in the ground. They provide nutrients, support in warding off or recovering from pests and disease; they can even act as exchange networks for the plants, passing important information between them. Regular churning of vast tracts of land through ploughing can destroy mycorrhizal fungal networks and expose microbes to light and temperature levels in which they cannot survive, with devastating consequences for this complex ecosystem that lives below our feet. Given time and organic matter, this underground world can recover from such disturbance, but repeated ploughing can deaden the land.

It is now widely understood that much of the whole foods we buy and eat today are considerably less nutrient-dense than those same foods grown and consumed as recently as the 1950s. This trend has been attributed to two factors. Firstly, we have developed crop varieties that offer greater yields, which deliver much-needed calories globally but are consequently less nutritious. Secondly, the advent of industrialised farming in the 1950s and its subsequent rampage across the world brought with it the modern era of large-scale monoculture farms, mechanisation, regular deep ploughing and the heavy use of synthetic fertilisers and pesticides. All of these practices have the potential to harm life in the soil. Without the necessary healthy relationships held between plant and soil life, our food crops are less able to access the mineral and nutrient resources they – and we – need.

But degraded soil can be tended back to health, and again the carbon cycle can assist. Living compost can be a medicine. It returns valuable decayed organic matter, carbon, which improves the quality of the soil and can provide food and forage for the life that should dwell there. This compost is in itself dynamic – it carries that vast collection of microorganisms and invertebrates which can inoculate and reinvigorate the soil.

The very same organic matter, or carbon, which can be turned to valuable compost, when treated as waste, can become toxic instead. Most shop-bought food arrives in our homes in packaging and bags, which are all too often plastic, and in the absence of a home compost system or a local food-recycling service, what isn't eaten departs in plastic bags too, this time destined for landfill (in 2021 the UK sent 6.8 million tonnes of decomposable waste to landfill. The quantity has been increasing every year). There, any organic matter begins to decompose but without the organisms and environment necessary for its metamorphosis into a precious resource, it becomes a pollutant. When organic matter decays anaerobically (without air), it releases methane into the atmosphere. Methane is one of the most potent drivers of climate change. Organic matter also tends to hold a huge amount of water, which seeps out of the putrefying waste and trickles through the landfill. Eventually it flows into underground rivers and streams. But this liquid that has journeyed through landfill is no longer innocuous water, it's now leachate, a contaminated fluid that pollutes any body of water it eventually reaches.

About 6 to 8 per cent of global greenhouse gas emissions comes from food waste. It occurs all along the supply chain, but domestic food waste in higher-income areas tends to be particularly high. We can *all* make a difference by valuing our food, buying only what we need when we need it, and using any leftover scraps to feed the soil.

Through this humble act, we can support nature to do what it does best, which is to waste nothing and generate abundant life. As a concept, composting can teach us about the circularity and regeneration of the earth's systems, and in practice we can become active participants in a reciprocal relationship with the land, responsible citizens rather than mere (over)consumers. Supporting cycles of life, giving back as much as we take, responsibility goes beyond sustainability (when something simply remains stable, as it is), and towards regeneration (when something heals and regrows). In a culture driven by overconsumption and waste, the principles of composting act as a guide to living well.

It wasn't long ago that our homes and gardens were closed-loop systems by default, with few ghost acres (acres used to produce or process resources required, in this case, by a garden), if any. In fact, it's only in the last seventy years or so that we have drifted so far from a lived experience of true sustainability and the power of regeneration.

As part of a burgage plot, my garden would have pretty much sustained the plot owners (aside from beans and grains which may have been bought) so very little became waste. Anything that wasn't eaten – eggshells, vegetable scraps – would have been returned to the garden to maintain it. As a result, many years of tending, care and recycled resources have turned the soil here a rich and fertile dark, crumbly black.

It was also once common to empty our own toilet, or 'privy', waste onto our gardens. Just like farmyard manure, it was considered a valuable fertiliser. In his *Five Hundred Points of Good Husbandry*, a month-by-month gardener's rhyming manual written in the 1500s, Thomas Tusser instructs gardeners to bury their toilet waste in the garden in trenches in November (perhaps because the cold weather would minimise the stench), and cover it with leaf mould. He also recommends carrying out this job at night-time, to spare others from witnessing or possibly smelling it.

If garden require it, now trench it ye may,
one trench not a yarde from another go lay:

NOVEMBER

Which being well filled with muck by and by,
go cover with mould for a season to ly.

Foule privies are now to be clensed and fide,
let night be appointed such baggage to hide:
Which buried in garden, in trenches alowe,
shall make very many things better to growe.

Human urine is also a rich fertiliser. It is high in nitrogen, one of the key ingredients required for decomposition and for plant growth, so I regularly use our own to kickstart the compost heap and to water the perennial beds as a homemade, organic liquid plant feed. And it's not uncommon for our friends to have wild wees when they come round, a sort of gift in exchange for our hosting!

For the longest time, people all around the world have tended gardens of utility, which both created resources and broke them down. These gardens were mostly born from necessity and the desire to live well. The cottage garden tradition in England grew out of this human need. From medieval times, they were places of subsistence, a plot of land tended by 'cottagers' (common people, not the poorest but far from being the richest). Most kept livestock, often a pig, perhaps some ducks. Depending on the local climate, resources and plants available, the gardens usually featured perennial plantings such as modest orchards, hedges and fruit bushes. The cottager would grow herbs and, as they became popular in England, vegetables, to supplement grains and meat. They might keep a hive of bees for honey, grow flowers for the bees and for joy. Diversity was woven in with plantings of native flowers and, before the widespread use of herbicides and pesticides, the gardens would have been organic by default. Since the purpose of these gardens was to sustain a family, traditionally they were managed cheaply and *had* to be sustainable. Gardeners fed kitchen waste to the pig, spread wood ash on the path in winter to deal with mud, and repurposed rocks – removed from the soil to grow veg – into stone walls.

Looking up from my compost heap today, I imagine my own

small garden, a portion of an original medieval burgage plot, tended in traditional cottage-garden style, one that I try to draw on. Seeing beauty meet utility is thrilling. I picture all that this patch once created and all that it has decomposed.

Without the process of decomposition, a garden can't be truly sustainable, healthy or fertile. The same can be true of a human, a society, a planet. By composting – the process of alchemising waste resources – I become part of the community of circularity. As I strive for independence from the culture of extraction, I feel pride at having helped to make this pile of black gold – and all from waste. My mind boggles. For me the transformation at work in my compost heap is more captivating than the germination of a seed, because a seed is the very beginning of life, you expect it to change and grow. While compost... well, it seems like it's at the end. But that's just linear thinking. Really, it's another beginning.

To go out for a walk and watch water drops gather on the tip of a leaf, to reach out my tongue to taste them; to kneel on the ground, to look below a log, to sniff the scent of decaying wood, all this helps me to remember I am connected to all life. But composting allows me to *actively contribute* to life. It literally rubs away at the edges of things, corroding the certainty with which I can claim my separateness. In composting, I simply but resolutely and repeatedly defy the path of linear extraction, waste and its ensuing destruction. I choose instead to participate in the greatest truth there is: the circularity of life's systems. To break that circle's flow is to break life. After all, compost made me and one day I will make compost.

So my first and most important piece of advice for anyone who is beginning to garden is this: build a compost heap. It can feed soil, society and soul.

COMPOST THREE WAYS

What follows is a simple guide to the three main methods of composting I employ: a compost heap (including fast, hot and slow, cold composting), bokashi and a worm farm. Choose methods that suit your context; for example, worm farms are particularly good for small spaces while bokashi allows you to compost even cooked foods!

COMPOST HEAP

If practising no-dig gardening, composting is really important as it reduces the need for 'ghost acres' to provide the mulch needed to create and maintain the beds. Composting takes time. Depending on the time of year, the method you follow and how much attention you give your compost heap, it will take at least three months and up to a year before your waste matter has decomposed sufficiently to be useful (though some highly efficient systems can produce compost even faster than this!). You can use your compost once it has fully broken down and no longer resembles what it once was. It will smell fresh and earthy, with a dark brown colour resembling chocolate-cake crumbs, and might have pieces of twig or very small fragments of eggshells still left in it.

WHAT CAN I PUT IN THE COMPOST?
Your compost heap needs a good balance of nitrogen-rich matter (greens) and carbon-rich matter (browns). Aim for a ratio of 2:1, 2 green to 1 brown.

The nitrogen in the greens will kickstart the decomposition process; the browns provide aeration and prevent the heap from becoming too wet. A very wet heap starts to decompose without air (anaerobically) and the compost will be sludgy, slimy and smelly, and may harbour nasty pathogens.

BROWNS: *From the home*
- Pet bedding e.g. straw, shredded paper, wood shavings
- Shredded cardboard and paper
- Hair, pet fur and nail clippings
- Crushed eggshells
- Untreated firewood ash

- Non-synthetic fabric (e.g. wool, linen, cotton) – ideally shredded for speedier decomposition

BROWNS: *From the garden*
- Wood chips
- Dry leaves
- Straw
- Small logs or branches can be included in a compost heap; their purpose is to encourage diversity of microbial life in the heap, but they will take a very long time to break down

GREENS: *From the home*
- Kitchen scraps of chopped raw fruit and vegetables, their peel and rinds. Citrus can be included but takes longer to decompose
- Coffee grinds, tea bags (if plastic-free) and loose tea leaves
- Houseplant prunings
- Pet rabbit, bird and other herbivore droppings
- Urine – and if you're brave and have the correct facilities to store and suitably decompose it, faeces! (Book recommendation: The Human Manure Handbook by Joseph Jenkins)
- Bokashi-fermented material

GREENS: *From the garden*
- Garden waste: trimmings, prunings and lawn cuttings
- Weeds: green parts and roots. Note: only include weeds if you are certain you will be able to smother and kill them under layers of other matter, or if you're sure the compost heap will get hot enough to kill them (see troubleshooting section below)
- Manure from rabbits, poultry and other herbivores

WHAT NOT TO INCLUDE ON YOUR COMPOST HEAP
- Raw or cooked meat and dairy products, and other cooked foods as they will smell and attract vermin
- Seeds or roots of aggressive weeds (unless your heap will get hot)
- Plastic, metal or glass
- Fats and oils

GETTING STARTED

Choose a shady corner of the garden. Allow a space of 1.5 m wide by 1.5 m long, minimum.

You will need a compost bin with an open bottom, or, if you prefer to create an open compost pile, a large piece of old natural-fibre carpeting, a rug, some thick cardboard, tarpaulin, or a sheet of wood to cover the pile.

You will also need a container to collect kitchen waste in.

METHOD

- Loosen the soil on your chosen site with a fork. Work towards yourself so you don't stand on the loosened earth – insert the fork into the soil, give it a wiggle, pull out and repeat. (If you are building a compost bay from scratch, do so before loosening the soil.)
- Place compost bin on the loosened earth.
- Spread an initial layer of browns, ideally twigs or straw, on the soil

SLOW COMPOST

- Add organic matter to your compost heap as it becomes available, ensuring you include the right ratio of roughly 2 green to 1 brown.
- Make sure to replace the lid or cover the heap each time you add to it.
- Occasionally turn or water the heap. If you have a compost bin it can be more awkward, but it is possible to do so by getting a garden fork in the bin and jiggling it around. If it is too difficult, turning can be forgone but the compost will take longer to breakdown and you will have to be vigilant that it does not become anaerobic.
- The compost may take up to a year before it's ready to use in the garden.

FAST COMPOST
Benefits
- Faster decomposition, producing compost in as little as a month and a half
- Kills pathogens
- Kills weed roots and some seeds

This accelerated option requires enough readily available green and brown material to fill your compost bay. You'll need a heap at least 1.5 m wide x 1.5 m high. Any smaller, and it will not get as hot. Products can be purchased, such as insulated and ventilated compost bins, to assist in hot composting in smaller spaces.

— Fill your compost container/bay. Layer green material on top of brown until the compost space is filled, following the 2:1 ration.
— Cover and turn the heap once or even twice a week.

NOTE:
If the temperature of your heap is dropping, turn the heap to incorporate more air or add more nitrogen in the form of greens or urine.

TROUBLESHOOTING
Moisture
Take a good look at the compost – you are aiming for a moist, deep brown colour.
- If the heap looks too pale and dry, your compost may not be rotting down.
- If it is dark black or green, it could be too wet and has moved into anaerobic decomposition.
- Take a handful and squeeze: you should not be able to squeeze out more than a couple of drops of water.

If the compost is too wet
- Add more browns and give the compost a turn to aerate it.

If the compost is too dry
- Add more greens to the heap and give the compost a good watering – give it a kickstart with your urine, if you like.

Managing the moisture levels
- Stick to a good greens to browns ratio. It can be helpful to store up a pile of browns beside your compost heap so you can add as much as you need in relation to the greens as they become available.
- Keep your compost heap covered. Exposure to rain causes waterlogging, and the sun and wind will dry it out.

TEMPERATURE

Ideally, aim to keep your compost heap at or above approx. 30°C – the temperature of a warm bath. If the temperature is lower, that's OK: the decomposition process will just happen more slowly. You can purchase a compost thermometer, or simply use your hand to judge the temperature yourself: the centre of the heap will be hottest. The microbes in your compost will be most active when the heap is warm.

At temperatures above 45°C, the compost will decompose more quickly, but the greater heat may kill or incapacitate many beneficial microorganisms and invertebrates, leading to a decline in microbial diversity.

COMPOST USES

- Once a year, spread on growing areas that require fertility, to condition and feed the soil.
- Incorporate into potting mixes.
- Sprinkle around crops as a soil and plant feed.
- Make a seed compost by sieving and mixing with sand or grit.

BOKASHI

Bokashi anaerobic fermentation is an ancient Asian method of pre-digesting, or pickling, organic matter before adding it to your compost heap, or burying it directly in the soil, to further decompose, it could also be given to a local community garden.

In our kitchen we have two bokashi buckets: one always filling and one fermenting. Any cooked food scraps that the chickens can't eat are packed tightly into a bucket and sprinkled with a layer of inoculated bokashi bran, holding the perfect combination of bacteria and yeast to begin to decompose the material through fermentation. This process takes about two weeks.

The pre-digested matter then becomes a delicacy for the inhabitants of my compost heap. When I turn bokashi-fermented matter into it, the compost can quickly become warm, or even hot. It takes about a month for the fermented matter to then decompose fully into compost.

YOU WILL NEED:
- A bokashi composting kit, including two airtight bins with taps and the inoculated bran. (You can make your own airtight bins with taps and follow a recipe to make the bran too – I have never done this but understand the process takes about two weeks.)
- Space to store your bins in a mild, stable temperature.

WHAT CAN I BOKASHI?
- Cooked food leftovers, e.g. bread, pasta, cake
- Meat
- Ground or broken bones
- Dairy foods
- Fresh or cooked fruit and veg
- Loose tea, plastic-free tea bags, coffee grounds
- Green garden waste
- Houseplant prunings
- Eggshells

WHAT NOT TO PUT IN YOUR BOKASHI BIN
- Mouldy or rotten foods
- Liquids, gravies, oil
- Paper, card, metal or plastic

STARTING THE BOKASHI PROCESS
Stage 1
- Sprinkle some bran at the bottom of the bin.
- Save up your 'waste' each day, storing it in an airtight container. Make sure to chop or break waste into small pieces.
- Pour your waste into the bokashi bin at the end of the day.
- Sprinkle with some more bran (roughly 1 tbs bran for each cup of waste).
- Firm down to ensure there are no air pockets.
- Replace container lid tightly.
- Drain the run-off liquid using the tap every few days.

Stage 2
- Once your first bokashi bin is full, seal the lid and store the bin out of the way.
- Leave the bin undisturbed to ferment for two weeks.
- Continue to drain the liquid every few days.
- While your first bin is fermenting, start to fill your second bin. This begins a cycle, with one fermenting and one filling at all times.

USES FOR BOKASHI FERMENT
- After two weeks, you can bury your finished fermentation in your compost heap as an activator and leave to quickly rot down into rich compost.
- Alternatively, bury the bokashi ferment directly in the garden: when it decomposes it becomes a soil conditioner and plant feed. Dig a trench at least 30 cm deep and pour in your bokashi waste. Cover over the trench and leave to rot down for two weeks. Plants grown into your trench will benefit from the enriched soil.

- The liquid by-product can be used as a plant or compost feed.

TROUBLESHOOTING
- A white fuzz may develop in your bokashi bin. That's OK! It's just the bacteria, yeast and fungi from the bran, living their lives.
- If your bucket starts to smell foul, throw the waste away, wash your bucket and try again. You may not be using enough bran. The fermentation should smell like sweet/sour yeasty vinegar. It shouldn't turn your stomach!

WORM FARM/VERMICULTURE

Ideal if you don't have a lot of space, or no outdoor space at all, the worm farm is a container which houses specialist composting worms – known variously as brandling worms, red wigglers, manure worms, red worms or tiger worms – which thrive in and feast on decaying organic matter. (These are not the common earthworms we find living in the soil; they like to burrow deep into the earth, and if relocated into a worm farm, will likely die.)

200 g compost worms can munch through 50–100 g waste matter a day. Figure out how much waste you produce and get hold of the appropriate number of worms.

The worm poop, 'vermicompost', is harvested every three months. It is teaming with microorganisms and micronutrients and can be used around the garden, much like compost. The wormery also naturally produces liquid plant feed every few days.

YOU WILL NEED:
- A container with one drainage point, such as a disused sink, bathtub or bucket with a hole drilled into it. Alternatively, you can purchase a ready-made worm-farm kit.

- A piece of metal gauze to cover the drainage hole, and a stone or brick to hold the gauze in place.
- A plank of wood or natural-fibre carpet to act as a lid.
- Bedding for the worms. This could be well-rotted manure, straw, hay, shredded paper or card.
- Composting worms. You can buy the worms on the internet, and they come in the post. Or someone you know may have a worm farm with some worms going spare.

WHAT TO FEED COMPOSTING WORMS
- Raw fruit and vegetable kitchen scraps
- Clippings from pot plants
- Garden matter, including soft prunings, lawn trimmings and weeds
- Crushed eggshells
- Coffee grounds (in small amounts) and loose tea
- Shredded paper and card

WHAT NOT TO FEED THE WORMS
- Citrus
- Onions, shallots, leeks or garlic
- Large pieces of tough woody material e.g. branches
- Cooked food
- Meat, dairy or fats. Avoid leftover salad unless you wash the dressing off first

HOW MUCH SHOULD I FEED MY WORMS?
- If the conditions are right, the worms can eat roughly half their body weight each day. If the weather is cold or hot, they may slow down.
- Feed your worms every couple of days, rather than daily, to give them time to work through the organic matter and to get a sense of how hungry they are. Overfeeding can lead to a sloppy build-up of smelly, anaerobically decaying organic matter.

HOW TO:
- If you have bought a worm farm, follow the instructions. If you are DIYing your worm farm, first cover the drainage hole in your chosen receptacle with the gauze and place a stone or brick on top.
- Using some old logs or bricks, raise the compost farm at an angle so that the drainage hole is at the lowest point. This will ensure gravity draws the liquids – 'worm tea' – down and out of the container so your worms don't get flooded.
- Place a receptacle under the drainage hole to collect the 'worm tea' that runs off.
- Spread a layer of bedding on the base of your worm home, then cover with an initial layer of organic matter for the worms to feed on.
- Place the worms in their new home, add a good splash of water and cover the container.
- Feed the worms every few days, and wait until you can see they have made a dent in it before adding more waste matter. They will eat more when they are at a comfortable temperature.
- Keep an eye on your new wormy helpers: make sure their home doesn't get too dry, too wet, too hot or too cold.
- Every few days, drain off the worm tea that gathers.
- After three months, the vermicompost can be harvested and you may be able to give some worms away.

WORM TEA
Harvest and use your worm tea as often as possible – an amazing plant feed, it's best used fresh. Like vermicompost, it contains lots of nutrients, minerals and microorganisms that will support soil life and the vitality of your plants. You can use worm tea neat or diluted up to 1 part worm tea to 3 parts water.

Water it directly to the root zone of plants, or spray onto leaves as a foliar feed (plants absorb nutrients through their leaves too).

HOW TO HARVEST YOUR COMPOST:
Simply dig into your worm farm with your hands or a trowel. Remove the dark worm castings, fish out any worms and put them back in their home.

Alternatively, wait until the worms have munched through all their food and bedding. On a sunny day, empty the whole bin out onto a tarpaulin and create a few mounds. The worms hate sunlight so will retreat into the centre from the edges. Harvest the worm-free compost from the edges and repeat until you are left with only a little pile of compost, housing lots of worms. Return them to their home, feed and give them a good watering.

Another option (again once the worms have eaten all their food and bedding) is to make some small holes in an old bag, fill it with fresh bedding and organic matter, then bury the bag in the worm farm. From between a few days to a couple weeks, most of the worms will have migrated into the bag to munch on the new food supply. Remove the bag, harvest your worm castings, then return the worms to their home with some fresh bedding. Give them a good feed and water them.

USES
- Spread vermicompost on growing areas to return fertility and condition the soil
- Incorporate into potting mixes
- Sprinkle or bury vermicompost around crops as a soil and plant feed

TROUBLESHOOTING
Moisture
The worms' living environment should look and feel moist to the touch, but there should also be no puddles of water.

If it is too wet
Make sure the drainage is working and add more shredded paper.

Organic matter is full of moisture, ease up on your feedings and wait for the worms to munch through their last feed before giving them more.

If it is too dry
Give the worms a good sprinkling of water and include more moist vegetables (e.g. cucumber peel, celery bums, leaves) to their feed.

SHORT DAYS, PATIENCE AND THE DARK MAGIC OF GARLIC

These last few weeks it's been cool and bright. The days are shorter now, that autumn is really here. Work at the community garden is now cut short by the sun slipping down to bed before we are tired. 'It's time to go home,' he says.

In the summer months we never saw the sun set over this land... or maybe we did, once or twice, when we had our dinners outside, but I don't remember the colours in the sky, just the food. The long days would warp out ahead of me. In the rhythm of chatter and work, time would stumble, both slipping away and standing still. In my mind, an hour would have passed, when in reality it was three, and I'd force myself home, feeling suddenly exhausted only once stepping foot through my door.

I remember cycling back one evening, my hot skin covered in gooseflesh as I flew under the blue dusk sky; warm on the inside from a sweaty day in the sun's gaze, cooled on the outside as the night air traced her cold fingers over my bare arms and legs. I think I heard a blackbird chirping in the roadside hedge. Sitting here now as I write, bundled up on the sofa with tea, wearing two layers of moth-eaten cashmere jumpers, heavy tracksuit bottoms, socks, slippers, a woollen blanket and our dog (aka the living hot-water bottle) on my lap, throwing my mind back is giving me goosebumps.

These last couple of weeks at the community garden, when the sun reminded us to go home, we obeyed. Without a source of artificial light, and with the little warmth dwindling, we'd gather up the food we'd grown in a hurry. Today we cleared the faded cut-flower bed and planted cloves of elephant garlic. We are transitioning the beds to a minimum till, or an 'as little dig as possible' system, in order to do best by the soil. So, we chopped down the flowers, pulled out the weeds, covered the bed with cardboard, then watered it down and sliced holes in it to plant the garlic through.

Since our compost isn't ready yet, we dress the newly cardboard-covered bed with clippings from the neighbouring meadow. It's a bit of an experiment, and besides, I love to think of all that diverse organic matter now feeding the soil not so far from where it grew. I don't think I'd dare try it with any new planting other than alliums, though. Slugs and snails simply love piles of this sort of moist matter, but alliums are less bothered by gastropods than many other plants.

Planting garlic is possibly one of my favourite jobs. I love garlic for its warm, sharp, sweetness, its seemingly infinite list of healing abilities, *and* because it can weather our winters. To me, it is a symbol of endurance. As I plant in autumn, I'm reaching into the future, dreaming of a hot dry June a whole seven months away when I'll be pulling plump new garlic bulbs back up again.

The cold dark soil of winter is essential for the garlic to form its cloves – without it, they simply remain as one slow-growing solid lump. The cold alchemises them into delicious segments of edible medicine, which in turn protects us from the coughs and sneezes that lurk in the long dark winter days.

There are two main types of garlic: hardneck and softneck. Hardneck garlic varieties which, generally, are best for colder climates, produce a 'scape' or flowering stem that grows up from the basal plate (the rooty bit at the flat end of a bulb of garlic), forming a sort of central pillar to the garlic bulb and making the neck (the pointy bit on top where the skin gathers) hard. These scapes are just one of the benefits of hardneck varieties, as you can harvest and eat them while the flower is in bud, a tasty appetiser while waiting to unearth the fat bulbs. Hardneck varieties also tend to have larger cloves and a stronger flavour, but don't store as long as softneck.

Softneck varieties don't tend to send up scapes, although they may do when stressed. They produce smaller cloves with a good storage life: autumn plantings harvested in summer can easily keep until the following winter. Softneck garlic is best suited to hotter climates, and with their malleable necks these are the varieties that you tend to find plaited into garlic braids. Despite growing in Devon, a place not famed for its heat, we will be filling another bed with this variety because we want to braid garlic in the sun.

My favourite type of garlic, however, is the variety we have just planted: elephant garlic.

Elephant garlic offers up those sweet scapes while also producing massive bulbs, some the size of my hand, split into giant cloves that are more than big enough for any meal (with smaller varieties I end up using half the bulb for most recipes).

Despite its name, appearance and flavour, elephant garlic is actually a closer relation of the leek than of garlic. It's Latin name *Allium ampeloprasum var ampeloprasum* ties it to its ancestor, the wild leek, *Allium ampeloprasum*, native to South-east Europe and Western Asia. True garlic, *Allium sativum*, on the other hand, has an uncertain ancestry, possibly originating in Central Asia, South-east Asia or the Middle East.

They say garlic wants to be planted in soil that will drain well, but here in the Devon community garden, we have just planted a whole bedful in heavy clay that drains fairly poorly and expect it to do just fine. As with all growing, it pays not to be too cautious of the rules, just try it and see. With garlic, so long as you're not planting into a bog, it will probably grow. What is for certain, though, is that garlic wants plenty of sunshine. Garlic can be planted through the autumn months, and even into December. They say some varieties can be planted in spring too, although I have never tried.

HOW TO PLANT GARLIC

Prepare a bed for your garlic (see page 43, 'How to Prepare a No-Dig Bed').

Break up the bulb and plant the cloves individually. Hard- and softneck varieties ought to be planted about 10–15 cm apart and about as deep as the bulb is tall, with the flat end at the bottom and the pointy bit at the top. The same goes for elephant garlic, though they want to be about 20–30 cm apart.

Once your bulbs are planted, there's really not much to do but weed regularly to ensure good airflow, plenty of light and reduced competition. Avoid hoeing too deep close to the plants as that can damage the bulbs.

Garlic is often recommended as a great companion plant due to its strong scent which can confuse pesky insects. If not harvested, it produces beautiful flowers loved by pollinators. It can be nice to intercrop garlic with lettuce or even strawberries, creating an additional harvest and also providing some root diversity and ground cover.

Elephant garlic can be treated as a perennial. Left in the ground, it will continue to multiply and bulbs can be pulled as needed. When harvesting, the little bulbils that are found on the outside of the main bulb can be replanted. In one year, they will become a single clove. In the second year, they form a bulb, making this variety ideal for a low maintenance but productive garden.

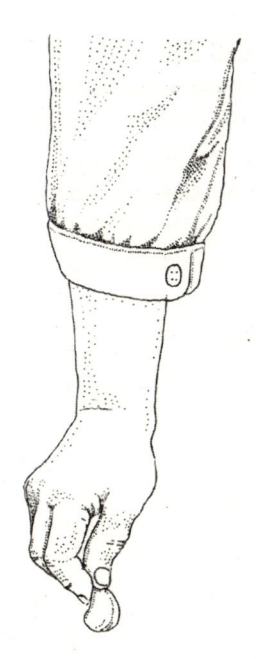

ROSE HIPS

After leaving South Africa, my brother, sister, Mum and I eventually settled in that small mouldy bungalow in a quaint village in Wiltshire; my siblings and I called the village 'the land of the thatched houses'. We'd driven through it a few times while staying with Grandma With The Nice Garden, and after years living in a city full of large modern buildings and dramatic tropical vegetation, the sight of all the cottages with their neat flowering gardens was somehow comical; they looked so pretty and small, like dolls' houses.

The village felt strange and quiet. On our walks home from adventures my siblings and I would often stop off at one particular old lady's bungalow. Along her low garden wall grew a gang of frilly rose bushes (*Rosa rugosa*). In the summertime, bright pink ruffled blooms sat snuggly amongst their greenery, and in the autumn, the bushes sported glossy red rose hips, the size of a £2 coin, plump and squishy with plenty of flesh surrounding the centre of hairy seeds. I have no idea how we first figured this out but those *Rosa rugosa* hips were delicious – tangy but sweet and tropical, a bit like pawpaw. We'd gently squeeze them until their sweet insides were forced out of the little hole in their skin where their stem once had been, then we'd lick the paste with our tongues or wipe it onto our fingers to deposit in our mouths. You had to be careful not to squeeze too hard or their nasty itchy seeds would pop out along with the flesh and that made for unpleasant eating. I think we enjoyed the element of danger. The wild dog rose hips in the hedgerows are small and hard and mainly full of itchy hairy seeds – not so good for fresh eating – I don't recall us ever even trying.

We used to squat below her low wall, one of us with our head sticking out to the side making sure no one was watching. The other two would bob up and down, reaching over the little brick wall to grab handfuls of hips, then we'd duck down again, out of sight, to munch on our hoard of sweeties. If the old lady spotted us, she never shooed us away or told us off. As we got to know the village better, we felt less at ease with the thought of a passerby catching us thieving, so we changed tactics. As we approached her garden we'd slow down then pluck as many little red nuggets as we could. We thought we were being subtle and stealthy.

Along with the crash course in how to conduct petty organised crime, eating those rose hips confirmed to us that we could interact with the living world around us, that we were part of it. In a strange way, arriving in this unfamiliar country – and even less familiar English village – where everyone apart from us seemed to have known one another for all eternity, our exchanges with those rose bushes became a significant relationship. Despite the wall, they welcomed us to this new place with sweets; they didn't care that we looked, sounded and behaved differently than everyone else.

Years later, those same roses were one of the first plants I added to my garden as little bare root whips in winter. I now love these roses, not just because they hold fond memories of my brother and sister, or for their generosity many years ago, but because they have now taken on new meaning as characters in this garden I am managing in a way that welcomes life in. I chose my old friend, *Rosa rugosa*, because she is beautiful, because, unlike many other roses, her blooms sit open as saucers, petals arranged invitingly around her pollen and nectar sources so that insects can find them. I chose her because her flowers and fruits are edible and because she is a perennial. Another very similar-looking rose, *Rosa gallica officinalis*, or the apothecary rose, was grown as a herb in gardens in England as far back as medieval times.

The planting in this garden is inspired by the beautiful utility of the cottage gardens of England, but it is also inspired by the ancient 'forest gardens' of the world. In such spaces people tend the wild plants around them alongside plantings of more useful plants that feed and support humans. In the Amazon rainforest, for example, some 4,500 years ago, parts of the forest would be cleared of trees with the help of low-level, controlled fires and then tended as a forest garden with edible domesticated crops like corn, maize and squash and medicinal plants given special care. Wild edible perennial species would be encouraged as natural succession followed, gradually allowing it to return to forest. The process would then begin again elsewhere.

This style of cultivation builds rather than depletes the soil and hosts vast biodiversity. Biodiversity is the *variety* of plant and animal life in the world or in a particular habitat, a high level of which is generally considered to be important for the health and resilience of the ecosystem. An ecosystem is a community of interacting organisms and their physical environment. A forest garden ecosystem would include the forest and all the biodiversity it supports.

As well as plant species that can be beneficial for humans, these sites often feature terre preta, Amazonian dark earth, soil so rich in organic matter and nutrients that it is visibly darker than the reddish, infertile earth of the surrounding rainforest. This soil was co-created over time as ash, charcoal, food scraps and gardening waste were allowed to decay. The people who continue to cultivate this soil today call it *eegepe*.

In forest gardens, plants are specially selected to support the gardener and their ecosystem; they may be edible, medicinal, useful for fibre, dye or fuel, or structure; some plants may be grown simply to produce biomass for composting and feeding the soil. To an untrained eye a forest garden may look wild and untended, as the plantings and maintenance so closely follow in the steps of an uncultivated landscape.

A forest garden, like a woodland, is filled with a diverse range of mainly perennial plants, all muddled together and growing in layers, filling every available niche in the space. The earth may hold roots and rhizomes, just above, the soil may be draped with a protective layer of ground cover plants. The gardener may cultivate a herbaceous layer of slightly larger plants, often herbs such as lemon balm, mint or more unusual edible perennials like ostrich fern (*Matteuccia struthiopteris*) or Solomon's seal (*Polygonatumn*). A shrubby layer may include plants like my *Rosa rugosa*. This layer is followed by small trees and large shrubs, like the small apple trees and sea buckthorn (*Hippophae rhamnoides*) that grow in my garden. Above them could sprawl the canopies of tall trees, perhaps sweet chestnuts, larger apples, mulberries, plums or pears. Finally, various vine plants twist and turn their way through the edible garden, perhaps grapes, kiwis or honeysuckle for beauty, wildlife, flavour and scent. Not all forest gardens contain all seven of these layers, but a uniting feature is the optimisation of space through growing plants like layers on a cake.

Plants are arranged to maximise mutual benefits, promoting positive interactions and minimising negative ones. Sun-loving herbs should be grown well away from the shade cast by shrubs and trees, vines may be supported by the structures of fruit trees, with fertility-building plants like comfrey grown at their base. The great diversity underpins the garden's health and resilience.

Collections of plants that accumulate nutrients and fix nitrogen in the soil, as well as ensuring that it is covered by living or dead organic matter at all times, allow the plants themselves to largely maintain the garden's ongoing fertility. Nutrient-accumulating plants draw up large quantities of minerals and other nourishment from deep in the soil, which they then store in their leaves, making them a wonderful addition to homemade fermented plant teas, compost and for use as a mulch. Through a relationship with bacteria in the soil, nitrogen-fixing plants can provide a source of nitrogen, which is essential for plant growth (more on this in 'Biodiversity' come Spring). The soil is tended by keeping it covered and largely undisturbed, just like a woodland floor. Some forest gardens may also be home to ducks, chickens, rabbits or other animals who help to manage weeds or pests and add fertility with their urine and droppings. Some, like my own, include open sunny spaces to grow useful annual vegetables, flowers and herbs, surrounded by perennial plantings.

Observing the living world, we see natural ecological succession, ecosystems shifting and developing over time. Imagine an area of bare ground or waste land: rain comes and seeds begin to germinate. At this stage, only the 'pioneer species' will survive. These annual plants (plants that live for one year), often regarded as weeds, tend to be opportunist. They can handle harsh living conditions and take advantage of this, growing very quickly to cloak the exposed soil, harvesting the sunlight, taking up as much nutrition as they can and then throwing out seed as quickly as possible before they are pushed out by other growth. These first fast-growers create more hospitable conditions for other plants to follow. Their roots hold the soil in place and also enliven microbial life, while the plants themselves act as a living mulch, sheltering the soil from harsh weather and providing a humid microclimate at the soil surface, reducing water loss through evaporation. When the pioneer plants die back, they break down and feed the soil. In the now-improved habitat, the vegetation advances, becomes more diverse, and as layers of growth emerge, some of the faster growing lower levels may eventually be shaded out by slower growing trees and shrubs. This is a simplified visualisation of plant succession.

In the UK, if a landscape is left to its own devices without the intervention of large animals like humans, cows or deer, it will gradually grow into a woodland. In most gardens, we humans are the largest mammals, interrupting this succession and stimulating the growth of all sorts of other ecosystems and habitats besides woodland. On a larger scale, at the 35,000-acre rewilding project on the Knepp Estate in the south-east of England, they call on small herds of herbivores to engage with the landscape and create a diverse range of habitats from scrubland to seasonal ponds.

In annual 'pioneer' plants, germination is often triggered by soil disturbance or even fire. Their short lives mean they tend to have shallow root systems, making them less drought-tolerant and sometimes unable to access nutrients found in deeper soil. But that suits these plants just fine – their aim is not longevity, but the fast and efficient use of available resources and space. Their ability to quickly blanket bare ground is their superpower and, in a way, their gift to the ecosystem. But when they are not allowed to deliver this gift by preparing the ground for the next wave of life, they have the potential to do the exact opposite, depleting rather than building the ecosystem.

Currently our diets and food systems are centred on annual crops like wheat, corn and rice; most of the vegetables we eat are annuals and many more are grown as animal feed. Too often growing monocultures of annual crops causes far-reaching environmental degradation. Biodiverse habitats are destroyed as vast areas of perennial systems, like our ancient rainforests, woodlands or hedgerows are cleared to give the annuals competition-free space.

In traditional horticulture and industrial agriculture this is done through repeated earth disturbance, whether digging or ploughing, causing soils to erode and become biologically inactive. In many no-dig or no-till 'regenerative' farms and gardens, soil disturbance is replaced with regular dousings of the carcinogenic herbicide glyphosate.

The ability of annual crops to quickly mop up any nutrition from the soil – originally so cleverly enabling them to grow rapidly in challenging conditions – has been bred into a greedy, grabby-ness. When monocultures of hungry annuals are planted in soil already damaged by repeated disturbance, they wolfishly take what they need; we then harvest them, but offer no organic matter back in return. And we repeat this cycle again and again.

To force this degraded soil to yield and to keep pests and disease at bay chemical inputs are called on. It is near impossible to farm industrial, large-scale monoculture without them. The promised result of synthetic fertilisers, pesticides, fungicides and herbicides is mind-boggling yields and a quick fix for problems that often indicate a lack of health in the plant or the growing space. The chemicals treat symptoms not causes, and once used a dependence develops. Depleted soil can only give a crop when drenched in fertilisers, becoming less and less able to do the job itself as the life-giving ecosystem it houses slowly dies.

The consequences are far-reaching. You can *hear* living landscapes, but when you trundle through these monocultures, they are silent, essentially dead zones for wildlife. There is an unsettling deadness in the earth itself too. Rivers and lakes are polluted by the run-off from the chemicals required to make the ravenous plants grow healthily in dysfunctional soil, and in agro-industrial settings, these sprawling monocultures have huge irrigation needs.

Industrial chemical farming has driven our biodiversity crisis. Britain is one of the most nature-depleted countries on Earth. Fields that would have fluttered with butterflies when my mum was a child now bloom silent and still. Industrial farming's widespread use of antimicrobials leads to antibiotic-resistant microbes and the chemicals it employs cause cancer. The list of ills goes on. This is so far from the balanced harmony and cascade of benefits that can arise from nature-led land work.

But in ecological succession within a healthy ecosystem, annual plants can be team players, I have witnessed it in market gardens with my own eyes and try to achieve it myself both in my home garden and on the community plot. Observing the living world around us can teach us that, by mimicking the healing conditions annual plants can provide, it is possible to grow them in a way that builds and sustains fertility and life.

Transitioning to agroforestry in all its varied forms (forest gardening is just one) is widely regarded as an important part of reforming modern, industrialised agriculture, providing a means to grow back carbon-rich soil and create valuable habitats while also feeding people. Our gardens can play their part too.

The further a garden is from a woodland, generally the more energy and input it will require to keep it that way, as the gardener is attempting to halt natural succession. Forest gardens, once established, are very stable ecosystems and so fairly low maintenance. The gardener is able to gather and graze, gently guiding the space towards utility, while also allowing it to express its own character. The wide range of crops provide the gardener with a healthily diverse, plant-rich diet.

In my veg garden, I ask myself what it is that annuals want to contribute. Simply, they want to cover and protect exposed ground, first with their living plant bodies, then when they are dead, they want to weave the soil together with their roots and to provide habitat and food, drawing in diverse life. In exchange, they require competition-free space, some moisture (much of which they provide by creating a humid microclimate at the soil surface where their roots hang out) and some nutrition, which they also contribute to, firstly by engaging with the soil biology, and secondly when they die down and their aerial parts become compost, their roots rotting into the ground. So I just let them do their thing: my task is just to keep the space clear. On a small scale, it is not always necessary to disturb the soil in order to do this. I reduce weeds and maintain fertility by keeping the soil covered with organic matter (be that compost, woodchip, a mulch of decaying organic matter or ground-cover plants), so those pioneering weed seeds are not triggered into germination and weedy perennials are smothered out. I hoe and hand weed regularly. I also cultivate less greedy heritage varieties, bred for greater resilience and less dependence on inputs. When looking to the wild for an answer to a problem, it is often pleasingly simple. On a larger scale, where no-dig may not be an option, annuals are called in as cover crops, sometimes taking up several years in a crop rotation.

Growing more perennials is another elegant solution. They have deep root systems, making them generally more drought-tolerant and able to access nutrients deep in the ground. As long-term fixtures in a landscape they are able to develop committed relationships with the soil biology and wider wildlife. Repeated soil disruption and annual plant replacement won't be required. Perennials can sequester huge quantities of carbon, both in the living plants and when they die back seasonally and decompose below and above ground. This helps to build healthy soils and to capture carbon.

Many perennial foods are incredibly nutritious. Per 100 g, the sweet rose hips I grow, for example, contain nearly five times more vitamin C than broccoli. Our bodies can't store or make our own vitamin C, so we need it in our diets every single day.

In Britain during the Second World War when citrus fruits could no longer be imported, there were fears that a home-grown winter diet would not deliver on the nation's nutritional needs. The Ministry of Health began to recommend that people, especially children, have a daily slurp of rose hip syrup, a medicine that grows wild and native to Britain. To supply enough syrup to go round, in 1941 a national hip collection week was introduced. School children, scouts and guides were encouraged to go out into the hedgerows and harvest the fruits and to deliver them to local collection points, usually organised by the Women's Institute. The foragers received a little cash for their efforts and soon Rose Hip Collectors Clubs emerged, with collectible badges to further incentivise children. Commercial syrup makers turned the bounty into the tasty liquid which was then sold cheaply in chemists all around the country. By

1943, following this initiative, 2.5 million bottles of rose hip syrup were being produced annually. It was so popular that the Rose Hip Collectors Club continued to give out badges well into the 1960s. I like to think that if the old lady in Wiltshire ever did spy us scrumping her hips on our way home from autumn adventures, she may have fondly recalled gathering rose hips herself when she was a child. Maybe that's why she never shooed us away.

Little did I know, head bobbing up over that little old lady's wall, that *Rosa rugosa* would one day become part of my own forest garden, a mixture of edible and medicinal perennials with annuals grown in cooperation with them. Those roses symbolise the practical beauty of such a garden: robust, giving and, above all, welcoming to life.

ROSE HIP SYRUP

- 1 kg rose hips
- 2 l water
- 500 g sugar

Optional: herbs and spices to flavour, e.g. ginger, clove, sage, rosemary, thyme, black pepper

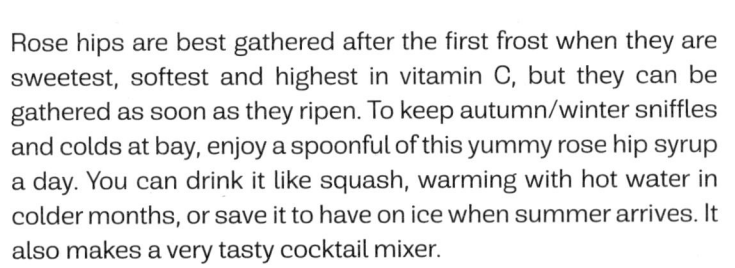

Rose hips are best gathered after the first frost when they are sweetest, softest and highest in vitamin C, but they can be gathered as soon as they ripen. To keep autumn/winter sniffles and colds at bay, enjoy a spoonful of this yummy rose hip syrup a day. You can drink it like squash, warming with hot water in colder months, or save it to have on ice when summer arrives. It also makes a very tasty cocktail mixer.

The whole syrup-making process takes about an hour and the recipe can be altered to taste – less sugar, more sugar, less hips or more hips.

— Place the rose hips in a large saucepan and cover with 1 litre water.

NOVEMBER

- Bring to the boil, turn the heat to medium and leave on a rolling boil for 20 minutes. Once the rose hips have softened, give them a good mash every now and then until they become a pulp.
- Remove from the heat and set aside to cool. Once more or less cool, drain the mushy mess into a bowl through a clean tea towel or muslin (I use an old T-shirt). You may have to put on some rubber gloves (to protect from the itchy rose hip insides which may irritate the skin) and encourage the last drops of rose hip juice through by squeezing.
- Return the leftover pulp to the saucepan and add another litre of water.
- Repeat stages two and three. You'll be left with lots of rust-coloured, rose hip-flavoured water. (And a T-shirt full of mushy pulp. Discard the pulp on the compost; put the T-shirt through the wash ready for next time.)
- Return the rose hip water to the saucepan, bring back to the boil and add the sugar. Give it a good stir and let it simmer until all the sugar has dissolved.
- Optional: At this stage, I add some herbs and spices to the syrup for flavour and medicinal value. I find ginger and rose hip flavours work wonderfully together. Suggested flavour combos are: ginger; ginger and clove; sage, ginger and clove; ginger, clove and rosemary; ginger and thyme; black pepper.
- I bundle these additional herbs and spices in a little square of cloth, secured with string to make a great big tea bag. Leave to steep in the hot syrup for 15–30 minutes, or longer if you like, tasting as you go and removing when you see fit.
- Meanwhile, sterilise the glass jars to store the syrup in. Put some water on to boil in a large saucepan and pop the jars (and their lids) into the water, open end down. The steam will rise up into the bottles, killing bacteria. Leave them this way until they're far too hot to touch.
- Remove the jars from their steam bath using oven mitts or dishcloths. Take care as they will be HOT.

- Pour the syrup into the jars – a metal funnel comes in handy here – and seal straight away. Leave to cool.
- Unopened, the syrup can be stored in a cupboard. Once opened, store in the fridge. The syrup can also be frozen as ice cubes or ice lollies.

ONE-POT FOOD FOREST

This recipe for a miniature food forest is inspired by the edible plant pots I grew while living on a canal boat in London. It's beautiful and practical in a small space and will help you to get to grips with the concept and efficiency of growing in a food-forest style.

All the seeds are sown at the same time and allowed to grow through the succession that will naturally arise. To create the layers, I have selected 'ground cover' and 'canopy' crops, and included a selection of each to contribute to diversity. You can also explore companion planting and include some species that will entice pollinators or deter pests (see Companion Planting Tips, page 261). The plants also need to have different maturity and harvest dates so that the planter will evolve over time, offering a constant yield once it gets going.

For the 'canopy' layer, I suggest broad beans, peas and mangetout. These plants will eventually grow to 3–4 foot tall, shading out the 'understorey' of leafy veg. While initially offering a harvest of leaves, they will eventually yield beans (harvested 14–32 weeks from planting) and peas (harvested 12–14 weeks from planting).

For the 'ground cover' level, you want a crop that will grow quickly to cover up the soil and act as a pioneer species, a placenta for the later crop, as well as giving a fast yield. I suggest rocket (6–8 weeks to harvest), loose leaf lettuce (8–10 weeks to harvest) and Asian salad seed mix (4 weeks to harvest).

You will need
- One large and deep pot – the bigger the better really!
- Compost

NOVEMBER

🌱 Seeds: broad beans, peas, mange-tout, rocket, loose leaf lettuce, Asian salad mix.

Method
— Fill your container with compost.
— Put in place supports for your peas, ideally some foraged branches with little twigs for the tendrils to grab on to. Hazel is traditional, but any suitable branches you find on a walk will do.
— Sow your seeds in early spring – March is a good time.
— Water and wait for your one-pot mini-food-forest to grow. Enjoy!

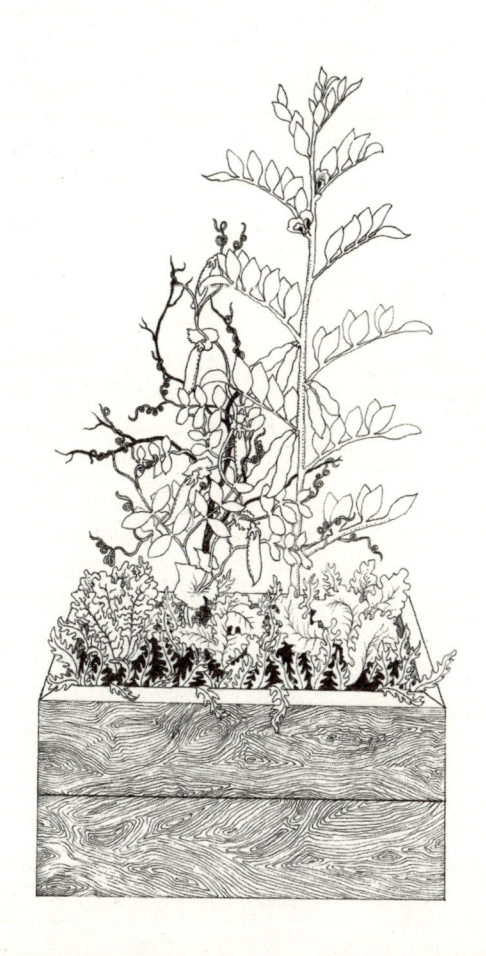

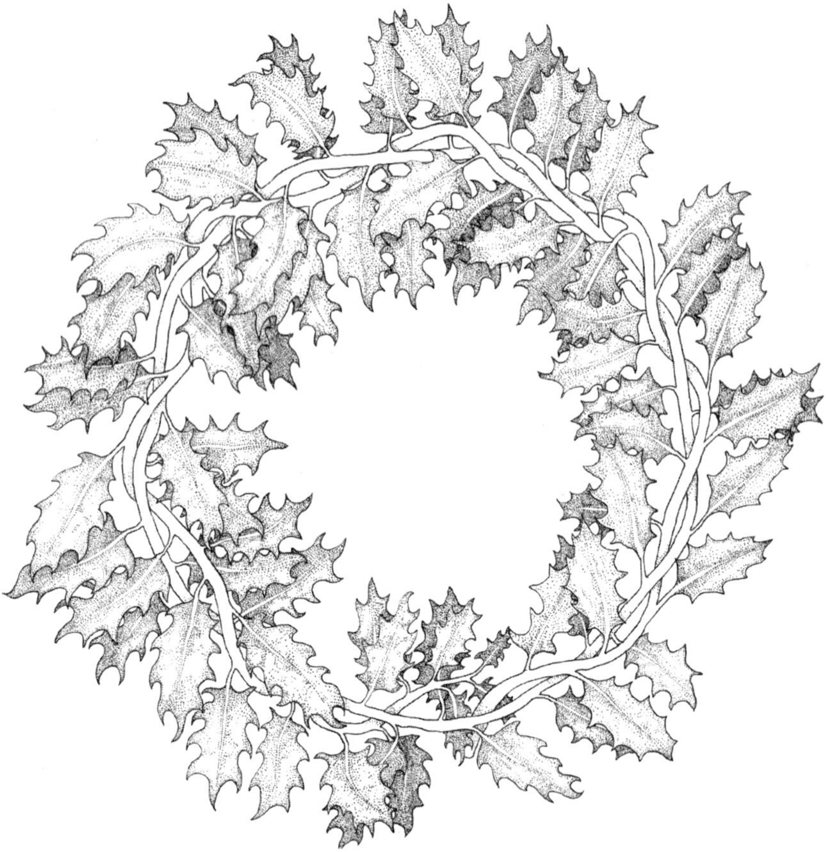

Winter

December

HIBERNATING INSECTS

As usual, I'm late to plant the spring bulbs – daffodils, tulips, grape hyacinth, snake's head fritillary and crocuses. Unusually, this year, I ordered them well in advance and the box thudded onto my doorstep in the middle of October. I left it in the porch to plant the bulbs out over the weekend. Now, two months later, they are finally in the soil.

I have stowed away many of the bulbs in the first section of the garden, the perennial patch dedicated to edibles, herbs, beautiful but poisonous plants, and plants that are edible but which nowadays you just wouldn't bother eating, like tulips. (In the Netherlands in the mid-1940s, tulip bulbs became a famine food, eaten out of desperation rather than delight. In my garden, I only eat my tulips with my eyes.)

Last summer, this patch of earth, now full of bulbs, was a swaying forest of herbaceous plants – the emerald green, feathery-leafed fennel (*Foeniculum vulgare*); proud goldenrod (*Solidago*), with its long lean leaves and towering stems that explode into cascades of fluffy, deep-yellow blooms. Like shooting stars, soft, silent fireworks, or, as their common name suggests, rods spraying out fountains of liquid gold. Wild marjoram (*Origanum vulgare*) which grows low, with small silvery rounded leaves forming mounds that rise up into constellations of delicate lilac flowers. Lemon balm (*Melissa officinalis*), a pale green stinging nettle lookalike that forms a lightly scented clump of leaves, covered in nursery web spiders in spring. Velvet-leaved marshmallow plants (*Althaea officinalis*) reach up tall, scattered with pale pink cups for blooms; and pineapple sage (*Salvia elegans*), with its vivid scarlet flowers that provide brushstrokes of vibrant colour against all the green. Much of this jungle towered well above my 5-foot 9-inch frame.

I don't clear this luscious part of the garden in the autumn; I simply leave the herbaceous plants to hang around (they offer wildlife and the soil protection from winter). Now a skeleton army of slender, brittle stems has taken their place. First their decadent flowers morphed into subtle seeds, then they cast off their greenery, only for their seeds to be stripped away too, blown on the wind or eaten by me and the birds. As the plants draw their sugars down and into their roots to overwinter, their stems dry out and turn to muted sepia.

I often stare out of our living room window, distracted by the crunchy, unruly texture of this long narrow swathe of bleached stems. To begin with I think it's beautiful; in autumn the fuzzy little seed heads of goldenrod are whimsical, they float on the breeze like fairies and hitchhike on my jumpers and in my hair as I move through the garden. I like that. When the garden is all over me, I feel part of it. Gangs of birds drift down to flit through the scraggly forest. They pause just for a moment, clawed feet firmly grasping the vertical canes, to pick at a seed or an insect and then twitch off again, perhaps onto another stalk, into one of the shrubs or back up over the wall and into the neighbour's garden. When the frost arrives, it dusts the brittle limbs in crisp, white crystals. It's all very romantic.

My sister comes to visit from London. We wrap up in scarves and wander over the little bridge into the garden to join the birds amongst the stems. We each carry a glass jar: Rosie fills hers with fennel seeds; I fill mine with snails. This garden is heaving with them, and I've noticed that the babies have a habit of sneaking right to the top of the fennel plants to hide in the nooks where the leaves meet the stems. So, each winter I go out and search through them, removing any specimens that look too big for the birds to handle, but which the chickens will devour.

The fennel seeds my sister gathers are small, like narrow grains of brown rice. In early winter, the seeds are a faint dusty green-grey, clustered at the top of the delicate stems that fan out from the end of the stalk. My sister's fingers roll and pull the seeds so they scatter into her glass, releasing their cool, airy scent. Satisfied with her work, she quickly challenges herself to fill the whole 500 ml jar. The light is falling, our fingers move faster, mine plucking baby snails, hers twisting and pulling at the fennel. Our jars full, we take my slimy offerings over to the chickens. They are delighted. Rosie less so.

The damp fennel seeds come inside to sit on the dehydrator on a low heat overnight. As winter draws in, they will be used to flavour roast potatoes, curries, teas, salad dressings, pasta sauces, cake icing, cocktails and so much more. When I pound them in the pestle and mortar, their smell rises in waves of summer sunshine and memories of that crisp evening outside with my sister.

As winter drags, all those brittle stems begin to look a bit beaten down, like a loose messy bird's nest, the fennel stems slanting at odd angles, blown over by the wind, and the tips of the goldenrod all snapped off. When visitors come, I find myself making excuses for this weird patch of loose ends. 'It's great habitat!' I hear myself say. 'You should see it in summer!' 'I'm gardening ecologically.' At this point, I have to hold my nerve... I am desperate to rid myself of this awkward lot. But I let it be, avert my gaze and try to see the chaos for what it really is – an ark. This disordered patch feeds the birds with its seeds, helps to protect the soil from eroding when it rains, and supplies winter homes for all sorts of creatures – and their eggs.

The first winter in our new home, I was delighted to find several ladybirds hibernating in the dead stems of evening primroses. Adult ladybirds and their larvae are very welcome here; I actively encourage them because they have a voracious appetite for aphids, tiny little vampire insects which drink the sap of plants. An aphid infestation weakens crops, reducing their productivity and vigour, and sometimes introducing disease. Ladybird larvae will eat upwards of fifty aphids a day!

Aphids also excrete honeydew, a sweet sticky liquid whose presence on leaves can lead to fungal diseases. Honeydew is simply delectable to ants. Some ants, called 'dairy ants', love it so much that they begin to 'farm' aphids, tending their herd with dedication, defending them from predators and picking them up and moving them around to safe locations to ensure efficient honey dew production. They sometimes even tickle the aphids to encourage them to excrete more honeydew.

The honeydew also attracts wasps, as we discovered when we moored our canal boat under three ancient crack willow trees in London. Each summer, their fresh green growth would become caked in aphids, who rained sticky honeydew on our boat and drew in armies of boisterous honeydew-drunk wasps. From the other side of the canal, I always thought what a strange little floating island it looked, buzzing with wasps and shiny with honeydew.

Often an abundance of one pest or disease is caused by a dysfunctional food chain. Without the correct predators, pests are able to multiply and thrive, hopping from one tasty plant to another. Cultivating diversity allows life to fall into a self-regulating balance. A balance that I find mesmerising. The purpose of this scruffy patch is what makes it beautiful. Its deadness supporting life.

After spotting those ladybirds sleeping snugly in the dead evening primrose stems, I began going out regularly to check on them. The chickens hadn't joined me in the garden yet, so there was no one around to see me intently gazing at a tiny spot on an old dead stem, no one to cluck at me and peck at my toes to break me out of my trance. I'd stand still a long while, another long thin brown stem amongst the others.

I hadn't changed anything in the garden back then so there wasn't much to do other than stare. I was still in my year-long period of observation, and in any case hadn't quiet processed the fact that this was *my* garden to *tend*. So even though I knew leaving these stems standing made the life in this garden happy, I'm not sure I would have cut them down even if I hadn't. I didn't feel I had the right to yet. If either of us should change or adapt to the other, I felt it should be me. I left the brittle brown forest standing, picking through it until I felt I really knew the place. In return, in spring, onto my freshly planted annual veg patch, the garden released a small army of ladybirds that had safely hibernated there.

Even now that I do actively tend this garden, I still won't cut the army down till temperatures consistently reach 10°C in spring. The warmer weather wakes any sleeping creatures so they can move on before their winter homes are demolished. Then I'll chip the stems in my electric chipper and return them to the soil as a carbonous mulch for the vegetable patch paths, feeding the fungi.

Part of cultivating a healthy ecosystem in a garden is not over-tidying, allowing dead things – dry old stems, leaf piles or log piles – to exist and just be. So, for now at least, my awkward skeleton army remains, towering proudly out of the earth that now heaves with bulbs. When the dry dead stems do finally come down in the spring, a host of vibrant bulb blooms will take their place.

SUNSHINE TEA

- ½ lemon, chopped
- ½ orange, chopped
- Thumb-sized piece of ginger root, grated
- Thumb-sized piece of turmeric root, chopped
- ½ scotch bonnet chilli, chopped
- 10 black peppercorns, approx.
- 1 cinnamon stick, roughly broken
- 5 whole cloves
- 2 tbsp raw cider vinegar
- Raw honey, to taste

NOTE:
It is possible to replace any fresh spices with dried ones.

Winter can be an endurance test for the body and soul. If I feel I'm coming down with a cold or if the monotonous view of the skeleton army against the grey of winter is getting me down, this soothing tea helps. My mum used to make it for my siblings and me when we were poorly. It's a nice warm hug on the inside.

The ingredients are antiviral, antibacterial, anti-inflammatory, brilliant for coughs, colds and sore throats. Always buy organic, ethically sourced Fairtrade spices where possible. And respect them: they may have travelled many, many miles to reach our shops.

- Combine all the ingredients in a teapot or heatproof jug, apart from the cider vinegar and honey.
- Cover in boiling water and pop on the lid (if using a jug, use a plate).
- Leave to steep.
- Once cooled to a drinkable temperature, add the cider vinegar and honey.
- Drink up!

FIRST FROST

In the past I have felt keenly the melancholy spell cast by winter's approach. The hopelessness and claustrophobic stagnation seemed like an inevitable part of life.

I used to be afraid of the cold. These days, I appreciate that winter makes new life possible. I now understand its mission and I trust that, like the hardy plants, I can cope with it. I see beauty in the resilience it calls for. There is a brave liberation in how the plants strip bare in defiance of winter; in their nudity they will survive the harshest months. Sometimes, in the height of summer, I even dream of winter.

I tend to think of the frost arriving as a firm hand, a hard wall, a full stop. A non-negotiable cut-off point. But when it does come, I'm often surprised by how gentle and delicate it is, like it's not even certain it wants to be here.

DECEMBER

This year, the first frost arrives on 8 December. Today it is like twinkling dust that has slipped through the moth-eaten holes in Jack Frost's pockets. In our attic bedroom the roof slants steep and low, and above our bed is a skylight. When I wake, I reach up and tug open the blind just a little. Light shines brightly through the chink. I let my eyes adjust, then yank the blind fully open. Briefly, I go blind and then I see the white sworls of frost on the pane of glass – strange magical symbols painted above our heads in the night while we slept. I push the window up and open and all the cold air in the world seems to come tumbling in. It's exhilarating, rushing into my lungs as I inhale. Outside, the world's colours have been dulled, greyish and yet it's still bright. It feels still, compared with my aliveness. It looks tidy. I like it.

I look out over our long narrow garden. Either side are our neighbours' plots, then an expanse of rooftops and, further beyond, the hill that surrounds part of our town. The town is built on a small headland that originally would have risen up out of tidal wetlands. I can't quite see it from here, but now all that is left of that marshland is a great tidal river that reaches high up onto Dartmoor and all the way down to the sea, passing our town on its way; the same river that can be seen from Meg's grave. The backdrop of the hill creates the illusion that I live in a soft mossy bowl.

Depending on the time of year, the surrounding valley is dotted with cows, lush with green trees, or rusty with autumn. From the skylight it looks like a distant land, a far off fantasy. I don't go walking up there often, but when I do it feels like I'm trespassing in my own daydreams.

Today the hill is subdued. There are no cows. There is no wind. Everyone and everything is cold and still. To my left, the winter sun is making his low, sleepy rise behind the town. Mervin the cockerel crows. I think he must be cold, so I decide to make an extra-large helping of porridge to take down to him and the ladies for breakfast.

When we first moved here, the frost thrilled me. I would run out barefoot to feel the crispness of it under my feet. London can be as much as 10ºC warmer than the surrounding rural areas, so it doesn't frost much. I had forgotten the thrill of frost, the way it transforms a muddy world to a crystal one. When it did occasionally get cold enough, we'd wake to the sound of ice cracking as canal boats navigated through the freezing water.

Large cities are affected by the 'urban heat island effect'. This is due to the many hard surfaces absorbing the sun's rays, the density of people, buildings, insulative materials and activities that create 'waste heat'. In the daytime, this heat is radiated out of hard surfaces as hot air. At night, the urban structures block the warmth stored in the ground, preventing it from dissipating into the cool night sky.

From a food growing perspective this was wonderful; my London crops came earlier, and tomatoes could easily be grown outside. But as climate change brings more extreme weather, temperatures in cities will soar. For many humans, it can make life hard. Hotter weather correlates with a rise in crime, while many struggle with their health. Urban greenery helps to keep cities cool, but all too often less economically well-off communities find themselves in urban deserts, devoid of vegetation, and so are more vulnerable to the high temperatures and the challenges they bring. I can't help wondering why governments and local councils don't put more energy into ensuring our cities are green. If the warmth of the city can grow food, then why not grow plenty of it, providing local produce, access and relationship to land and a cooler, safer and more beautiful environment while we're at it?

Today, I step into the cold, hoping the ground will crunch. It doesn't. The dusting is too powdery and is silently crushed below my shoes instead. I trudge down the garden. The strawberry leaves have been laced in white. I always wish they had fruit on them in winter, they would look so beautiful: red fruit, green leaves and white lace. The yet-to-germinate broad bean seeds will be chilly despite being covered with great sheets of bubble wrap. Feeling glad I covered them, I send them a good luck wish, hoping they make it through the cold snap. My weather app tells me it is here for a while.

Mervin alerts the others that what I've brought them is worth getting out of bed for. Carefully, he plucks warm sweet porridge oats out of the bowl and passes them to his sisters as he cuck, cuck, cucks.

The first frost has been kind.

DECEMBER

*

The second day of frost, 9 December, is a little firmer. After its first uncertain outing yesterday, it is starting to feel at home. I can feel it set in and expect that strong hand to be with us soon. When I go out to feed our flock, Freddy the dog, always mildly anxious when not out on a walk, comes lopping down the garden after me. Freddy is our pedigree Cavalier King Charles Spaniel, we inherited him from Meg; I harbour some shame in this fact since I had always imagined that when we did eventually adopt a dog, we would take on a great big wolf of an animal, clever, a bit wild, independent and with a bloodline as mixed as mine. When he first arrived, he couldn't believe his luck that there were chickens in our garden: 'Live playmates, just for me?!'

It took a few failed attacks followed by imprisonment in the bathroom before he learnt they were our friends and not to be bothered. So, these days, he's devised a cunning way of getting his kicks without officially breaking any rules. He barrels along the path as though headed straight for the chickens, sending the flock into a chaotic flutter, then at the last minute veers off into a flower bed or veg patch and begins sniffing feverishly, as if he hadn't even noticed the angrily cackling birds. He does this nearly every time he goes out, and I can't bring myself to stop him because, as well as this being quite an (uncharacteristically) intelligent workaround on his part, I could swear he's hiding his secret thrill from me, and there's something quite clever and endearing in that too. (I like to encourage clever in him because, well, as I said, he so rarely demonstrates that trait!) Having watched this performance unfold several times I'm now equally convinced that although the chickens don't half make a fuss, they quite like the excitement the faux attacks add to their otherwise safe and fairly mundane existence. For breakfast today, they get suet from the butcher melted into their porridge with a topping of frozen berries. Toby tells me I spoil them. I don't care.

After feeding the chickens, Freddy and I set off for the community plot. All soft smiles and unwavering love, our silly little thoroughbred boy trots alongside me, his breath puffing clouds in the frigid air. Our river steams.

I spend the rest of the day with my fellow community gardeners, shovelling frozen mulch onto the weeded beds, while Freddy snuffles about on a secret mission. By 4.30 p.m. the light is dropping and Freddy has icicles growing from his ears. By 4.45 p.m. we are all at the pub warming up with cider and a fire. It doesn't take long before Freddy's ears have thawed and we are peeling off layer after layer of thermals and jumpers.

By 11 December, the frost is hard. At home our ponds have frozen and I have to thaw the chickens' water with boiled water from the kettle. At 8.30 a.m. the sun is low and still hasn't risen above the town, when it does eventually land in the garden, its rays aren't strong or long enough to melt the frozen ponds. Today everything is a crisp white, no longer dusty grey, and the ground crunches under my feet. There is no mud: it has frozen rock-hard. Out in the fields, aside from the birds, Freddy and I seem to be the only living things that can still move. All other life is holding its breath. Put under a spell, the world has been crystallised.

With the garden frozen as hard as this, I don't attempt to weed or clear the beds because creatures who don't have a warm indoors to retreat to will be hibernating in there or eating what they can. I don't sow seeds. I don't even harvest until the crops thaw out. I don't prune either. I just wait.

Lots of plants deal with this time by drawing their energy down from their extremities. They reduce, focus, pull in. Others distil their energy into seed. Tiny bundles of life on pause, still breathing but very, very slowly, they lie in wait for the sun's warmth and the rain to tell them it is safe to reach up and out once more.

The cold forces life to focus. Winter doesn't lie. Without the distraction of luscious life, the flirtation of spring's blossoms or the lustre of summer's greens, it can be harsh. But the dying back gives space to see. The frost dances on the skeletons of the garden pointing out and highlighting all its features – without interruption, we can gaze directly in and through, spy what's underneath. I wonder if this is why so many of us struggle with winter – stripped bare, perhaps, there is nowhere to hide.

On 20 December, the frost has thawed, for now. But after twelve days of frozen stillness, we have been firmly pushed into winter.

*

When we lived on our boat in London, if we let the fire go out in winter, we would feel the cold. It was the sort of cold that clasps you, wrapping itself all around, seeping in out of the water through the thin metal hull. Growing up, when we couldn't run the heating, as I ripped out of bed and ran to the hot shower, no matter how fast I dashed, that cold would hug and hold onto me too, slickly enfolding me, happy to see me again, hungry for me to warmly hug her back.

I don't like or want to be cold *inside*, but now I do love to experience winter outside; to go out and feel that crisp bite, to feel the turning of time, to understand the meaning of the sun's hot kisses so much better for having embraced the ice. I am grateful for the timely winter cold. It is essential for the abundance of summer and spring.

The cold of winter is like 'turning it off and on again'. It can restore health and balance. When deciduous trees undergo the prolonged cold of winter, they essentially reset the ecosystem in their branches. Freezing temperatures help to manage pests, pausing or halting their breeding cycles, killing a fair few in the process. Many pesky dependents are killed off or at least reduced in number by the lack of leaf cover, and food supplied by the trees' blossoms, flowing sap and delicious foliage. A mild winter on the other hand can welcome hordes of slugs, snails and even disease.

Many fruit and nut trees, from apples to pears, plums, cherries, hazelnuts, walnuts and more, actually need a period of cold to produce their crop. This followed by gradual warming in spring triggers their flowers (and catkins in the case of the nut trees) to burst forth. If temperatures don't fall low enough, blossoms can fail to open; unopened blooms can't be pollinated, and unpollinated flowers give no fruit.

Many seeds – foxgloves, echinacea, hollyhocks, valerian, chamomile, some roses, apples, raspberries, plums and more – require or prefer a period of winter rest before they are able to germinate. This is due to a process called 'cold stratification'. Some seeds only need a week or two of cold weather, others need several months. Other seeds, like blackberries, like to be eaten by birds, to pass through their digestive system, which helps to break down the hard outer coating of the seed, as well as a period of cold before germination. The garden always weaves complex webs of interconnection. Fruit, food, bird, seed, cold – all linked up as one.

If the cold of winter lingers for too long into spring its frost can kill off blossoms and fresh young growth. Plants and creatures alike have adapted to the general consistency of gradual cooling and gentle warming, giving them time to adjust. Climate change, however, is bringing with it balmy days in the winter and sudden freezes in spring. Life, both in our gardens and in the wild, is not accustomed to such wayward weather. A great number of British native plants need this timely cold to complete their life cycles.

As the climate shifts, we will likely see the living world that surrounds us shift as well. Some plants may be able to move their territories northwards, following the cold. But those with long, slow lifespans may not move fast enough. Knowing this, I've come to cherish the cold, taking in every moment with it and the landscape it creates, like watching a lover who may someday have to go.

BIRDFEED FAT-BRICK

- 1 cup oat groats or rolled oats
- ½ cup sunflower seeds, ideally black ones
- ½ cup unmilled wheat grain
- ½ cup hemp groats
- ½ cup millet
- ½ cup cracked corn
- ¼ cup lentils
- ¼ cup sesame seed
- ¼ cup flaxseed
- ¼ cup pearl barley
- ¼ cup dried kelp flakes

- 1 cup fat – suet (this can be vegan), coconut oil or lard (I like to use lard that the butcher practically gives away, putting a 'waste' product to use)

I make this treat for the chickens from time to time through the winter. The wild birds like it too. The quantities above are given in cups so you have an idea of volume ratio and feel confident to experiment. I tend to vary the ingredients depending on what I have in the house.

- Mix the dry grains and seeds together in a large bowl.
- Melt the fat in a pan on a gentle heat.
- Once the fat has melted, add it to the bowl and mix to thoroughly combine it with the seeds.
- Pour the fatty mixture into a loaf tin, or muffin tray, ideally made of silicone as it's easier to turn out.
- Leave in a cool place to allow the fat to harden.
- Once completely hard, after a few hours (I leave mine overnight) turn out your oily brick, or scoop it out with a spatula.
- Leave outside on a bird table or in the coop as a feast for your feathered friends.

EVERGREENS

On 21 December, moving heavy and slow in its own cold darkness, the longest night of the year rolls out. This is the winter solstice. For a few nights, the season engulfs us in its inky world. Time seems to stand still as the days remain eerily short. Then, as imperceptible as it may be, the scales tip and very gradually the days begin to lengthen, slowly stretching themselves out like a contented cat basking in the sun's return.

For many pre-Christian Northern Europeans the unfurling of winter into spring was a period of huge significance. Their very survival, life and death, were tethered to the elements in a way most of us living in this region can hardly imagine today. Longer days did more than simply ease seasonal blues: they signified the return of greater safety and comfort in the grace of the sun's warmth and light. Many communities practised rituals and festivities throughout this darkest period of the year, starting around Halloween or Samhain, to ensure the sun *did* choose to return to them after all. Its return wasn't taken for granted.

One ancient – and still sometimes practised – Northern European tradition includes the burning of a great yule log, which then smoulders in a hearth for days coaxing, welcoming or perhaps even guiding the sun back to Earth. The ashes would later be scattered on the fields; a cleansing gift to the soil.

In our bright, centrally heated homes, where we turn lights on and off with the flick of a switch and feast on tropical summer fruits plucked from supermarket fridges all through winter, it's no surprise that many of us may not experience the same visceral interconnection with the cosmic balance of the living world. Our relationship with the earth is abstract; many of us no longer feel the need to coax life back into the land that sustains us through ritual offerings and acts. Instead, in this time known as the 'Anthropocene', an epoch dominated by the power of the human, in mid-winter we give gifts of gratitude and love to each other.

I find an irony in celebrating Christmas, a holiday now synonymous with vast overconsumption, in a season that seems to whisper of the significance of valuing subtle joys and the resilience of life despite its perceived bareness. My garden's inhabitants appear grateful to make the most of sharing a very scant landscape, while inside we make the least of a decadence the kings and queens of the past could barely begin to imagine. Giving gifts and sharing food are some of life's great pleasures. But these days, excess makes me afraid.

Our planet is regenerative, but many of its resources are finite. It cannot support perpetual and widespread overconsumption. We need to consume less, the world's richest urgently so. As Oxfam's report 'Climate Equality: A planet for the 99%' explains: 'In 2019, the super-rich 1% were responsible for 16% of global carbon emissions, which is the same as the emissions of the poorest 66% (5 billion people).' Extend that to the richest 10% globally and this population is thought to be responsible for 50% of emissions. Having more than $1 million in net wealth earns you a spot in the global 1% according to Credit Suisse. The poorest 50% are only responsible for 8% of emissions. Currently, wealth is linked to overconsumption.

Perhaps we can learn from our winter gardens and put aside some of our wants wrapped up as needs, instead sharing the comfort many of us find ourselves living in. Effective taxation of the super-rich and sensible public spending could be a good start to effective sharing.

In the winter garden, my friend the robin never fails to show up, coming to gather any invertebrates I uncover as I work. It's just us two, and we become intimate in a way we are not in the abundance of spring and summer. When the distraction of excess is removed, our bonds can come into focus, along with our relationships with what we *do* have.

*

Folktales and pagan myths of midwinter describe the Sun King being reborn at this time, returning from his journeys in the underworld, bringing with him prosperity and longer days.

Writing in 700 CE, the monk and scholar Bede the Venerable recorded that before their conversion to Christianity, around midwinter time the pagan Anglo-Saxons of Britain celebrated 'Mother's Night'. The folklorist Dr Terry Gunnell writes of an ancient link between woman, death and winter, pointing to Northern European winter festivals for women and gods perceived as female (or gods in their female form), who governed death. In nature-based faith systems, he speculates, this link could have been born out of the common perception that birth and death are not so far apart, that they are one and the same, intertwined. And that women, capable of ushering in new human life, symbolise this reality.

I've heard and read countless stories describing the act of giving birth as a death of sorts. Many mothers tell me that in the process of birthing, part of them drifted away, leaving their body to labour alone, or even that a part of them died, perhaps 'the maiden', as they became a mother. The experiences that accompany inhabiting a female body do seem to make 'womanhood' the perfect symbol for the dichotomies of winter, the cosy yet uncomfortable, expectant emptiness.

Bede's 'Mother's Night' was held on what is now Christmas Eve. It's not hard to spot the parallel between this ancient pagan winter celebration and Christian Christmas. For the first few hundred years of Christianity there was no official or standardised date for Jesus' birth – it might be celebrated any time between January and September. It wasn't until the fourth century that the Pope of Rome set the date as 25 December, embedding it in a period of widespread European winter rituals, including the pagan Roman feasts for Saturn, the god of agriculture and time. Saturnalia celebrations spanned several days, and featured many festive traditions we still recognise today: sharing food, gift giving and song. Placing Christmas among pre-existing festivities no doubt was a strategy to ease the population into celebrating a new occasion, again a birth, but now of a magical child rather than our solar system's sun.

*

At Christmas, despite the darkness and cold, we fill our homes with evergreens that seem to invite life inside. To me, evergreens embody resilience, reminding me that even in the darkest months life can persist. In Devon, this period of long nights brings storms, and I've built my own tradition of walking out to the woods to collect evergreen tree limbs that have fallen in the winds. In the garden at this time of year I give the pair of bay trees and the holly a prune too. I twist all these spare bits of tree into one another, weaving them around and around until one branch holds in the other, which holds in the next, and together they form a green circle. A structure dependent on the force exerted by each participating branch. I bring back handfuls of ivy from my walks with Fred and wrap it around the wreath, binding the branches in its coils. Just as the ivy supports the structure of dying trees, it holds this structure together too.

As I work around and around, I think of Eke Ogba Ijeke, the python eating his own tail, wound into an internal cycle, and I think of Eke weaving her cloth while Chi builds his great house. It is said that after her transformation Eke's weaving lies discarded until a skilled weaver, the spider known as 'Ududo Okwanka', finds it and decides to complete the work. Ududo Okwanka carries the cloth high above the cosmos where he settles down to forever weave the incomplete fabric of the universe. This ever-expanding cloth engulfs the body of Eke resurrected as Ala, The Earth. On and on Ududo Okwanka spins, weaving infinite interconnected spirals of the story of all creation and time.

Shaping my own wreath from offcuts of the world has become a little magic practice to me. As I twist the ivy, I think of my loved ones and wrap them into the wreath in a hug of evergreens. This is a mundane moment of co-creation with the plants who gave me their branches, which I have attributed significance to. As I weave a symbol of life from their dead limbs, I'm reminded that life and death are intertwined.

SAGE AND PARSNIP NUT ROAST

- 100 g brown rice
- 2–3 parsnips
- 1 tbsp maple syrup
- ½ tsp cinnamon
- 1 onion
- 4–5 cloves garlic
- 3–5 sticks celery
- 175 g mushrooms
- Sprig of fresh rosemary
- Handful fresh parsley
- Small bunch fresh sage
- 110 g chopped walnuts
- 110 g chopped chestnuts
- 250 g silken tofu
- 1 tbsp Dijon mustard
- ½ tsp mace
- Salt and pepper, to taste
- 2–3 tbsp olive oil
- Fresh rosemary, sage and parsley sprigs, to garnish
- Garlic oil, to drizzle

Optional: 1 red pepper

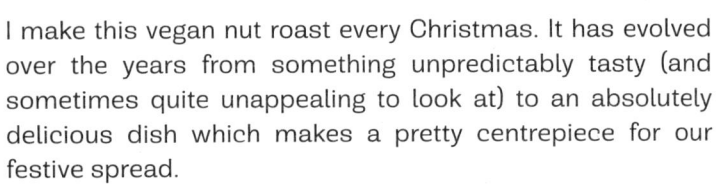

I make this vegan nut roast every Christmas. It has evolved over the years from something unpredictably tasty (and sometimes quite unappealing to look at) to an absolutely delicious dish which makes a pretty centrepiece for our festive spread.

Packed with protein and iron and with a sweet nutty flavour, texture-wise it is moist but firm with a crispy crunchy outside. Inspired by a wonderful veggie nut roast recipe from Julia Ponsonby's *Gaia's Kitchen*, this has become such a favourite that Toby and I cooked it in bulk for our wedding.

DECEMBER

You can bake this nut roast in advance to reheat and turn out at a later date. Leave it in the loaf tin to cool thoroughly and store in the fridge or freezer.

- Preheat the oven to gas mark 6 or 200°C. Grease and line a large loaf tin with greaseproof paper.
- Put the rice on to boil.
- Slice the parsnips into lengths and arrange at the base of the baking dish as you'd like them to appear when the bake is turned out. Place the chosen parsnip pieces into a pan of boiling water and parboil for about two minutes (i.e., until softened but not fully cooked).
- Drain and transfer the parsnips to a bowl. Drizzle over a tablespoon of the olive oil, add the maple syrup and cinnamon. Agitate the bowl to fully coat the parsnips with the sweet spiced oily mixture. Set aside.
- Finely chop the onions, garlic and celery (this can also be done with a food processor), add to a pan with a tablespoon of olive oil and gently fry until soft. In the meantime, finely chop or process the mushrooms and red pepper, then add to the frying pan along with a little more olive oil, if necessary.
- Finely chop the herbs and add to the pan.
- Season well with salt and pepper.
- Continue to cook over a gentle heat until the veg is soft and fragrant.
- Chop or crush the nuts to resemble a textured flour or crumble mix.
- Remove the veg from the heat and add the nuts. Mix to combine well.
- Drain the rice and mix this in along with the mace and Dijon mustard.
- Add the silken tofu and thoroughly mix everything together (you can whizz the tofu in a processor first, so it is smooth and easy to incorporate).

- Arrange the cooked, maple-syrup-oil-coated parsnips on the base of the prepared loaf tin, as before. Pour in the nut roast mixture, firming it down with a spoon as you go. This helps the mixture to hold well together once cooked.
- Place the nut roast in the pre-heated oven for an hour to ninety minutes. To test if the roast is cooked through, pierce it with a knife at the centre – if the knife comes out clean and the loaf looks lightly browned on top, it's done.
- Leave to cool slightly, then turn the roast out onto a serving plate like an upside-down cake so that the parsnip base is visible.
- Garnish with a few sprigs of fresh herbs and serve with cranberry sauce and a drizzle of garlic oil.

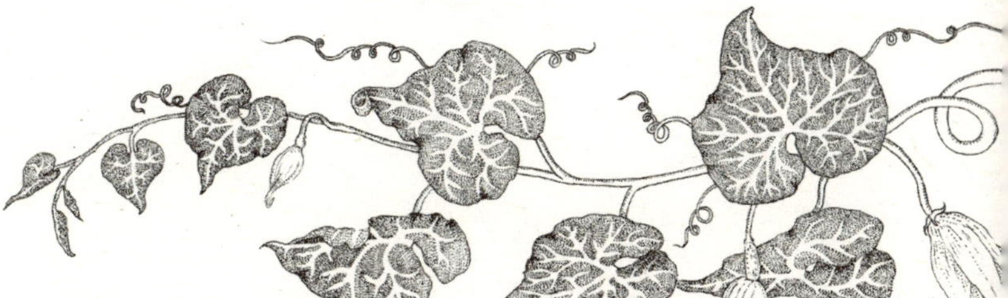

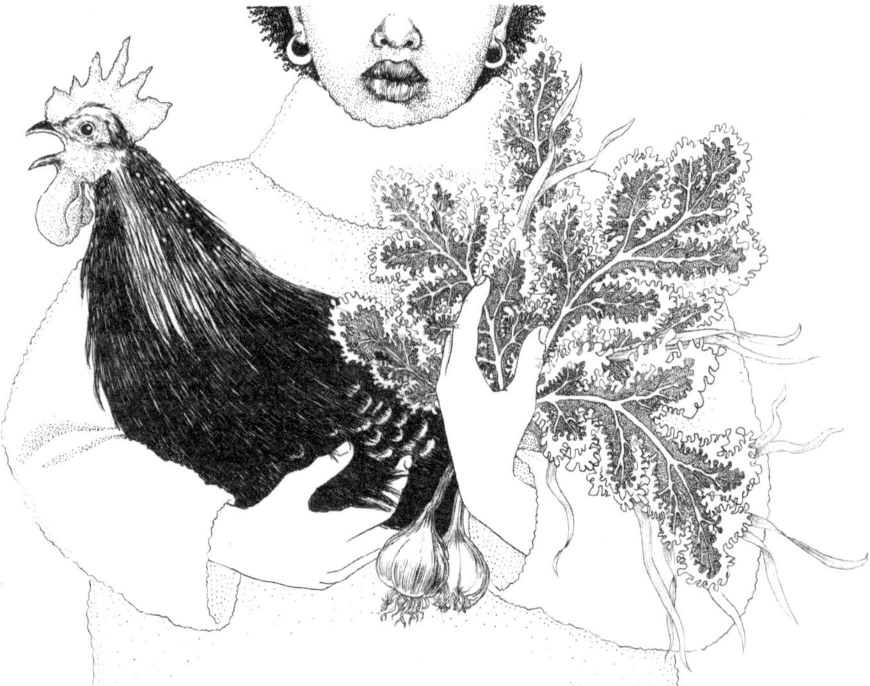

January

WE LOSE OUR BROAD BEANS

At the community garden, after December's cold snap, we lose our autumn-sown broad beans (*Vicia faba* 'Aquadulce'). They may be hardy but they're not quite hardy enough, it seems, to stand up to the extremes of this Devon winter and that heavy clay soil.

Thanks to all sorts of clever physiological feats, hardy plants like these broad beans can normally withstand extreme cold. ('Aquadulce' can supposedly survive temperatures as low as about -10°C.) Tender plants, on the other hand, don't like the cold at all – they won't survive below zero and would prefer to be well above 5°C. (I always think that if I'm cold, then my tender plants are too.)

Plants are made up of about 95 per cent water. And when temperatures fall, turning the earth's surface moisture to twinkling ice crystals, the water within the plants isn't spared. This can create all sorts of problems in how a plant functions: bursting cells, creating bubbles in the passages that carry water and minerals up from the roots, and reducing or halting the flow of that water in the plant entirely.

When temperatures drop, mysterious mechanisms kick into play inside plants that can weather the cold. The water *between* the plant's cells begins to freeze, but the water *within* the cells themselves does not. The fluid in the plant's cells (cytoplasm) is rich with components essential for the plant to function, and liquid containing a high concentration of dissolved chemicals has a lower freezing point than pure water. As the in-between water crystallizes, the water held within the cells is drawn out through osmosis, leaving the cytoplasm with an even higher concentration of dissolved chemicals. This movement of fluids in the plant guards their precious cells from freezing.

When water is lost from the plant's cells, we see this as wilting, just like when a plant is dehydrated. But as the rising sun warms the day and thaws the frosts, in hardy plants the water gradually returns to the cells and the plants regain their turgidity, standing tall once more.

Some hardy plants have further tricks up their sleeves. Evergreens like holly and bay trees have a thick waxy layer on their leaves called a cuticle. Frosts can reduce movement of water into and around the plant, but this cuticle reduces evaporation from the leaf's surface, protecting the plant from dehydration. Other plants have anti-freeze proteins which are deployed to reduce the formation of damaging ice crystals, and some pre-emptively reduce the fluid in vulnerable cells, moving it to areas out of cold's reach, like their roots. Winter sends life inside itself.

We can actually taste some plants' responses to cold. In a protective move, to lower the freezing point of the cytoplasm, kale stuffs its leaf cells full of sugars. Carrots perform a similar trick, converting the starches stored in their roots into sugar so that this biennial root, known botanically as an 'organ of perennation', can survive the winter to sprout back up and flower the following year. This wonderful response gives us deliciously sweet carrot roots and kale leaves to gather in the icy cold.

I find myself marvelling at the perfect timing of plants becoming richer in sugars exactly when our bodies need more calories to keep us warm. Eating out-of-season food grown on the other side of the world in the comfort of our warm homes, it is so easy to miss the magical details of how our needs, the biology of plants and the shifting of the seasons are so intertwined. But out in the garden, the connections are there, waiting.

The weather may have been cold and wet, but with the broad beans our fatal error was to sow them in a part of the field which we now know to be a frost pocket. This was my first winter growing in that spot, and I curse myself for not having noticed the way the land swoops down a hill to a high hedge, creating the fatal combination of day-long winter shade and a pooling place for cold air flowing downhill at night. Consequently, our broad bean patch was frozen solid for days. The cold weather knocked the bean plants hard, but what really did them in was the battering, torrential icy rain that followed. Already weak from the effects of the freeze, they were properly pummelled to a slimy mess. By the end of it all, there was nothing left. It's as if they were never there at all. I lie in bed imagining the stealthy cold gently rolling down the hill, down and down, until the bottom of the hedge was enveloped in ice. I sigh the frosty vision away and pull the heavy duvet up to my chin, wishing we had thought to tuck the broad beans in a warm bed too.

The IPCC's Special Report on Climate Change and Land acknowledges that the shift from a subsistence lifestyle in modern cultures has led to a loss of local knowledge of how to live with respect for natural resources. But as I am experiencing first hand, this shift has also led to a loss of appreciation for the sheer know-how and effort required to produce good food, particularly in the face of progressively unpredictable weather events.

As 'consumers' we are generally so far removed from the farmers and producers that the real cost – and thus value – of food can so easily be obscured. Crop loss at any scale, for example, is a reality few of us in the WEIRD countries (Western, Educated, Industrialised, Rich and Democratic) ever truly have to confront beyond a slight price hike. This reality may change with climate breakdown, when ensuing conflict and biodiversity loss drive instability in our food systems.

Our beans were lovingly planted in early autumn, weeded and tended for a quarter of a year. Alongside them we had grown visions of ourselves harvesting the bounty in early summer, the sun on our shoulders, filling our baskets and later our bellies. As a collective we do not face a financial consequence from the loss of our crop beyond that of our time and seed. We were not *dependent* on the success of the beans, but we did tiptoe a little closer to grasping the reality of losing a great deal of food to a weather event. And all it took was a moment of incomplete observation.

Had we planted the beans at the top of the hill the winter sun may have warmed them just enough. Had we realised we were planting into a frost pocket we could have tucked them up under fleece so they still had a chance of growing strong.

As I stand above the now-empty broad bean patch in the drizzle, my arms folded, rain dripping through my hood and down the back of my neck, my mind is elsewhere. I'm marvelling at the art, skill and deep value in ecological food growing. In my family, generations of growers came before me – right up until my paternal grandparents left their village, and my grandfather's grandparents on my mother's side. As children, planting and growing would have been just another language to them, one in which they would naturally become fluent, confident. Yet here I am, standing in the rain, looking at a bare patch of ground where once the broad beans grew, attempting to relearn that language, or at least some of it. Two steps forward, one step back.

Every plant we sow and grow is nothing short of a miracle. A seed may not germinate; a tender shoot may be whipped out by a slug; the emerging plant may be crushed by a frost or devoured by a pigeon. Given all the pitfalls, the ability to successfully grow plants that actually become food is a marvel to me.

Perhaps the hands-on experience of growing food should be an essential part of all of our lives. I imagine government-funded community gardens, garden shares and growing groups springing up around the country. Everyone would contribute, take a day in their week to work on the plot and to learn the reality of what it takes to grow life-giving food. I wonder how this proximity to process would change how we relate to one another and to our local environment; how it could improve our well-being and help us to appreciate the true value of food and the ecosystems that help us produce it.

JANUARY

Something a man I met in a food forest in India told me comes to mind: 'Life is about growing good food with good people, sharing the food and then dancing in celebration.' Sounds good to me. I suppose to this philosophy I'd add, 'Dancing in celebration and gratitude that the cold and rain hadn't swept away the harvest.'

ZERO-WASTE VEGETABLE STOCK

Base Ingredients
- Celery (including leaf)
- Celeriac (including leaf)
- Carrot root
- Parsnip root
- Leeks
- Onion and garlic (not peel)
- Swede
- Mushrooms

Ingredients to add sparingly for extra flavour
- Carrot tops
- Onion and garlic peels
- Herbs such as bay leaves, rosemary, sage, thyme, parsley, ginger

---

This is a guide to how to make your own ever-changing stock, depending on what 'waste' vegetables you have on your hands – offcuts that would otherwise go on the compost (I use clean vegetable peels, bottoms and tops); leaves of veg including celery, celeriac and carrots; sad-looking veg that you're not sure what to do with; or perfectly good veg, if you like (and useful if you have a surplus of something to use up).

Use the finished stock to add depth to pasta sauces, soups, stews and gravies.

To get a good balance of flavour, save up any veg scraps in

a bag in the freezer, then once you have a nice, ample collection, boil them up. Since it takes some time to boil the stock, it warms the kitchen with steam, which is cosy in winter.

Not all vegetables are tasty in a stock, I find the best flavours come from earthy roots and celery. Above is a list of my favourites.

- Chop your veg collection into rough chunks and add to a large pan. Cover with boiling water and season well with salt and a handful of peppercorns.
- Place a lid on the pan and bring to boil on a medium heat.
- Leave to bubble for 30 minutes to an hour. The flavour of the stock will evolve as it cooks, so taste as you go, topping up with boiling water as required.
- Strain into a clean container, putting the boiled veg aside (I give it to the chickens or put it in the bokashi composter). Add more salt and freshly ground pepper to taste and leave to cool.
- Once cool, store in the fridge or freezer, or use it to cook with right away.

HENS IN WINTER DON'T LAY

Well, some do, if they are young or are given plenty of food, warmth and extra light. But our hens – who live outside all year round, foraging from the garden and eating kitchen scraps (with some supplementary soy-free organic grain) – don't lay in wintertime. When our original hens, Prim and Florette, stopped laying in our first winter with them, I was concerned. I looked in my chicken books, thinking they might be ill, or backed up (hens can become 'egg-bound' when an egg gets stuck and won't come out – this can be fatal as the hens can go into shock and die). To my relief and surprise, they were not poorly. They were just taking a break.

Left to their own devices without much human intervention, most hens (like ours) will lay from mid-spring to autumn.

Their egg-laying rhythm is governed by sunlight. For the relevant hormones and egg development to be stimulated, they need about fourteen hours of light each day. Sensibly, if they don't feel safe, they also stop laying. Insufficient warmth, food, water or a fox attack can put them off. Their egg-laying is closely linked to the world around them to conserve vital energy in times of danger, and to ensure that they don't mother chicks in conditions that aren't conducive to survival.

Hens only hatch their eggs when they go broody, and this also follows a seasonal pattern. A broody hen gathers up all the eggs she can, sometimes popping other hens' eggs under her wings and carrying them off to wherever she decides to nest! She stops laying and sits on her clutch, keeping her eggs warm and turning them day and night. You can tell a broody hen by the look in her eye: in the process of nesting, she becomes very intense, sometimes with dilated pupils; and she can be quite grumpy, neglecting her own needs for food and water. When the nesting hen does eventually emerge, she often moves about differently too, dropping lower to the ground and fluffing up. There are ways to coax hens out of broodiness, but if left undisturbed, even if their eggs don't ultimately hatch (or if they have no eggs at all!), it will last for about three weeks, the time it takes for chicks to emerge. However, if the hen doesn't actually have a clutch to hatch and there is no emerging brood to snap her out of her mothering trance, broodiness can continue for as long as six weeks.

We have five Pekin Bantam chickens. Prim and Florette arrived in our first spring here. Florette went broody in her second summer, so we bought her some fertilised eggs to sit on and our flock grew to five, to include Mervin the cockerel. Now with a cockerel in the flock, the ladies have the potential to build up a clutch of eggs, go broody and hatch any of the eggs they lay. For us, this is playing with fire since we don't have the space for the flock to just keep expanding of its own accord. Too many chickens with not enough space will scratch and peck a place bare, harming an ecosystem rather than helping it.

Early last summer we had a heatwave, and despite the dappled shade below the apple trees, the chickens were hot. I often saw them panting, dust bathing and sitting about with their wings lightly fanned out, trying to cool off. On my morning egg hunts in the days following, I discovered fewer and fewer eggs, and then eventually there were none at all. I suspected the extreme heat was bad laying weather. Indeed, when temperatures cooled off a little, I started finding eggs again.

But three weeks later, when the weather had fully broken and the rain finally came, I went out to feed the chickens and noted that Prim was missing. Squatting down beside them in my yellow rain jacket, I scanned below the trees. I heard a peeping. I kept very still, not wanting to believe my ears, but the peeping came again, and this time there was a whole choir of cheeps.

The suspicious noise was coming from inside a grassy hummock. I stepped towards it, slipped my hand between the wet fronds and felt Prim's warm soft body. Parting the grass, she sat looking incredibly low and broad, wings slightly fanned out. The peeping came again, this time from right beneath her. I gently lifted her wing and more chicks than I could count came tumbling out, chirping and falling over one another as they tried to bury themselves back in their mother's warmth. I fell back on my heels and stared in shock. All those missing eggs I hadn't gathered during the hot weather *had* been laid after all! Prim had simply gathered them up and hatched them!

I fetched a big basket and filled it with newspaper and some grain, planning to move Prim and her brood into the shed's dry warmth. I gathered Prim up in my hands and popped her in the basket. She exploded out in a flap, perplexed at being separated from her chicks, even if just for a minute. So instead, I began to scoop up her babies and deposit handfuls of them in my basket. I counted ten! I couldn't help commending Prim on her sneaky feat. Once all the chicks were safely stowed, Prim hopped into the basket of her own accord and I carried the little family into the shed.

Toby was away at a music festival, so I sent him a photo with no explanation. His response pinged back instantly, 'Wait, what?' And then a beat later, 'WTF?', followed quickly by, 'Are you joking!? Oh

JANUARY

babe! This is hilarious.' And then what I was hoping he wouldn't say, but knew that he would: 'We can't possibly keep them!'

He was obviously right. My dad's calm solution was: 'Don't worry, we will eat them later. Honestly, Toby and I will eat them.'

Spurred on by Dad's suggestion, in the end I managed to find good homes for all the little chicks. So our flock went back down to five (and we'd like to keep it that way).

After this palaver, I was quite relieved when the days started to shorten and I no longer had to worry about hordes of fluffy little chicks suddenly appearing from the undergrowth. Now come winter the hens have genuinely stopped laying.

*

I send my dad a video of Mervin the cockerel, the father of all ten of those chicks. He's perched on the frosty roof of the compost heap, neck stretched high to the cloudless winter sky, crowing with all his might. He looks satisfied with the sound he's made and does it again. Dad sends me back a video of 'the local chicken posse' that wanders the village he is currently staying in. This multigenerational flock is left to expand at will. They look different to our chickens, but not unrecognisable. I think our chickens would envy their warm weather and dust. Being winter the ground here is cold and moist under their warm little feet. 'How do you say chicken in Igbo?' I text. He messages back: '*Okuko*.' I ask him to send me a voice note, so I know how to pronounce it.

My dad is far away; he has been for most of my life. The few times he has been geographically close by he has often still felt distant. As I grow older, I have empathy for this remoteness. He has things he needs to do in this lifetime, peace he needs to find, lessons he wants to learn. As far apart as we are, these days one of the things that helps us bridge the many miles are the chickens. We both love these gentle and nurturing birds. Dad doesn't tend a flock of his own, but he hopes he will someday, and in the meantime he watches the posses which roam the streets, birds that will feed many people. Where he lives, many of the processes of sustenance are still a visible part of everyday life. When I think on this, he feels even further away.

In this country, by contrast, our exploitation and abuse of these animals is carefully hidden in plain sight. Travelling on the train recently, we sped past a vast chicken bunker. The kind that packs hens in as tight as is legal and churns out such quantities of manure that our waterways, like the River Wye, become toxic to swim in and dead of life. I only glimpsed the tidy new roof and walls surrounding the imprisoned hens, but I still had to look away. I can't stomach the reality of industrial-scale chicken farming, looking after our little flock has made my heart vulnerable – I know their complexity, their capacity for character, thoughtfulness and affection, and I've witnessed their pleasure, discomfort and pain. We have fun and there is a relationship of trust, sharing and support. I call Prim and Florette my friends. We adopted them when someone we knew couldn't keep them anymore. Toby built their house below the apple trees at the end of the garden. They were immediately curious to get to know us. On their first morning in the garden, Toby and I ate our breakfast in a hammock strung between the fruit trees. Florette jumped in beside us and stared intently into Toby's eyes, head cocked to one side, her searching eyeballs just centimetres from his. She was fearless and inquisitive.

JANUARY

Having been vegan throughout my twenties, these days I am mostly vegetarian (due to the land use and emissions associated with rearing livestock, plant-rich diets are necessary for a comfortable future on this planet). As children, we were raised practically vegetarian, not out of ethics or politics but because there was no money and Mum knew how to feed us well and cheaply without meat. We ate a lot of beans, but we also occasionally ate chicken. Despite this, I've still spent most of my life eating animals (like Prim and Florette) without knowing the first thing about them.

Now that I've gotten to know these little feathered creatures, it feels shameful that I was previously so ignorant of something as simple as their life cycle. In the crisp, glistening cold it seems common sense that they would stop laying, saving their energy to keep themselves warm and saving their chicks from entering an inhospitable world. The fact that I could have overlooked this now obvious fact shows me just how far removed I was, and actually largely still am, from the subtle interconnections between life and our environment. I have so much to learn.

Caring for this flock through all their and the earth's seasons, I realise just how much chickens had been tethered to their commodified output in my mind. Although I consider myself an animal lover, I knew chicken as a product – as meat or eggs – far better than I knew *chickens*, okuko, the creatures. When I was younger, my dad told us that some children raised in cities thought that spaghetti grew on trees. 'Know where your food comes from,' he'd tell us. And I thought I did – but then I met the chickens. In *Witches, Witch-Hunting and Women*, Silvia Federici explores how our relationship with animals was altered by the rise of capitalism. This, she writes, is how a new social ethos was born that prized self-discipline and the ability to override one's instincts, essentially becoming a human machine, capable of contributing efficiently to the labour force. A 'cultural revolution' took place in which *control* became a defining characteristic of what it is to be human.

Consequently, a chasm began to open between humans and animals. Animals were no longer considered intelligent creatures in their own right, but seen to embody an 'instinctiveness' and wildness that threatened 'civilised' industrialisation. As Descartes' philosophy (which cast humans as the only rational beings on Earth, superior to the rest of the living world; animals, he decided, were mindless self-operating machines) gained traction in the popular conscience, animals were further downgraded in the collective imagination to mere commodities lacking all sentience, ignorant objects to be exploited and consumed. No wonder I had thought of chickens as edible commercial goods and nothing more.

Growing a garden has shown me that all of our food depends on complex relationships with place, seasons and other life forms that we may not even be able to imagine. I thought I understood and was sensitive to seasonality, but then the hens stopped laying in winter, teaching me a reality of nature that without them I would never have noticed. In theory I got it, but in practice I had failed to understand that in the living world, in a very literal sense, winter is not a time for creating new life. It's a time to stock up, bed in and rest. Clever chickens. Clever birds.

EARTHLY DELIGHTS

Every winter I'm tempted by the plump out-of-season tomatoes sitting on supermarket shelves. I gingerly think of my summer self swearing off the fruits when out of season, but it's easier said than done, when winter comes around and they're right there in front of you. I feel like Eve in the supermarket garden of Eden, enticed by the promised pleasures of the rosy toms. 'They'll only taste of water', I remind myself and wistfully move on, yearning for the soft sweet tomatoes my garden will grow come summer. Other times I'm less resolute and pick up a packet labelled: 'organic, origin: Spain'. Back in the garden I scout round for plants to accompany my purchase.

These tomatoes will have travelled many miles from the soil they grew up out of (or more likely substrate as most are grown hydroponically). If they had been British tomatoes, I'd have known they were grown in heated greenhouses. Eating fresh tomatoes in the winter in Britain is a luxury, one that comes at a great cost we aren't aware of. Just as the lives of chickens are obscured by their commodification, so too is the story of how these fresh fruits come to sit on our shelves in the dead of winter.

To understand this, we're going to travel a long way away from my little winter garden in Devon. We are going to follow the tomato trail around Europe.

*

We'll start here in the UK where heating a greenhouse through winter requires gas. Currently, the majority of gas we use is imported from Norway. In Norway, to access this gas, state-sanctioned extraction projects (as well as oil mining and green colonialism in the shape of wind farms) have been non-consensually carving up the Land of the Midnight Sun, Sapmi, the Arctic landscape that is the homeland of the Sami people, heralded as the last indigenous community in Europe. Sapmi curls up out of the top of Norway and through Sweden, rising up into the north of Finland and dropping down into the northernmost lands of Russia.

The Sami lifestyle is nomadic, based on reindeer husbandry. Reindeer are central to their way of life, providing food, milk, clothing, shelter and cultural identity, their bones and antlers crafted into tools and art, they help to manage the land and so much more. Herders move many thousands of miles with their many thousands of reindeer and a deep understanding of how to work with the seasons and the renewable resources available in what many of us would consider harsh and extreme conditions. This land-based wisdom, accompanying a worldview that was and still is largely rooted in animism, has allowed the Sami people to reside in Sapmi, sustaining themselves and the land for thousands of years.

Like so many other Indigenous peoples, the Sami have faced pressures to convert to a mainstream, politically useful religion, one that leaves no room for their rich heritage of animistic traditions and attempts to quail the perception of deep planetary interconnection and of the world as alive, as companion or Mother, not to be used and abused. Since the seventeenth century, when lines were drawn out on pieces of paper marking the invisible boundaries of the Nordic states, the Sami have faced persecution, land grabbing and displacement.

Sapmi is rich in valuable non-renewable resources, like tomato-greenhouse-heating gas. The spread of industrialisation, including gas extraction, into the Sami territories over the years compromises their way of life, disrupting reindeer migration routes, damaging grazing lands, waterways and biodiversity, while bringing pollution and deforestation.

But the extracted gas does not leave Sapmi forever, it attempts to return to its homelands and its peoples, changed beyond recognition. It returns as climate change, bringing unruly weather events, causing rains in the winter when there should only be snow. Rains that then freeze hard, encasing the reindeer's feeding sources behind impenetrable glass cabinets and letting them starve. It returns as long summers and mild winters which are gradually eroding the eight seasons of Sapmi into just four, and it comes home as inedible moss that is comfortable in the warmer climate, driving out the reindeer's main food source – lichen.

Our warming planet and progressively unpredictable weather events are compromising the Sami's ability to depend on their landscape, which is now changing beyond their experience. To mitigate against their reindeer's starvation, more and more Sami are resorting to keeping their herds enclosed over winter and feeding them themselves. This is a huge shift for a culture rooted in a nomadic way of life, with a delicate and interdependent relationship with their land based on movement to reduce overuse of any one resource. Bringing in feed for the reindeer creates a considerable economic burden on the herder and enclosure makes it easier for disease to spread amongst the stagnant herd. A way of life rooted in renewable resources that sustained them for 10,000 years is being compromised by a few centuries of exploitation.

We might not have known it but the land of the Sami people, many thousands of miles away, is feeding us tomatoes in wintertime. The heated greenhouses growing flavourless, plump winter tomatoes for our delight, cold and firm out of the fridge rather than fresh, sweet and warm from the summer sun, are in part powered by the gas which flows out of Sapmi, and so we are connected.

But what of the tomatoes grown in warm, sunny Spain? The primary exporters of tomatoes into the UK.

If you type Almeria into an online map and turn on the satellite function, you would be forgiven for thinking you were looking down at snow-capped mountains. In reality, the swathe of white is sheets and sheets of plastic fashioned into a city of houses growing tomatoes, peppers, cucumbers, green beans and more, all year round. This is 'el mar de plastico' or 'the sea of plastic'.

This sea of industrial farms, roughly three times the size of Manchester, has become rife with human rights abuses, with migrant workers facing unsafe and exploitative working conditions, payment below the legal minimum wage and even forced labour.

Almeria is one of the driest regions in Europe. Until the 1960s farming in the area was adapted to the arid environment, with farmers focusing on growing the Mediterranean triad: grains, olives and grapes. But the range of crops expanded with the discovery of rain-filled aquifers. Today those aquifers are being emptied faster than the rains can refill them. Exploitation of these coastal aquifers has led to the water becoming salinised, and this, along with the run-off from the farms, is degrading the groundwater source, compromising drinking water quality, habitats and thus the species which have occupied these landscapes.

So we can see that in the case of the much-loved and unassuming tomato, there is a long snaking chain – a chain of people, animals, water, insects, air, soil, trees – that has contributed to bringing tomatoes to British supermarket shelves in winter. Ultimately it's a total miracle that now feels entirely ordinary, and the immense and impressively complex system that allows this miracle to occur turns out to also produce outcomes that are harming us all. It is a system that is not firmly rooted in a balanced relationship between all parts of the chain.

In Almeria, the industry has brought prosperity to the area for some, and it does allow us Northern Europeans year-round access to a range of affordable produce grown without the need for energy-intensive heating. But part of the food's affordability is due to the exploitation of people, land and resources. Some farms are switching to organic practices, harvesting rainwater from the greenhouse roofs and increasing the efficiency of irrigation, yet there is a long way to go to achieve sustainability. Giving industries like this a social licence to operate and a demand to meet is partly why they continue to exist, rather than evolve.

Growing some of our own food in the face of this overwhelmingly complex web of exploitation is radical. It allows us to divest from the system, feeds us, teaches us how it *could* be done and empowers us. It grows in us a curiosity about our food system which is vital if we are going to transform the way we farm, shop, eat and ultimately reform what is arguably one of the most destructive industries on earth.

We can start to notice in our wider lives the web of interconnection we observe in the garden. Tending a little patch of the earth encourages us to care. It's these shifts that can link us to one another and lead to real positive change. The choices we make, opportunities we see and our visions for the future can be coloured by a shifted world-view. Gardens can grow all this in us alongside earthly delights such the satisfaction of sweet summer tomato fruits.

In recent years gardening, foraging and 'nature connection' have become trendy, but in this they can lose some of their grit and power. All too often the pretty pastoral aesthetic is harnessed as an empty story or marketing tool rather than a means to understand and challenge the exploitation that is wrecking so many human and non-human lives on Earth. When our gardens only serve as aesthetic oases for us individuals to enjoy, they may be lovely, but they're not radical.

*

Back in my garden I pick a handful of kale, some rocket and coriander from the unheated greenhouse. I massage the kale, making it soft and moist. I press a clove of garden garlic and scrape the sweet sharp pulp into some garden cider vinegar and olive oil. I toss it together with salt and pepper, tumbling the Spanish tomatoes in with the tastes of my winter garden. I think knowing what a feat tomatoes in winter really are makes them taste better (they are still quite watery, though).

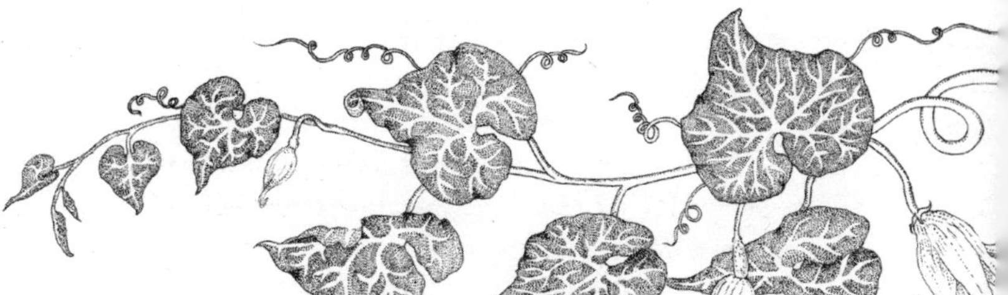

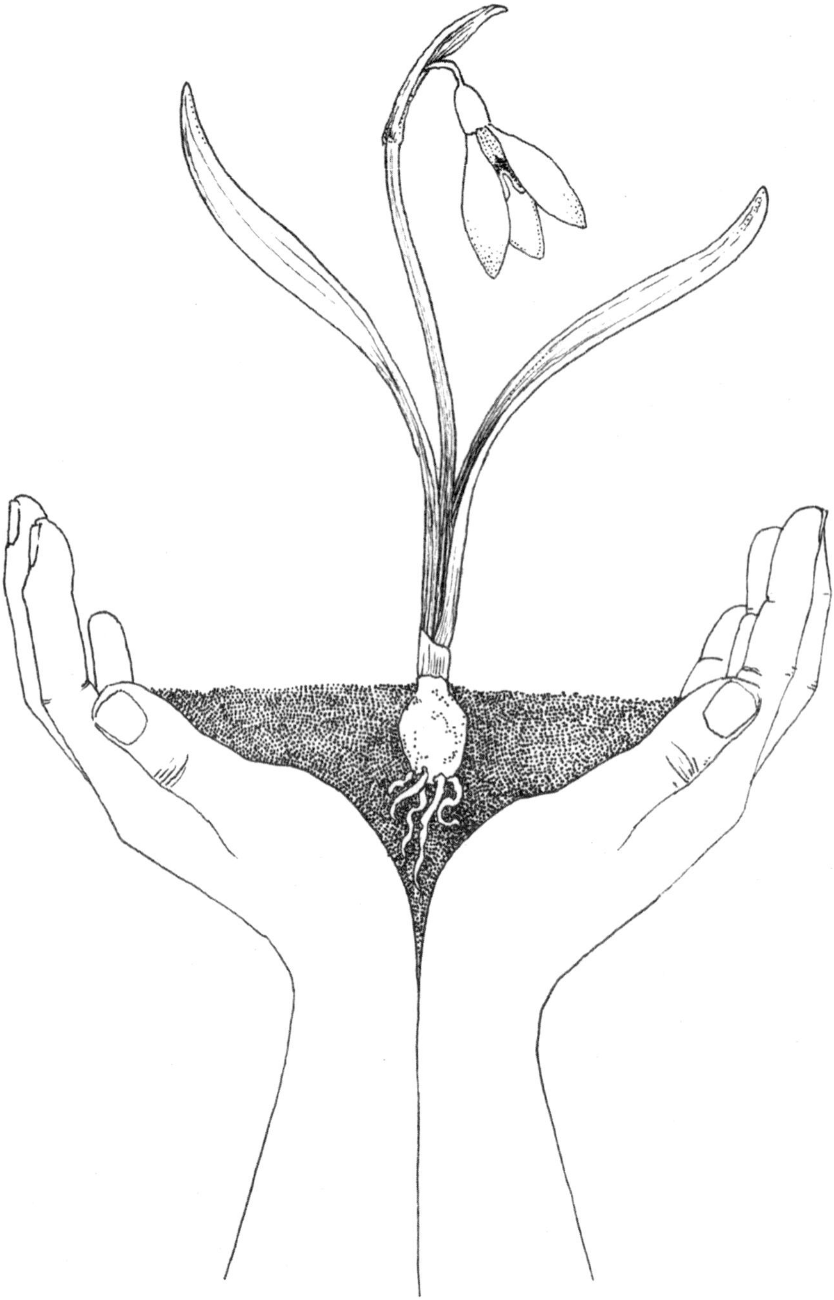

February

BARE ROOT PLANTING

Outside the valley is enveloped in a still, grey dampness. The world feels small and close; the dense, moist air and blanket of soft clouds have bundled us all up and put us away. On days like these I could be convinced that this garden in this town floating about in this valley is all there is.

After several weeks of crisp, dry winter sun, the soil had become dusty and I was starting to worry. For a spring sighing with beautiful life, the crucial ingredients in late winter and early spring are plenty of rain, mild temperatures and occasional patches of sunshine. So the cosy dampness that's descended on us is very welcome.

Today I will show the bare root blackberries their new home. I was inspired when, last year, the neighbours planted blackberries all along the fence surrounding their vegetable patch. They grew high, a few adventurous limbs curling up and over into our garden where a couple of these welcome trespassers flowered. In late summer the berries were delicious. So now here I am, standing in a light drizzle with four pathetic looking twigs, about the length of my forearm and with some straggly roots at one end. They look unpromising, in fact they look more like something I might chop up and condemn to the compost pile. But once safely in the ground, come spring, green shoots will tentatively emerge. In summer they will explode into young blackberry bushes crowned with miniature rose-like flowers, which will buzz with an entourage of winged insects foraging for sweet nectar and protein-rich pollen. And, later, beady-eyed birds will race me for their sweet, dark, juicy berries.

My hands carefully handle the skinny blackberry canes while my mind time travels. My mouth puckers thinking of the tartness of the firm, unripe green-purple fruits and my tummy tickles with anticipation for the plump, shiny black ones that slip easily into my palm, taut or squishy with juice. Ripe, warm, sun-kissed blackberries don't like to be eaten inside; after just a few hours' neglect on the kitchen counter, they go mushy and can start to turn mouldy. They are a treat to be enjoyed as you find them, right then and there.

*

Bare root plants are deciduous, woody perennials that have been lifted from the earth between autumn and early spring when they are dormant and sold to us totally naked, just little twigs without any soil on their roots. You can plant bare root perennials all through winter right up until early spring. Although I have never planted them later than February, they say planting as late as March is possible. This is the best, lowest maintenance and most economical way to grow perennials. They are watered by the seasonal rains and can find their feet before spring and summer come along, and without the need for pots or compost, the plants require far less resources and are easy to move about.

I get a kick out of putting bare root plants in the ground in winter, fantasising about the renaissance of something so very unassuming. Like sowing seeds, it's an action driven by active hope. Someone else might see these plants as ugly, pathetic-looking twigs. But I know the secret of the potential bounty and beauty they hold. I know that really, they are magic.

My life has been so deeply enriched by growing and learning from the garden, I can no longer recall what once would have satisfied me as much as planting these four sorry-looking twigs does now. I sometimes wonder if there was just a void in me waiting to be filled. I do know that for much of my life I felt like I was searching, feeling around in the dark for... something, I didn't know what. My hands would grope and then out of somewhere someone would offer me something: a new pair of shoes, an expensive skincare product, one flight then another and another and another. To find something, somewhere and feel... something... perhaps home?

Now I feel home is *here*, in my small damp garden, planting these bare sticks that plan to grow up big and green and strong and transform themselves into beautiful food. I can support these blackberry roots in their mission, and in so doing they will support me too.

I push my sharp old spade into the ground. Wiggling it forwards and backwards I create a slit in the earth, kneel down and slide straggly blackberry twig number one into its new home, tuck it in and silently wish it well. A quiet ritual. I used to mumble my well wishes out loud, attempting to feel confident in my awkward prayer. But these days I don't open my mouth at all. I suppose now that these actions are familiar, it is more of a feeling and less of a performance.

I say 'prayer' because ecological gardening can, at times, have all the characteristics of a religion. It has sets of beliefs, there are directions for best practice and these are used by many, many people all around the world. It can also often be accompanied by a deep faith that we are working alongside, with, or even *for* forces of nature far greater than ourselves. Tending, gardening, growing can very easily feel like an act of worship. And if not religious then, at the bare minimum, spiritual.

When I was a little girl, our family attended church semi-regularly. In South Africa, around the age of ten, my dad took me to a gospel church in Johannesburg. The mood at the church we normally attended was thoughtful and reserved. This new church was the opposite. The congregation were Black South Africans, a community who had weathered apartheid and who now found themselves marginalised in the country that had been their home for generations. But their religion was vividly alive and kicking. As the service began, the building was heaving with song; people sweated, shouted, cried and danced and danced and danced. That church seemed to hum with their prayers, woes, hopes and dreams. Out of what may have been incredibly challenging lives, this powerful faith had exploded into something so incredibly beautiful and nurturing. Born of struggle, it was fluid and life-giving. It was beautiful and real and of the people. In that gospel church something in me was fed. And now, when I dwell on my relationship with the land or work in the garden, I get the same feeling of energised peace.

Until not so long ago, most of us humans believed that all 'things' – rivers, rocks, trees – were alive, animated. As ecologist Stephan Harding writes: 'Even the ground underfoot was a repository of divine power and intelligence.' This 'animism' underpinned most ancient spirituality and religions.

In Odinala, Ala, the goddess of the Earth and the Earth's body itself is an *alusi*. It is said that when the universe had only just risen from Eke's body, Chukwu sent down a bird to check on creation. The bird carried her mother and father on her back so they could come see it too. But the journey was long and her father died along the way. At this time, the Earth, Ala, was wrapped in the original darkness of uwa and covered in the waters of oshimmiri. With nowhere to bury him, the bird laid her father to rest in her own head. Soon her mother also passed away, and again the bird could find nowhere to lay her to rest but in her head. Eventually, amongst all the water and darkness, the bird found a tree. Having perched there, she laid an egg; the egg cracked open and out came Onwa, the goddess of the moon, and Anyanwu (the male or sometimes female), god of the sun: her mother and father. The bird had displayed such dedicated love for them that Chukwu sent them into the sky to watch over Ala and the universe for the rest of time.

In Odinala, the entirety of the living world is viewed as a type of embodied divinity, since Chukwu, the ultimate genderless energy, or God, is everywhere and in all things – animals, plants, soil, ponds, bacteria – in the form of Chi. Chi is the guardian spirit, animation, aliveness, or God-like nature found in *everything*. It is said that when we interact with the world around us, or hold a loved one close, our Chis also interact. In Odinala, there is an understanding of the ultimate oneness of all things through the Chi.

As a gardener, this presentation of the world as a complex web of life feels familiar and sensible. I see it in the garden, and I feel it too. This garden is small, but it is a mirror of the wider world. I unpack and digest so much of what happens out there when I'm working in my garden, and the garden's lessons often accompany me into the world beyond its walls. As I learn Odinala, I find myself cobbling together a new world-view based on garden lore and the myths and legends of my ancestors who lived in a time when a balanced relationship with the earth was the norm. I like to think that my garden has a Chi, and that feeling of purposeful peace I experience when I am out working with the garden, that's our Chis communing.

My small patch of Earth offers me a dirty religion, a gloriously complicated one that gives as much as it takes. It has teachings on life and death, on care, reciprocity and sharing, dedication and discipline, and on hard work. It has taught me resilience and optimism like nothing else. That you can plant little miracle twigs in damp grey winters and harvest warm ripe fruits eight months later. That if I am a good disciple, *my* God, this force of life and death, will spill secrets into my ears and pour seeds into my hands. This garden guides and anchors me. It fills me with something that I now need to stay balanced and sane. It has replaced the hands reaching out of the dark offering me all sorts of inanimate distractions, things that I can't nurture or accidentally kill. Things that can't teach me about life and death and joy. This garden does so much; it gives me the biggest, brightest views from the most inconsequential soggy, grey moments.

HOW TO PLANT A BARE ROOT PERENNIAL

Some examples of perennials that can be planted bare root:
- Roses (I recommend Rosa rugosa for sweet juicy rose hips, see page 84)
- Sea buckthorn
- Hedging plants like hazel, elder and hawthorn
- Berries like blackberry, raspberry and gooseberry
- Fruit trees like plums, cherries, apples and pears

Most bare root plants are ordered to arrive by post. It is really important to keep the roots moist and the plant cool, so don't leave them hanging around in a warm house. It is best to plant them out as soon as possible, but if you can't, heel them in.

'Heeling in' is what it says on the tin: use a spade to make a slit at an angle in the ground, pop the plant in and firm it down with your heel. Heeling the root in at an angle helps you to identify which plants are in their permanent homes and which are temporarily being kept cool and hydrated.

To plant out permanently, dig a hole or make a slit deep enough to comfortably house the plant's roots, then slide it into the soil, up to its nursery line – i.e., the line of soil you will see on the plant's stem, which marks the point to which it was buried before being sent to you.

Firm the plant in and water to keep it moist, though this shouldn't be a problem when planting in winter!

IMBOLC

In the garden, time doesn't play by the rules. I can't trust seconds, minutes, hours or even days because sometimes sixty seconds feels like a lifetime, and at other times a whole summer like a day. Instead, I measure time by growth, by when the birds sing and when the sun drops low. I can also measure time by how long it takes my seeds to germinate. If it's cold that could be three weeks, but if it's warm it could be a matter of only days. Time becomes an *experience* rather than a structure outside of myself. When the world feels like it's whizzing, or too dreary and slow, this is a very handy tool. Outside amongst the chickens and the veg beds, I can choose which timeline to dip into – the zippy life of the gnat darting in the sun, or the slow upwards stretch of the grandma apple trees.

One thing I can rely on in garden time is returning. Our gardens teach us that we can come back. Each year, each day, we repeat, we try again, feel again, remember, practise, watch, over and over and over. Time here spirals around and around and around, it loops and it hoops, whisking us all up, the dead, the yet to be and the now. Held in time's great arms, we do not leave our actions behind us: we harvest them in the future and we compost them in the past. Everything feeds everyone and time continues to turn.

When time twirls rather than stomps, life feels different – spacious and yet grounded. We cannot drift away from what we do into the ever-distant future. We must revisit it. And that holds us accountable. There is a direct connection between our actions and the experiences to follow, since we will find ourselves back again. We reap what we sow. Will we have left the soil depleted or fertile? In the garden, the connection between action and future outlook is tangible; fertility and abundance literally grows or dwindles based on our seasonal, repeated actions.

While the looping of time holds us accountable, it also gives us grace. A garden is a generative system with capacity to grow, heal and evolve, so mistakes are welcome. We have the opportunity to come back and try again. This is very different to the experience of goal-oriented, linear time, a concept on which we have built our modern lives. In linear thinking, we are taught that we have an end destination and one chance to get there. When you shift this kind of thinking, the world seems to expand. It becomes possible to experiment and make mistakes because they are no longer considered wasted energy, but fuel for learning or a new process. This shift in perception helped me to transition from feeling disempowered and helpless in the face of the injustices of the world to feeling entitled to try to create change, even if I wasn't sure exactly *how*. In the spaciousness of a circular world-view, it's OK if my efforts don't work the first time, or the second or third. It gives me freedom to dream and experiment. Because I will be back here, one way or another, to try again. There is no final 'complete' distraction. Only the constant doing.

Moving through time in the garden is like moving through a house each year, through different parts of the rooms each day. This room has a thick carpet of snow. I look again and the snow grows nodding heads, bobbing on slender green stems. The carpet of snow is really a covering of white flowers – I've arrived at the room where the snowdrops grow.

Snowdrops, *Galanthus nivalis*, meaning 'milk white flower resembling the snow', are one of the first flowers out of bed in late winter, typically flowering around the festival of Imbolc. After winter's peak at Yule, Imbolc, meaning 'in the belly', is the first of the festivals to mark the gradual emergence of life as we move away from the dark of winter solstice and towards the light of the spring equinox. Though the snowdrops have risen, most other life is still just a promise, gestating below the ground, in the belly of Ala.

Noting Imbolc, traditionally celebrated on 1 February, has really helped to change my perception of time moving through winter. The dark stillness of these months can bring a claustrophobic feeling of motionlessness. But the festivals of Samhain, Yule and Imbolc help to mark out the season in stages, giving it a momentum. The shuffles in time and subtle shifts in the world around me become more evident: I know what to look out for and what the signs mean. These annual festivals can act as a map. When I follow it, something more is revealed each year.

I used to run long distance. By the end of each run, simply knowing the end was near brought with it an elation and a final burst of energy which often saw me finishing those final kilometres at my fastest. I used to find this part of winter – the bit at the end which drags on – the hardest. But seeing the snowdrops at Imbolc gives me that same burst of energy. It is still a dark, slow and peaceful time but now it is filled with excited anticipation. Seeds not yet sown and plants still dormant, the whole garden is pure potential. The return of life is so near. I've never marked Imbolc with anything more than going to look for the snowdrops, but *that* now has become my ritual.

WINTER'S EDGE

With my head lolled back, eyes wide open, I take in the edges: the skeletons of the trees' interlaced fingers overhead. It's not long before the cold forces my eyes to fill with tears, squint and shut again.

When I emerge from the woodland, the whole wide world spreads out in front of me. Twinkling white grass flows from one field to the next; outlines of trees rise up from the angular lines of the fences which divide up the land. In the distance the crisp grass runs into a dense knot of twisting trees, their fine naked lines making up what once was a hedge. I know that behind those bare branches are further fields still, falling down to the wide river that rushes from Dartmoor past our town. Today it will be icy cold. Beyond are hills that, from afar, seem to merge into low, palest of pale lavender clouds. Then above the clouds is the cool sun. Milky yellow, nearly white, Anyanwu (the Odinala *alusi* of the Sun) lifts themself into a peachy sky. All the colours are muted. All things are either softly smudged or sharply outlined – there is no in-between. The cold feels light. My breath swirls from my mouth. My ears sting and my cheeks feel hot. This will be one of the last frosts. I take it all in.

Now even on the coldest, darkest, wettest of days, I can feel spring drawing near. Gushing and gurgling towards us like a rushing stream, near ready to break her banks, she will not wait for anyone. I try not to brace for impact. Spring will bring a sweet, breathy whirlwind, quickly tipping into sweaty midsummer evenings, weeding with hot sun-kissed skin and cool early mornings picking herbs and flowers. But right now, the world is quiet and we watch one another, neither moving, not wanting to break the spell. I'm teetering on winter's edge. I soak up the peace.

Winter's dark days and nights provide ample time for thoughtful planning and scheming. Back at home, in my mind's eye I transform the bare garden into explosive, warm, bright colour, the beds full of life. It never turns out quite how I imagine, fine by me. As long as, in my imagination, for these few weeks I can gaze at my colourful fantasy, living in two worlds for a while.

That might be what unites all of us gardeners, perhaps – an infatuation with anticipation, that little tickle of the beauty that's still to come, that we can coax into being. A feeling that holds hands with hope, I think. We hope for spring. The hope grows and grows, then rushes up through us, like sap rising, until the leaves burst through, a green firework display in slow motion. By the end of February my fingers are itching to meddle with life again!

As winter's spell wears off and restlessness grows, I use my garden fantasies as a guide for what I want to grow in the season to come. I list the plants I see in my imagination, flick through garden books and seed catalogues, and go for nosies around other people's summer gardens through the wizardry that is the internet.

To make this vision a reality, I try my best to source the ingredients from suppliers who share my ethos of centring people- and earth-care. In growing a beautiful garden for myself, I want to avoid inadvertently harming the far-off environments of others. Generally, I first try to source anything I might need second-hand. For seed, I hunt down those that are agro-ecologically produced. For me, that's seed that was grown as locally as possible and as ethically as possible. If I'm purchasing the seed, I look for organic or biodynamic (Demeter) certification; better yet, I swap seeds with small-scale local growers. For produce to be certified organic, the Soil Association requires it to be grown from organic seed, unless the seed is unavailable on the market for one reason or another. So, when growing organically in our gardens, it's worth considering the seeds' origin, too. (More on origin of seed in early autumn's 'Seed Saving'.)

In preparation for spring, I no longer buy special seed-sowing compost; I simply use the garden soil, sieved of any large clumps, stones or weeds. (I first started doing this suspecting that it was probably a good thing for the seeds to start their lives in the same sort of medium they will end up in). For me, in my domestic setting, it works excellently. Previously, I bought compost that was both peat-free and also organic.

Peat is formed of organic matter that has partly decomposed in wetlands. It builds up slowly over thousands of years to form peat bogs, which, area for area, store more carbon than rainforests. In fact, the UK's peat bogs hold more carbon than all the forests in Britain, France and Germany combined. The bogs soak up lots of water like a great big sponge, and so help to protect against flooding. They release the water gradually, and because peat acts as a natural filter, the bog water is purified. Peat bogs are also important nature hotspots, housing flora and fauna that depend on this unique habitat. When we dig up our bogs to use the peat in horticulture, we release carbon and destroy an incredibly significant landscape in the process.

Ultimately, the issue of peat use in horticulture is so pressing that it requires legislation to restrict its use entirely. There are many campaigns you can support to hurry this process along. Until that day comes, we can refuse to buy any product that contains it, sending a clear message that we do not want or need peat to be removed from the landscapes it has belonged to for many thousands of years.

When I have tended to the foundations of the garden, spread compost, harvested as much water as I can, put my bare root plants and bulbs in the ground, and given and taken rest, I feel I can enter spring well prepared for the whirlwind of life to come.

In winter I built the structure, in spring and summer I will grow into it.

SOWING CHILLIES IN WINTER

You will need
- Chilli seeds
- Compost
- Seed tray and/or small plant pots

I begin my first seed sowings after Valentine's Day, towards the end of February. Where I live, days have lengthened by this time and though it's still nippy, spring is very near.

Chillies are tender plants, so in winter I keep them indoors to germinate in the warm, and they stay inside until the temperature rises. A cold snap can kill them. But they also need a long growing season to yield their spicy fruits. Some people start their seedlings as early as January, but I personally find that without a grow-light, this can lead to 'leggy plants' – plants which, starved of light and with plenty of warmth, grow lanky and thin, arching towards whatever light source they can find.

There are so many different varieties of chilli to choose from, some mind-blowingly hot and some milder and sweeter. I use a lot of Scotch bonnet and cayenne in my cooking, so these are the ones I grow. Have a look in your kitchen cupboards to see what sorts of chilli you tend to cook with and consider growing those. Or if you want to taste something new, have a read around to discover weird and wonderful varieties to try.

STEP 1: Sowing

1. Fill your seed tray or pots with compost.
2. Sprinkle your seeds on top.
3. Sprinkle a little more compost on top of your seeds and firm down to ensure contact with their growing medium.
4. Place your tray on a plate, in a bowl or second tray which you can fill with water.
5. Pour water into whatever vessel your chilli tray is resting in. The compost will drink up the water from below creating a nice moist environment for your seeds without knocking them about by watering from above.
6. Remove your tray or pots from the water after about five minutes, or once you see the moisture has reached the surface of the compost.
7. Place the pots or tray somewhere sunny and warm, ideally a bright windowsill where they will get plenty of light.
8. Now just watch and wait for germination, making sure your compost remains moist but never waterlogged. To water your seeds just pop them back into a tray of water.

NOTE:
The temperature and moisture level will determine the speed at which your seeds wake up. To speed things up, put your seed tray/pots inside a large, clear plastic bag and seal them in, creating a mini greenhouse. Or try covering your pots or tray with a clear plastic tray to form a lid (like the ones used in some supermarket packaging). You might also purchase or borrow an electric propagator to keep them warm.

STEP 2: Pricking out chilli seedlings
If you have sown multiple seeds together in a tray or pots, once your seedlings have risen and opened up their first leaves, it's time to move them into separate pots of their own. When moving your seedlings, be very careful not to damage the stem. The delicate baby plants can handle some damage to roots and leaves, but a broken stem means game over.

1. Fill some 9 cm pots with compost.
2. To remove your seed babies, gently hold a seedling by one of its leaves, then, using a pencil or twig, carefully excavate the soil around and below the seedling. Carefully tug at the plant and it should slip out with most of its roots intact.
3. With your finger, pencil or dibber, make a little hole in the compost in the prepared pot and slip the seedling in – guide its fragile roots using the pencil too. Firm the compost around the seedling, being careful not to cause any damage.
4. Water from below, as before.
5. Leave somewhere warm and bright. Light is even more important at this stage as the chilli plant continues to grow.

TIPS:
If you move your seedlings when they are very small with only their first set of leaves, it is possible to plant them deep into the pot, right over their stem and up to their leaves. The stem is so young it will happily switch to producing roots. This is a handy trick when pricking out very leggy seedlings. Bear in

mind, though, some plants, like courgettes and squash, don't respond well to this approach. It's best reserved for plants that produce small, delicate seedings.

- Feed your chilli babies with an organic liquid feed while they are in pots. I water mine weekly with a chicken manure and nettle home brew.
- As your plants continue to grow, you will eventually want to move them to bigger pots or into the ground. As lovers of warmth, chillies do best when grown somewhere toasty – in a greenhouse, polytunnel, against a hot wall, in a conservatory, or even on a windowsill in a large pot.

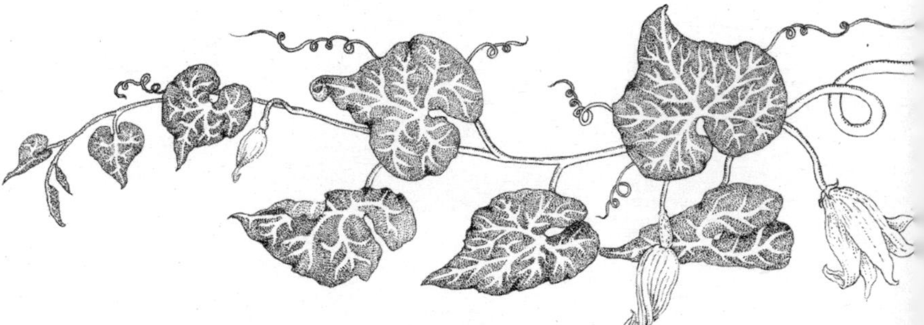

Feb
Mar
April
May
June
July
Aug
Sept
Oct
Nov
SOW
TRANSPLANT
HARVEST
Basil
SOW
TRANSPLANT
HARVEST
HARVEST
SOW
TRANSPLANT
HARVEST
SOW
TRANSPLANT
HARVEST

March

TIME TO SOW

Just as they did last year, and all the years before, the days are now noticeably growing longer. Growing days grow plants. They have what can only be described as an encouraging effect on them, as though the plants think to themselves, 'Well, if the day can do it, so can I.'

Tentatively, the germinated chillies are becoming young plants, crowding my living room windowsill. They arch towards the sun in a slow-motion side stretch – it looks like it would feel nice, slowly extending up and over, leaves flung open, unfurling a little more day by day, to catch every last bit of that great star's glow. It's almost as if they're bowing before it. When I do my stretches, reaching my hands up and open to the sky, I often think of them. Every few days, I rotate the baby plants so they don't overdo it on one side and become crooked.

They will stay in the living room with us a while longer; outside isn't warm enough for these tender sun worshippers just yet.

The world around tells me it's time to start my spring sowings. I'm noticing more and more wild seedlings germinating, in the cracks of the pavement, on muddy verges, at the edges of paths. Tiny soft green leaves emerging, braving the still brisk weather, woken by the sun's gentle gaze. Taking cues from the 'wild' is one of the most valuable gardening lessons I've learnt. I say 'wild', but I always find it funny referring to any part of Britain as such. Though less tended than public parks and verges, the woodland paths, rivers and hedgerows I walk along are not completely devoid of human impact and management. They are the result of many years of human interaction and cultivation. But they are outside my garden and mostly left to their own devices, so to me they are 'the wild'.

No two locations are exactly the same, and no two seasons the same either. What we read in books and hear from fellow gardeners, who may tell us to sow seeds on a certain calendar date, must always be adapted to our own local conditions. When we tune into how the life outside our garden is responding to the change in weather and season, it becomes a sort of personal compass helping us to navigate through the year. And after spending some time in a place, that relationship becomes instinctual; for example, we may know to begin sowing when the first daffodils show in a local park or street. I have found that through bringing what I learn in the wild back into the garden, I act as a bridge between the two worlds, and I feel a deeper connection to them both.

Before I had a greenhouse, despite watching seedlings popping up all around me outdoors, I would sit on my hands and wait until the early tulips bloomed at the end of March, or even the start of April, to sow any hardy veg. I simply didn't have the indoor space to accommodate hundreds of seedling housemates each spring. Only a select few could stay inside, the rest had to brave the outdoors, where March's chills would slow their growth, giving them a sluggish start. Trying to gently coax life out of plants that would far rather just wait a few weeks longer and get on with less fussing seemed a waste of my energy. Now the seedlings and I have a compact, unheated, glasshouse, which changes everything. It can provide enough warmth for speedy germination and enough protection for the plants to put on plenty of growth while it is still very cold outdoors.

I love this liminal period in the garden – we are between seasons, winter not quite shrugged off and spring not quite here. The faint March sun is calling me outside. I bundle up, although not too much, because I'm headed for the greenhouse, which, on a day like today, will be warm.

The garden looks mostly brown still, but green is rising. Like a watercolour splodge on damp paper, it slowly seeps up and out from the earth, first covering the ground, then climbing a little higher and higher until eventually deciduous trees are covered in leaves. But for now, spring is small and unassuming, at the moment the drop of paint lands on the paper. The lower growing plants take advantage of this time to soak up the soft spring sun's rays before the days become hotter and taller plants begin to cast shade. I'm glad the trees wait to put on their leaves. I like shade in the summer, but in spring I want the thawing touch of direct sun.

Inside the greenhouse, I scan my sowing calendar. I've spent the last few days getting ready for this moment, tidying and sorting in preparation for the arrival of lots of new babies. Washing, clearing, weeding, mulching, arranging. It's a kind of nesting. A second-hand, slatted wooden potting bench runs along the greenhouse's left side. While I mother my plants, its useful slats allow stray soil to fall through to the ground to be easily collected and reused – any excess water can escape too. Right now, my bench is dusted down, clean and ready with an unusually neat pile of pots and trays.

From the pile I select a small tray about the size of a paperback book.

Beside the pile of pots on the bench sits a metal bucket filled with sifted, moist dark garden soil, with any weeds, stones and twigs picked out. I scoop a few trowelfuls into my tray, tap it down on the bench so the soil settles and add another trowelful, then press the soil down with my fingers and gently ruffle its surface so it's not too flat. Next, I divide the tray into three sections, using wooden lollipop sticks as walls running from side to side. I sprinkle a heap of tiny pale tomato seeds into my palm (these are a variety called Moonglow that I saved last year). A whole field of tomatoes in the palm of my hand.

I find seeds untiringly remarkable. These miraculous minuscule grains are alive biologically, but don't appear so; in fact, you would be forgiven for mistaking them for tiny bits of grit, or flecks of dust. They seem to exist in an in-between world, somewhere between life and death, between potentiality, impossibility and actuality.

Plants are autotrophs. They create food from sunlight and carbon. And because of this feat, we exist. Plant life supports so many other forms of life with food and shelter. I scatter a few Moonglow seeds into the first third of the tray. In my mind's eye, when I plant a seed I'm drawing a dot on a blank piece of paper. Infinitely complex webs radiate out from that dot, into the past and future, linking up with life the plant's ancestors once supported, and the lives its kin will one day support in turn. Seed is a wonderful and precious gift.

I dust a handful of soil over the top of the seeds and pop another lollypop stick into the tray, this time a label: 'Tomato Moonglow, 5 March'. The other two sections of the tray will house further tomato varieties. I'll have more plants than I need, but that's the beauty of seed. Any spares can be given away. When gardening ecologically, it doesn't take long to create an abundance of just about everything. There's plenty to share.

The tray will come into the house with me so the tomato seeds can germinate on the warmth of a windowsill. Once they have germinated, I will prick the seedlings out into their own little pots. Being tender plants, they will remain inside till temperatures rise, then I'll move them to the greenhouse soil. The tomatoes and the chillies are the two plants we tolerate co-living with. The rest of the seeds I sow today are hardy; they will stay here, in their glass home, till they are big enough to plant out in the garden beds.

Gardening is hitching a ride on the rhythm of the year – spring will carry us along; the seeds we sow will grow. But this same rhythm can become our enemy. When I apply linear thinking while gardening, the threat of missing the boat can fill me with dread. At this time of year, before the greenhouse made early sowings possible, I often felt as though I was trailing behind. I'd panic, worried that spring was leaving the station without my seedlings and me onboard.

Garden time, however, says otherwise. The garden isn't thinking about a final destination to be reached by running along a straight track. Carbon-based life is born, grows, dies, decays, is born, grows, dies, decays, and so on and on and on. Spring, summer, autumn, winter, on and on and on. I remind myself that this isn't the only train and there is no final destination, no need to rush.

SOWING TIMETABLE

The moment Valentine's Day has passed, it takes all my discipline not to sow every seed I have. I want to throw all of them at the visions of vibrant beds in my head. With so many different crops and varieties to choose from, it's easy to get carried away. Over the years I've found that less is more. It's easy to sow a seed. The real challenge comes with continued commitment to caring for what emerges, and at times I can feel overwhelmed by the armies of seedlings sown in excitement but which I don't actually have the ability or space to nurture. To reduce overwhelm, I stagger my sowings through February, March and April, growing a little at a time.

Below is my sowing timetable for this garden. I tend to keep it to hand as a guide, following it loosely rather than letting it dictate what I do. You may be able to follow it more or less precisely, depending on where you live, or you may want to simply use it as inspiration and adapt it to your local climate.

	JAN	FEB	MAR	APR	MAY
Amaranth leaf			SOW	TRANSPLANT	
Basil		SOW	TRANSPLANT		HARVEST
Bean – *Dwarf French*			SOW	TRANSPLANT	
Bean – *Broad*	SOW / TRANSPLANT				HARVEST
Bean – *French Climbing*			SOW		TRANSPLANT
Bean – *Runner Bean*			SOW	TRANSPLANT	
Beetroot			SOW	TRANSPLANT	HARVEST
Cabbage – *Spring*			HARVEST		
Cabbage – *Summer*		SOW	TRANSPLANT		
Cabbage – *Winter*				SOW	TRANSPLANT
Chard	HARVEST		SOW		TRANSPLANT
Chilli	SOW	HARVEST	TRANSPLANT		

	JUN	JUL	AUG	SEPT	OCT	NOV	DEC
	HARVEST						
				UNDERCOVER HARVEST			
	DIRECT SOW						
		HARVEST					
					SOW		
						TRANSPLANT	
		HARVEST					
	DIRECT SOW						
		HARVEST					
	SOW						
		TRANSPLANT					
		HARVEST					
				HARVEST			
						SOW	
		UNDERCOVER HARVEST					

	JAN	FEB	MAR	APR	MAY
Chicory				TRANSPLANT	
Chives			SOW		TRANSPLANT
	HARVEST				
Coriander			SOW	TRANSPLANT	
	UNDERCOVER HARVEST			HARVEST	
Courgettes			SOW		TRANSPLANT
Cucumbers			SOW	TRANSPLANT	
Fenugreek				DIRECT SOW	
Fennel			SOW	TRANSPLANT	
Garlic	PLANT				
Kale			SOW	TRANSPLANT	
	HARVEST				
Leeks		SOW		TRANSPLANT	
	HARVEST				
Lettuce		SOW	TRANSPLANT		
	UNDERCOVER HARVEST			HARVEST	
Asian Greens		SOW	TRANSPLANT		
	UNDERCOVER HARVEST			HARVEST	

	JUN	JUL	AUG	SEPT	OCT	NOV	DEC
		SOW					
	HARVEST						
						UNDERCOVER HARVEST	
	DIRECT SOW						
	HARVEST						
		UNDERCOVER HARVEST					
	HARVEST						
	HARVEST						
					PLANT		
	HARVEST						
		HARVEST					
						HARVEST	
						UNDERCOVER HARVEST	
						UNDERCOVER HARVEST	

	JAN	FEB	MAR	APR	MAY
Parsley	HARVEST	SOW		TRANSPLANT	
Peas		SOW	TRANSPLANT		HARVEST
Radish		DIRECT SOW			HARVEST
Rocket		DIRECT SOW	HARVEST		
Spinach		SOW	TRANSPLANT	HARVEST	
Squash – *Summer*			SOW	TRANSPLANT	DIRECT SOW
Squash – *Summer*			SOW	TRANSPLANT	DIRECT SOW
Tomato		SOW		TRANSPLANT	

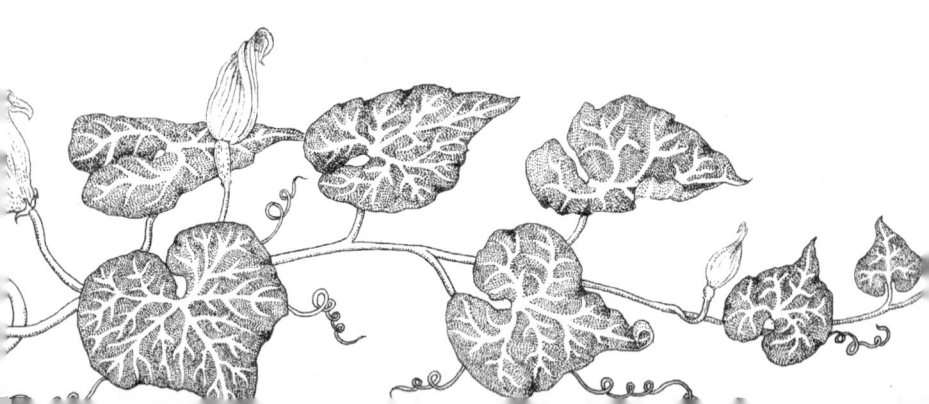

	JUN	JUL	AUG	SEPT	OCT	NOV	DEC
					SOW		
						UNDERCOVER HARVEST	
						UNDERCOVER HARVEST	
		HARVEST					
		HARVEST					
		HARVEST					

UNINVITED GUESTS

Last night it rained; today we have Devon mist. The temperature is mild and the air is heavy with water that seems to linger, never quite falling. It's like living in a cloud. Toby, who grew up first on Bodmin Moor in north Cornwall and then in Devon, is no stranger to living in clouds. Before we moved here, he warned me of the damp. 'It's very wet down there in Devon,' he'd say again and again. I'd shrug it off. I mean, just how wet could it really be? In any case, when I was a child, my grandmother had told me not to worry about the rain, since I'm not made of salt.

My measure of 'very wet' was the sudden torrential downpours in the rainy season in South Africa. Cracking lightning ripping the sky, ear-splitting thunder, buckets and buckets of water falling all at once... and then it would pass. The rainwater would soak or drain away, and you'd get on with your day. I was tough enough for that kind of wet when I was a little girl. 'I can handle the rain,' I'd tell him.

But as it turns out, Devon wet is different. It's not thrilling, explosive and enlivening like South Africa's rainstorms. It's slow and stealthy and it lingers, sometimes for weeks. One early spring here, it was wet every single day for an entire month. You don't need to be tough, just to have enduring patience. In winter, when the seemingly endless wetness is combined with a blank landscape of greys and browns, it becomes a test of mental resilience.

Nevertheless, even when I hate the Devon wet, I love it. I love that it asks us to dig deep: its nothingness gives so much room for our somethingness. I love to watch out the window as the world drips. I love the soft greenness of a landscape sprinkled with life-giving moisture, the jungle of ferns, navel wort and moss that it grows on the upper side of the branches of great big trees. When it's not winter, Devon wet can be beautiful. Tiny droplets of water balance on every surface; if the day is bright, they glow. My dark skin and Afro hair, prone to dryness, adore it. Sometimes I can watch the Devon mist advance upon us, roll down over the hills, across the valley and into our little town. When it descends, the valley is obscured from view.

MARCH

Outside, as I wander through the garden, the tiny gravity-defying droplets cling to me, all the plants are coated with delicate crystal balls, and when I brush past them my clothing gets drenched. Inexplicably, this mist is only wet if you touch it. If you let it be, let the droplets hang gently wherever they form, they remain a spattering of lovely little orbs. But the moment they are touched, they burst, trickle into wet rivers, form damp patches, soak into socks and skin. Wet-weather gear is recommended. On particularly mild days, the alternative is as few clothes as possible. There's nothing worse than sodden clothing; skin dries faster than fabric; and I love the sight of the watery orbs gathering amongst the soft hairs on my arms and legs.

This morning I'm heading out into the mist for two reasons: firstly, to fill my mug with nettle tops from under the apple trees; secondly, to check on the lettuces I planted out yesterday.

The lettuces are all still here, good. But in the bed opposite, I notice that one of the young cabbages has vanished. I squat down to make sure I'm not mistaken. No, definitely, certainly, the plant which last night stood a good 15 cm tall with several healthy leaves is now nowhere to be seen. I lean in, frown and count the cabbages again just to be sure. There must at least be a stump remaining. There isn't.

An enchanted garden coated in water crystals that are not wet and vanishing cabbages. These clues point to only two things – slugs and snails, the gastropods.

I planted the cabbages out about five days ago. At night, I'd carefully covered each of them with a garden cloche or an old glass jar from the kitchen. But this last evening, I'd forgotten, and one of them didn't make it through the night, devoured by the horde of gastropods who live in the garden and who appear, clearly ravenous, by night.

The slugs and snails have excellent taste; they also love Devon wet, in fact they might die without it. Like me, they too adore the ancient stone wall that runs the length of the garden. They love compost, mulch, wild areas that offer a garden a touch of lovely chaos and the edges to veg beds made from old scaffolding boards, bricks, rocks and slate found around the garden. We both dislike slug and snail pellets but love homegrown veg and cannot get enough of fresh strawberries (although I prefer mine sun-warmed while they like their soft fruit wet). The list could go on. With so much in common, to some degree it's hard not to respect them.

Some of my earliest garden memories include gathering buckets of snails in our garden in London and Grandma With The Nice Garden telling me they were a nuisance in hers. I have always found their doughy, almost cow-like faces cute, and, controversial, I know, but there's something about their soft, slow slipperiness that is endearing to me. I like the way they shrink away into their shell when startled and then tentatively send out their little tentacles to feel around, check the coast is clear and then slowly re-emerge from their mobile homes. They are so strangely different from us, but also alike. They too have lungs, a liver, stomach, heart. They too are dependent on healthy ecosystems for their survival.

I am less fond of slugs. I don't like how, when I pick them up, their slime clings to my skin and I have to scrub with a rough brush and soapy hot water to get it off. The little ones can sometimes be sort of sweet, but I find the big ones cumbersome and grotesque in their portly slime. I don't hate them, though. In any case, I am fairly certain the bulk of the damage in my garden is down to snails. Only nine out of the forty-four slug species in the UK eat living plants. Most slugs in the UK are 'detritivores'; they are cleaners and tidy-uppers, which makes them incredibly helpful in our gardens. Snails will also help with clearing up dead or decaying matter, aiding the process of keeping the nutrients cycling in a loop within the garden, but their favourite activity is devouring fresh green growth.

When I go out with a torch at night, it's snails I see sneaking about everywhere I turn. When we come home late and walk up the alleyway to our garden, it's snail shells we feel crunching under every step. Once we returned from dinner with friends to find the path so crunchy that we drunkenly decided to go out and gather as many as we could. We filled a whole bucket that evening!

Like most gardeners, I mainly encounter the classic brown garden snails (*Cornu aspersum*) and a few of the smaller branded snails

(*Cepaea* species), the ones with smooth, shiny shells and stripes of dull creamy yellow and brown. Of the two, the common garden snail is most likely to be responsible for any damage in growing spaces, from gardens to farms and allotments.

When we arrived here, the vast colony of snails reflected the fact that the garden had been left wild for several years. Since the garden is small and surrounded by other gardens in the town, it lacks a concentration of the natural predators who help to keep snail numbers down. Some human intervention is required.

This thriving snail community warmly welcomed my first attempts to grow veg. Even though I had suspected for a while that most 'natural' quick-fix slug and snail control methods don't work, I doggedly tried them all – copper tape around the tops of all the raised beds, eggshells, grit, sand and beer traps. Then the RHS conducted a trial which confirmed my suspicion, finding that wool, eggshells, copper tape, sharp horticultural grit and pine bark mulches don't work at all. Another study has shown that a barrier of rough, plastic bristles around the plant reduces snail attention in the short term. I find this to be the case with the eggshells and wool also. They seem to put them off momentarily, but I once watched a snail slide over a ring of wool pellets, and have seen many glistening trails left over crushed eggshells, because no sooner does one snail make it through than the others follow. Snails track the slime trails of others in the hope of finding food, and juvenile snails tend to follow the bigger ones for the same reason. They also have the habit of returning to successful feeding sites. All it takes is one big brave snail to cross the textured boundary once, locate the tasty young plant, and then night after night all the other snails follow suit.

It was with relief that I finally decided to stop faffing around with half-solutions. But knowing my slimy folk management toolkit was officially pointless, I also felt a bit helpless. So, I do still – perhaps superstitiously – lay sheep's wool and eggshells around plants, though now more for the health benefits the added organic matter can bring to the plants than as an effective physical deterrent. Instead, I now take no chances and keep all young plants covered with jars and cloches every night and on damp days too. I keep this up until the plant has grown big and healthy and usually don't let them go a night alone till a dry spell arrives, sending the slimy folk off in search of cool, moist shelter. Except last night. And now one of my cabbages is being digested by the garden's not-so-small army of snails.

For me, the use of pesticides in the garden is out of the question. Chemical warfare may kill these slimy beasts, but it harms other life in the process. Thankfully the pesticide metaldehyde, typically used to kill gastropods, was finally banned from use in the UK in 2022, due to rising concerns of the ripple effect it was having on wildlife and the wider landscape. Slugs and snails were recognised as being a vitally important food supply for many creatures and so critical for the health of an ecosystem. Poisoning them was poisoning creatures further up the food chain as well as reducing their food supply.

Tempting as it might be to embark on the nigh-impossible task of eradicating all slugs, snails and other crop-munching creatures from the garden, it would in any case be a fool's mission. Reducing a garden to a space devoid of gastropod hangouts will dissuade most other life from taking up residence in the garden too, turning it into a barren space, lacking the biodiversity necessary for resilience, beauty and health. We humans can spend a lot of time and energy (two very precious resources) trying to rid our land of any so-called pests, but the moment that space is liberated from this constant upkeep, the slimy fellows will return, along with a tangle of weeds, decaying organic matter and a touch of vibrant chaos.

Slugs and snails help to break down organic matter, assisting in building healthy soils and supporting the process of locking carbon in the ground. Their nutrient-rich faeces also increases fertility in the soil. Snails are particularly important in calcium cycling – concentrating the calcium they consume in their shells which can then be eaten by other creatures or broken back down into the soil. If, by some horrid miracle, I was actually able to wipe them out, the impact it would have on the rest of the ecosystem – and so me – would be terrible.

Nature-friendly gardening, though, does not mean simply letting slugs and snails have all the fun. Instead, it invites a holistic approach. Rather than focusing on the problem as an isolated issue, I see it as part of a network of interactions. When walking on a damp afternoon in the woods, it would be strange not to see snails and slugs going about their business, and yet the woodland is not harmed by them because this habitat is biodiverse, healthy and balanced. There is ample surplus plant matter to feed the slugs and snails without causing destruction and there are enough natural predators to keep their populations in check. In fact, the woodland positively benefits from the activities of the slugs and snails and the web of life they support.

This healthy balance is my aim in the garden – to cultivate a space abundant enough that it can tolerate a reasonable number of gastropods and offer their predators an ample food source. If the balance is right, then those predators will keep the gastropod colonies in check and ensure that they don't munch through everything that can photosynthesise.

Slugs, snails and their eggs are food for all sorts of creatures – birds, hedgehogs, slowworms, toads, frogs, foxes, badgers, shrews, rats, mice, moles, ground beetles, glow worm larvae and nematodes (microscopic parasites found in the soil), to name but a few. When we arrived, the wild plot was already home to a whole collection of helpful species. So I added a couple of ponds and was mindful not to over-tame the space to ensure it remained welcoming for the organisms that predate on gastropods. I have found several stashes of empty snail shells in quiet corners of my garden, under log piles, below shrubs or beneath piles of dry brown matter destined for the compost heap. These collections are likely leftovers from mouse banquets, or possibly rats.

Some gastropod predators have developed ingenious techniques for hunting their prey. Thrushes pick snails up in their beaks and flick them down hard onto a specially selected rock or stone, called a 'thrush anvil', which they return to. I've found hard, protruding tree roots on quiet footpaths used for this purpose, evidenced by the piles of smashed snail shells around roots that had been made shiny from the dried snail slime. Ground beetles are known to use their mandibles to break through snail shells, cracking along the shells' spiral. Hedgehogs, who usually prefer to snack on insects that are less slimy, surmount the problem of a slug's stickiness (which makes them inedible to many creatures) by rolling them in the earth and then wiping the gloopy soil off, rendering them more palatable.

Glow-worm beetle larvae have a particularly gruesome way of devouring their strict diet of slugs and snails. Their bite administers a paralysing poison which prevents any chance of escape and begins the digestion process, turning the slug or snail into a sort of soup which the larvae can then easily slurp up. The slug or snail is often alive during the process. Though a grim way to go, death by glow-worm larvae is actually quite an effective slug and snail management strategy. The larvae of most glow-worm species are specialised predators, adapted to prey on slugs and snails alone. A UK study published in 2020 showed that over the course of 18 years, glow-worm numbers have dropped by 75 per cent. This is due to habitat loss, increasingly warm summers driven by climate change (like slugs and snails, glow-worms enjoy cool damp conditions), and the widespread use of pesticides and herbicides which impact the glow worms directly as well as their habitats and prey. The steady increase in light pollution is also attributed to their decline. Female glow-worms 'glow' to attract a mate, but male glow-worms are attracted to *all* sources of light and so can be easily drawn off course by a garden or security light. Current healthy populations of glow-worms exist predominantly in locations less affected by light pollution. By housing a healthy number of slugs and snails in our gardens and cultivating spaces that are appealing and safe for wildlife, we create the conditions necessary for many other creatures to take up residence too. Imagine having glow-worms supporting your night-time slug and snail garden patrol?

Due to the garden's size, location and the fact that I'm in it often, there is a limit to the predators present. And there are only so many slugs and snails I can gather myself, so I have recruited some extra helpers, the Pekin Bantam chickens. Chickens might not be as efficient at managing gastropods as ducks, and they have the annoying habit of scratching everywhere they go, but the flock has helped me create a better balance in the garden. Predominantly predating on smaller specimens, they have no interest in the larger slugs, and they require my help to get at the bigger snails with strong shells. Thrush-style, I break them open on a stone and the chickens swiftly swallow the exposed morsel in one gulp.

I briefly considered buying in further backup in the form of predator nematodes – microscopic worms that exist naturally in the soil, some of which are parasitic on slugs and snails. Although effective, nematodes target *all* slugs and snails they come into contact with, including the thirty-five detritivore slugs and harmless branded snails. If there is a sudden crash in an area's gastropod population, their other habitual predators are forced to seek out food elsewhere. When the nematode numbers eventually and inevitably subside and a normal population size is restored, with fewer other natural predators to keep slugs and snails in check, the ensuing gastropod explosion could be considerable. This would start a cycle of dependence on a product. In any case, I don't want to eradicate the *entire* slug and snail population – only *some*.

I look up from my missing cabbage at the muddle of weeds inhabiting the patch right beside the bed. I know the gastropods are living there, because I see their night-time trails running across from the greenery. But this wild corner also houses their predators. The undergrowth obscures a pile of pruned apple branches that were too girthy for my chipper, and a thick layer of decaying organic matter on the soil surface. There is also a pond in there, home to at least two hungry frogs and in spring their spawn and tadpoles. Only the night before I found a hedgehog snuffling around too.

The health of this soil also plays a lead role in the battle against the gastropods. Healthy soil grows healthy plants, and healthy plants, just like healthy humans, are more resilient. Over millions of years, plants have evolved various strategies to ward off attack – from slugs, snails, deer and caterpillars, to mealy bugs and mites – such as a thick bark, thorns or waxy leaves. But they also have mysterious and unseen weapons at their disposal – their biochemical defence.

Just as in humans, the plant's microbiome (a vast collection of microorganisms, some helpful, some harmful, many neutral and others which choose a side depending on the dominant characters) plays an essential role in defending against disease, parasites, pests and herbivores. A plant's microbiome is largely found in the rhizosphere, the small zone around its roots which is teeming with tiny lives. Rhizospheres are thought to be some of the most complex ecosystems on Earth. The organisms inhabiting this space are generally recruited from the surrounding soil and are attracted by the high levels of nutritious fluid, called exudates, which the plants release from their roots. A plant's rhizosphere also plays a part in a dynamic underground communication network, exchanging signals between neighbouring plant roots, bacteria and fungi.

Beneficial organisms in the rhizosphere can act as the plant's first line of defence. They promote healthy growth by delivering vital nutrients; they out-compete pathogenic bacteria for nutrients and space; they antagonise harmful microbes by producing toxins and antibiotics which protect the plant and ward off disease; and, incredibly, they also activate disease-resistant genes in their host plant. When the healthy plant, supported by its microbiome, is under attack, it triggers the production of chemical compounds called secondary metabolites. A plant's metabolites can repel herbivores or attract predators for the pests troubling it, heal injuries, communicate with other organisms, and so much more.

Plants supported by healthy soil biology and a beneficial rhizosphere are more likely to have access to the resources required for them to produce the secondary metabolites they need to deploy their biochemical defence.

Take the cabbage white butterfly and its caterpillar's dinner of choice – the cabbage. A healthy cabbage is able to produce secondary metabolites which both repel cabbage white butterflies from laying their eggs on the plant and also attract a parasitic wasp to come and deal with any existing grazers. The wasp, drawn in by the cabbage plant, lays its eggs inside the caterpillars and then, on hatching, the wasp larvae consume their hosts alive.

New evidence suggests that insects are crucial vectors for the spread of plant-beneficial microbiomes. Pollinators become district nurses on wings. Strawberries, bees and beneficial bacteria known as Streptomyces globisporus SP6C4 (I'll call it 'Tomy' for short) are a beautiful example of one such relationship. When present in the strawberry's rhizosphere, Tomy protects it from soil-borne pathogens. This bacteria also travels up from the rhizosphere to the plant's flowers, where it protects the tiny white blooms from harmful fungi. Honeybees who gather pollen and nectar from the strawberry flowers, pollinating as they go, also unknowingly collect the Tomy bacteria, which in turn protects its new bee host from harmful microorganisms. As the bees visit each flower, they spread the healthful bacteria from bloom to bloom. On the bees' return to their hive, Tomy spreads through the colony and is subsequently passed to many other strawberry plants far and wide. Once delivered to a new flower via the bees, Tomy migrates back down to the rhizosphere where it continues to live in symbiosis with the plant.

I find this incredible, complex relationship, invisible to the naked eye, so very humbling. Plants, insects, bacteria and fungi have been co-evolving for many millions of years, and undoubtedly have more tricks up their sleeves, more relationships of support and co-creation, than we will ever know.

Through the complex webs of life in the garden, the insects pollinating the plants may also be helping to spread microbes which can support those plants in responding to and bouncing back from disease and attacks by all pests, including slugs and snails. Growing organically with ecology in mind, we foster these miraculous relationships *and* cultivate healthy plants.

The recipe for lively soil biology calls for a diverse range of living plant roots, which pump out rich exudates into the rhizosphere and so engage in symbiotic relationships with soil-dwelling bacteria and fungi by feeding them. The life in the soil needs that all-important decaying organic matter to live in and feast on too. So a soil surface protected and fed by diverse living, dead and dying vegetation above ground and held together by roots below contributes to a diverse and thriving universe beneath our feet.

I endeavour to recreate a similar environment in the garden. In a way, by laying sheep's wool and eggshells on the soil to ward off the slimy folk, I am also contributing to the unseen forcefield of protection offered by the plant-beneficial microorganisms in the earth. The added organic matter helps provide the humidity, stable temperatures and carbon required for the soil life to thrive.

Finally, as an added precaution, I religiously follow the wisdom of a memorable gardener's rhyme first recorded in the mid-1800s, though most likely it's as old as old can be. It reminds us to:

Sow four seeds in a row,
one for the mouse,
one for the crow,
one will wither
and the other will grow.

For my garden, however, I have adapted the rhyme to:

Sow four seeds in a row,
one for the snail,
one for the crow,
one will be slugged
and the other will grow.

Following the example of the woodlands, I build capacity and generosity into the system. In sowing and growing more than I need, I ensure that if all else fails, I'll always have a few plants to spare for the uninvited guests.

I accept that my young plants will not only feed me, they'll feed the snails too. And no matter how much the snails touch my heart, I am very happy that, in turn, they will become food for the chickens and any other creatures that help to keep them in check.

I plant out a replacement cabbage and wander back to the house, my tightly coiled hair now glittering with watery orbs of Devon wet. I take a detour and step into the warmth of the greenhouse. Bending over to inspect the seedlings, I move my head. Rain falls as all those tiny droplets of water in my hair shower down on the seedlings.

SPRING EQUINOX

The garden has giant nests scattered about it; they are narrow, maybe an arm's-length wide, but high. I made the nests when I chopped down all the brittle, sepia-toned growth from last year's plants, the stuff that insects would have been overwintering in, and gathered it into these huge bundles. If it was just me in this garden, I would leave the nests where they stand – there's something whimsical about them, as though they've been fashioned by some enchanted giant birds, and I imagine finding their enormous eggs nestled inside. But reluctantly, as I do annually, usually around Easter, I lug the electric chipper from the shed and start the long, slow task of processing each pile of old growth. I don't know exactly how long my chipping chore took this year, but if I measure time by events, like my Igbo ancestors would, I'd say it took me long enough to require a snack break, a tea break and a stand-there-staring-at-nothing break. A large bucket under the chipper catches the fragments of stem, branch and twig, and every time it fills up, I empty its contents onto the paths between the veg beds. The chippings will slowly break down, locking carbon in the soil and encouraging fungal activity. Last autumn, the old chippings were caught in a net of white mycelium.

A few days ago, a ladybird moseyed off a dead stem and onto my finger for closer inspection. This was my clue that temperatures had warmed enough for the insects to wake from hibernation. The ark had done its job – it's always a great relief to chop it all down. The young bulbs popping up, sweet and soft and bright, were showing up the forlorn jungle of last year's spindly growth. Clearing the lot is a springtime ritual, it feels like shaking off a heavy winter coat. The garden feels bigger now, lighter, emptier, with more room for potential. The jackdaws are back, too. I stand at the living room window and watch them plucking up the sheep's wool mulch on the veg beds to take back to their nests. It's the day before Easter and so it feels fitting to see these birds prepare for new life. This time there are two couples – word must have got out that there's good nesting material here.

After such a wet early spring, suspecting we will have a hot dry summer, I recently laid the wool on the beds to insulate the soil, keeping it cool and humid in the soon-to-come summer sun. Sheep's wool used to be highly sought after by gardeners, but I had no idea where to get hold of any. I asked around and a friend said his family had some stored up in the roof of their ancient barn, that it had been up there for at least fifteen years. I arranged to go and fetch it, and he advised me to bring a mask for the dust. I arrived at the orchard, put on my mask and followed my friend up a wobbly ladder. The cobwebby loft smelled like time. Together we fill up a few old compost sacks with the most beautiful Jacob sheep wool. Now the beds smell like sheep and look like someone has carpeted them with an expensive rug. It's lovely. I like imagining how pretty the jackdaw nests will be, lined with this soft fleece, their speckled blue eggs resting snuggly.

With the paths chipped and the beds mulched I feel like spring is really here, and the garden is ready. The chickens feel it too – they started laying again a couple of weeks ago.

Having eggs appear once more just a few weeks before Easter has given me a whole new perspective on the traditional Easter egg hunt.

In the Christian calendar, Easter is possibly the most important event of the year as it commemorates Jesus's resurrection. And it is possibly my favourite festival because it is when the world around us seems to come back from the dead too.

In most European languages the word for Easter is derived from the Jewish Passover, *Pascha* in Latin. But German and English chose a different word, reaching back to a shared beginning. Germany has *Ostra*, and in English we, of course, have Easter, or as it's known in *The Wheel of the Year*, Ostara.

The history of this word is shrouded in mystery. Though it was common for pagan festivals to be blended into Christian ones, it was less common for Christian festivals to be blended into pagan ones. Our old friend Bede wrote that Easter was named after the Anglo-Saxon lunar month Eosturmonath, and that this month in turn had been named in honour of an adored Anglo-Saxon goddess, Eostre. This month marked the time that she was celebrated. Today,

Eosturnmonath would coincide with our April.

I once came across a very popular and poetic tale claiming that Eostra was the origin of the word 'oestrogen', but sadly I have discovered that is not the case. Oestrogen is derived from the Greek words for 'mad desire' or 'frenzy' (fitting) and 'to produce'. Many scholars believe Eostra was a goddess of fertility and the dawn, since some claim the name is linked to the Old German word for 'east', evoking spring sunrise and new beginnings. At one time the word 'easter' was also used to mean 'moving towards the east'. I think of the warm, dry easterly wind that sometimes blows into Devon from the continent. We will probably never know the truth of what the ancient pagans were honouring in Eosturnmonath, but I like to daydream about this goddess, so loved and respected that she had a whole month named after her and ended up having the day of Jesus's resurrection named after her too.

Every year since I can remember, I have painted eggs at Easter. I can't imagine welcoming spring without them. On Easter morning, when I go out to gather the eggs from our hens, I hide chocolate eggs for our godchildren, too. I am both on an egg hunt and creating one. In my pocket are some loose squash seeds I intend to sow in the coming weeks, but for now they just jangle about and play with my fingers whenever I put my hand in there. I feel surrounded by promises of new life, eggs, seeds, the leaf buds swelling on the apple trees.

It's not hard to imagine eggs playing a part in veneration for a goddess of the dawn. Eggs are new life and have come to symbolise it too. They have long been used as ritual offerings and gifts, and it's not hard to be enchanted by them: smooth, beautifully curved, full of life, whether in sustenance for another or an actual new chick that grows inside the shell, warmed and turned by a dedicated hen for twenty-one days. Eggs often played a central part in feasts of the poor, who may not have been able to afford the decadence of meat. I read that in 1290 Edward I bought 450 eggs which were decorated in gold leaf and hidden around the household for the delight of the royal entourage.

The traditional egg hunts we enjoy today are thought to have originated in Germany in the 1500s. Men would hide eggs for the women and children to find, a re-enactment of the women discovering the risen body of Christ. As a child, Queen Victoria enjoyed the egg hunts which her German mother organised, and she went on to devise egg hunts for her children too. This Easter entertainment gained popularity and in the 1850s artificial eggs first arrived for sale. But it wasn't until the 1950s that the confectionary industry cottoned on and recognised that Easter was a perfect opportunity to sell chocolate and sugary eggs, a market now worth in excess of £220 million in the UK annually.

For me egg hunts are not limited to Easter; most days when the hens are laying (from now right through to Halloween), I'm scouting eggs. The hens often hide them, cunningly, in the compost heap and tufty grass hillocks. I send my Dad a picture of an egg I found this morning. Perfectly smooth, soft brown, clean, it glows in the sunlight against the backdrop of the garden's green. It's beautiful. I hold it up between my thumb and middle finger, a precious gift. 'How do I say egg?' I ask Dad in a text. He voice-notes back: 'Akwa'. It sounds like the Latin for water, aqua.

In my household, the Easter morning opening event is a celebratory start to the new egg-hunting season.

EASTER BISCUITS

- 80g fat – vegan butter, coconut oil or sunflower oil, for example. Remember that the fat will contribute to final flavour
- 3 tsp honey, maple syrup
- 230g oat flour or whole oats
- 60g flour (I use buckwheat or spelt)
- 7 tbsp plant milk (oat milk is fab)
- 1 tsp ground nutmeg
- 2 tsp ground ginger
- 2 tsp ground cinnamon
- 1 tsp allspice

- Handful of raisins
- 1 capful vanilla extract
- 1 capful orange essence or zest of 1 orange
- Pinch of salt

For me there's no such thing as a celebration without a feast, and at Easter in our house, we feast like it's Christmas. These biscuits have become part of our Easter tradition. Feel free to mix up and experiment with the spices in this recipe: use some, all, or a combo of your choice.

You can also adapt this recipe to make really yummy chocolate digestives – simply skip the spices and top with melted chocolate after the biscuits have cooled.

- Pre-heat the oven to 180°C or gas mark 4 and line a baking sheet with greaseproof paper.
- If using whole oats, blend them to a floury consistency in a food processor.
- Combine all the dry ingredients in a large mixing bowl. Make a well in the centre and gradually work in the fat and other wet ingredients to form a smooth dough.
- Spoon dollops of the dough onto a greaseproof paper-lined baking tray. With the spoon – or your fingers – mould the dollops into flat round biscuit shapes. Place these on the baking tray and bake on the top shelf of the pre-heated oven for 10–20 minutes till they are golden, or until they look tasty to you.

EASTER BRANCH WITH PAINTED EGGS

First go out and find yourself a nice branch – I like to choose one that has fallen in the wind, or one that 'wants' to be pruned or cut back anyway. The branch walk can become quite a ritual; hunting out a perfectly sized limb with great egg-hanging potential is an engrossing task. I go with Toby and Freddy dog on these expeditions and we usually find lots of potential candidates, without fail ending up in lengthy debates over our branches.

In the past we have made eggs from papier mâché, which is a lovely vegan option if you can't access ethically raised eggs (organic and free range, or home reared).

The Victorians often boiled their eggs with gorse flowers to dye them yellow, or with onion skins to colour them a dull gold.

In my family, the night before Easter we blow the eggs. Very carefully, we make a little hole at the top and bottom of the egg with a corkscrew or darning needle. Then we blow with all our might into one hole until the yolk and white come shooting out the other. We save it all up to make an Easter omelette the next day.

On Easter day, we stick our eggs on twigs we find in the garden, or kebab sticks found in the kitchen, securing them in place with Blu Tack (if anyone has remembered to buy any).

Then we get painting with acrylics. Once the illustrated shells have dried, we string them up by tying a short piece of twig or kebab stick to the end of some thread and feeding it through one of the holes. The twig catches in the egg, securing the thread in place. We then hang them on our annual Easter branch to sit alongside others painted in previous years, some from as many as thirty-five years ago, and some by loved ones who are no longer with us.

SEEING THE FAERIE FOLK AT EASTER

The primrose gets her name from the Latin for 'first rose' because she shows her face so early in spring. This is a flower I associate with Easter.

Folklore connects the primrose with the faerie folk. People would leave bunches of the delicately fragranced pale yellow blossoms in cowsheds so that faeries would not steal their milk. It's also said that if you hold the correct number of primroses and touch a faerie rock you will be shown to the faerie kingdom. Better yet if you eat the flowers, you will be gifted with faerie sight and see them all around!

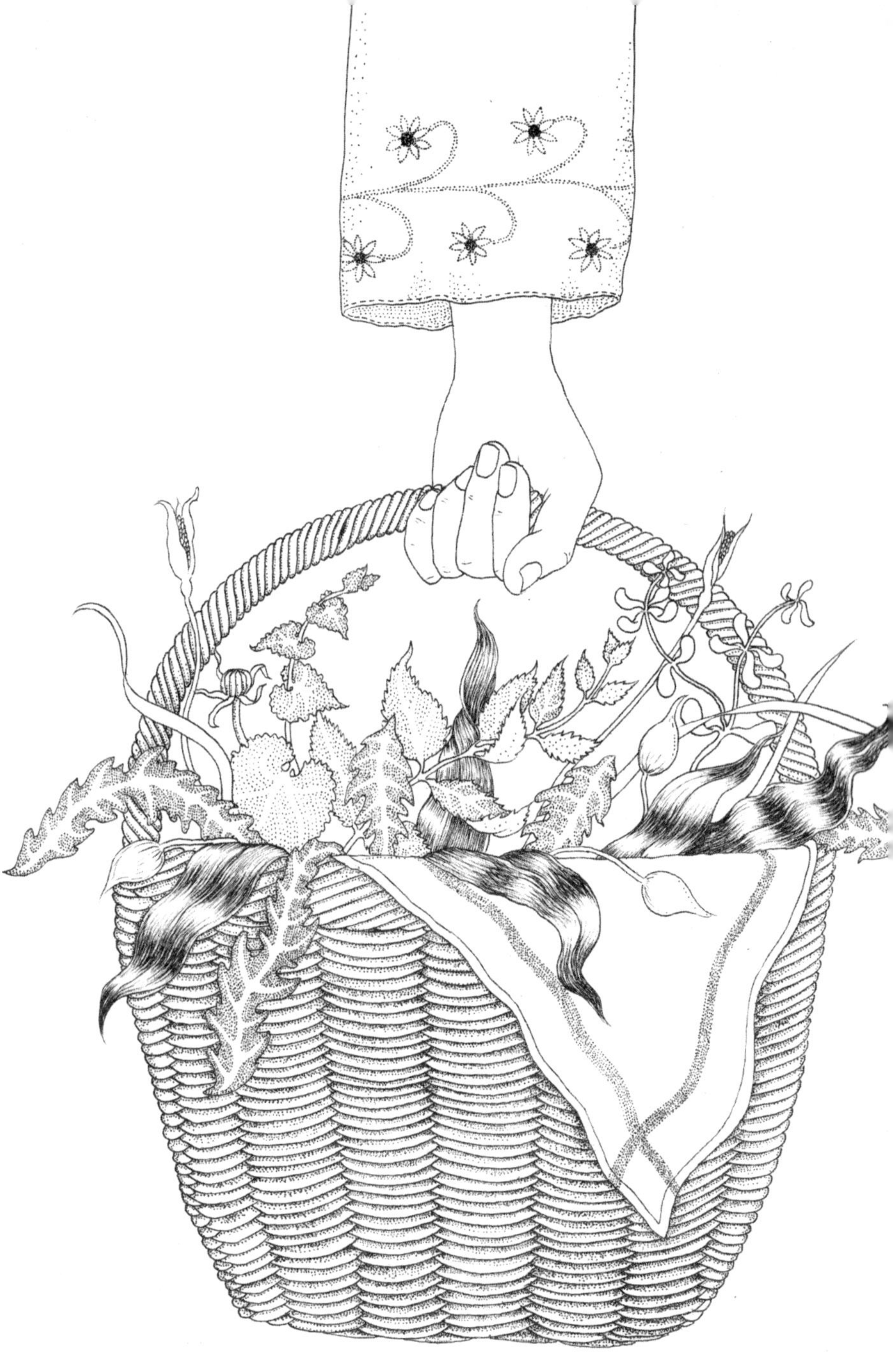

Sweete April showers,
Doo spring Maie flowers.
Thomas Tusser, Five Hundred
Points of Good Husbandry,
1573

April

THE HUNGRY GAP – AN ODE TO WEEDS

I venture into the garden after days of rain. Whoever has been pouring water out of the sky with such grave dedication has taken a break, for now at least. It's late morning, the garden is lit in a watery light but it's not necessarily cold. I look to the beds for something for my lunch; they look back at me, unyielding and glum. The plants here are either past their best or not quite ready yet, like guests ill-timed to a party. Some have only just arrived, look gorgeous and fresh but aren't giving much away. Others came earlier, have had an excellent time but, having given their all, are now crashing, looking a bit worse for wear and missing some key items of clothing – most certainly nearly ready for bed.

The newer guests include a block of green pod-less broad beans at the back, like a square in a giant's colour chart; the garlic, which won't be ready to pull until the heat of the summer sun has warmed its bulbs; various frilly little herbs and salads, soft and wet after the rain; the snail-munched cabbages; some kale, chard and spring onions. The middle bed holds sleepy strawberry plants just putting on new green growth, and the fresh, sinuous pea shoots which wriggled up out of the ground only a few weeks ago.

The early and now exhausted guests include more chard, spinach and the kale plants – all bolting. The warm spring has invited these overwintered crops to bloom and they have obliged, abandoning their previous mission to grow big tasty leaves and putting their energy instead into flowering and setting seed.

I picked some of kale's juvenile flowering stems last week. They look and taste like soft delicate purple sprouting broccoli. I left several to open into acid yellow blooms. First, the flowers will provide food to a gaggle of flying insects, and then, if we have a repeat of the last couple of years, as the flowers morph into soft seed pods, aphids will engulf them entirely and the plant's raggedy remaining lower leaves will become drenched in sweet, sticky honeydew (see page 100).

This time of year is a curious contrast of abundance and scarcity. We are settling into 'The Hungry Gap' – a moment through the seasons when gardens and farms in the UK run the risk of offering nothing much substantial for the kitchen. From April to June, our winter crops tend to come to an end, and as temperatures warm, they begin to bolt. Meanwhile spring and summer crops, like broad beans, peas and new potatoes, have not quite got off the ground. There actually is some food here, that is if you like eating tough old kale leaves, bitter spinach and chard, or if you treat your herbs, legumes and salads as microgreens and shoots. The broad bean leaves are delicious, but I hold back from stripping the plants which would sacrifice fat future pods. I know there's tastier fare to be found elsewhere. So I go back inside, gather up Freddy and a bag, and head out beyond the garden to gather some nourishment from the wild.

Outside the veggie patch, the hungry gap closes; all around us is green and alive. As I walk, I fill my bag with gifts from the land. Wild garlic, crisp purslane and her pretty pink flowers, velvety young primrose leaves, fat hen, tender young dandelions, three-cornered leeks and their floppy white flowers, jack-by-the-hedge, field sorrel and hawthorn leaf buds – commonly called 'bread and butter', as my mum told us as children. (Much to our disappointment they don't taste much like their name! I think it probably refers to their prevalence rather than their texture and taste.) And of course, as always, nettles. This tasty gaggle of weeds covering the hedgerows, parks, messy borders and abandoned gardens arrives early. These plants enjoy the damp cool springtime, taking advantage of the ample light, not yet dappled by the leaves of tall trees, resiliently braving the cold nights so as not to miss out on this window of opportunity.

When I was a child, Mum would take us foraging, but we didn't call it that, we didn't call it anything. We just went 'blackberry picking', 'to look for elderflowers' or we went for a walk, along the footpaths that traced the canal, climbed over hills, twisted through woods, along roads, streams and swimming holes, without any intention of gathering anything at all, only to be offered up plump elderberries to take home and transform into crumble. Without interrupting our discussions, we'd simply gravitate towards them, tugging and snapping the bunches of tiny blackberries. I suppose because the activity didn't have a name it didn't seem significant, we didn't feel the need to talk about it.

This simple activity which once seemed so mundane now means a great deal to me. It is both humbling and mesmerising how, if uninterrupted, wild spaces simply offer up not just food, but safety, shade, clean water, flood mitigation, beauty, medicines, fibre, dyes, nice smells, well, almost everything we could need. It is particularly humbling when the garden, tended by me, lies so bare. Gathering from these wild places helps me to feel my garden as part of a whole and myself as a part of that whole too. Not islands, walled and fenced in. Resources and life flow from the wild into my garden and from my garden out into the wild. I'm not just the tender of my little patch; I'm Earth's gardener too.

The banks, muddy verges, footpaths and their edges – these liminal spaces – feel like ours. Maybe owned, maybe not; maybe forgotten, maybe not. I don't know and I don't try to find out, no one seems to try to find me out either, so the wild harvest from these untended, in-between parts feeds me during the hungry gap. It also feeds my mind. It shows me just how much is possible with so little. As I fill my bag I watch and I learn. I see how the plants like to grow together in layers; I see how resources are cycled, how water is conserved, how soil is built, how life collaborates, creates beauty and everything else. Gathering food for free is a joyful reminder of the abundance of nature.

In the end, these wild places fill up my garden too, a space somewhere between wild and tended. I make a point of welcoming these untamed plants into the garden, especially in the spring. They provide early food and forage for me and many other creatures too. My ethos is, if I have nothing better to put there, a weed can have the spot: I just might eat it later, and if I don't, the creatures of the compost heap almost certainly will.

FORAGED PLANT FEED

- Nettles and/or dandelions. Comfrey is a great addition and it's also a great way of using bindweed, which I don't put on the compost heap. The more material the merrier, but two or three handfuls of each should suffice.
- Water (ideally rainwater)
- A bucket with a lid (this can be makeshift)

This DIY plant feed is free, organic and can either be foraged or homegrown. It is a wonderfully simple example of circularity and how to utilise local resources.

In spring, with many plant babies either in pots waiting to be planted out or just getting comfy in the ground outside, it is a great time to gather wild nettles and dandelion leaves on foraging walks to brew into a nourishing liquid feed – they contain the full spectrum of nutrients that plants need to thrive. When I go on my rambles, I like to bring home food for me and for the garden.

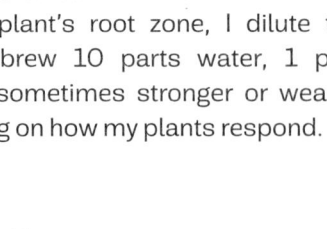

For use as a foliar feed or for watering into the plant's root zone, I dilute the foraged brew 10 parts water, 1 part feed, or sometimes stronger or weaker depending on how my plants respond. It's not possible to kill your plants with this feed, even if you don't dilute it.

- Place the plant material in a bucket and add water to cover. Weigh down the greens with a brick or stone to keep them submerged.
- Cover the bucket with a lid and leave somewhere out of the way to decompose (be warned, it is a stinky process!).
- Return to stir daily.
- The extraction can be left for anything from three days to six weeks or more. The warmer the weather, the faster the decomposition and extraction process. You can also keep a brew on the go indefinitely, adding more greenery and topping up with water as necessary.

TIP:
I like to add chicken manure to my brew as it's full of goodness the plants really love! If you have rabbits, hamsters or guinea pigs their droppings can be added too. Some people like to stir in worm castings, either at the beginning of the extraction or just before watering the diluted feed onto the plants.

KNOWING A PLACE

In spring, more perhaps than at other times in the year, I feel beckoned to explore and learn my wilder surroundings. Spring is the year's honeymoon period: all is potential, myself included, so I like to imagine a version of myself that knows this place with the depth of time.

I came to Devon to set down roots. I wanted to sit still long enough for my edges to blur and become part of somewhere. Like the old glass bottleneck I found buried in the garden, its sharp edges smoothed by the constant gentle rubbing of the earth, a parsley taproot growing straight through it. Presumably it had travelled to this garden from elsewhere, but with time it had become part of this place.

I arrived in this damp county in early summer. I walked about, out along the river, hedgerows and woodland paths, and imagined I was seeing it all with the eyes of someone whose grandmother had shown her the best spots for blackberries, meadow sweet and yarrow. I imagined my garden through the eyes of someone who had lived here a lifetime and who held the stories, visions, hopes and dreams of ancestors who had grown old in this house.

I have come to realise that the sort of belonging I'm hankering for is actually a sense of *knowing*. A strange, slippery-slidy kind of knowing that accepts that it can never *fully* know a place. Only stretching time can offer the sort of gentle and organic observation that opens the world up to the viewer, making them a *knower*.

*

In that first spring in Devon, I found it surprisingly destabilising and alienating to no longer have the same plants around me or have access to my former London foraging spots. Essentially, I didn't know the land and the land did not know me.

When you have spent some time letting your mind loose on the plants in a certain environment, you begin to absorb an incredible, fluid kind of local knowledge. Things like which elderberry trees blossom earlier in the summer and which later. You know which bushes have blackberries that are easier to gather and which you need to bring your long-armed partner with you to reach. Most importantly, you just know where all the plants are.

In this new landscape, I didn't have that sense anymore and I felt very bare without it. I was faced with the task of learning about unfamiliar plants and was missing the ones I knew and loved. The trouble with the seasons is that things do not wait for you before they change. So I started to feel like I was rushing about to find my plant friends, to catch them in the moments I needed to find them in – ripe, in bloom, or juvenile. Foraging became a frantic sport.

I had chosen to come here, I felt welcome. I wasn't dependent on these plants for food or medicine and yet I was really struggling without them. The idea that many of us living stable lives in the places we call home are in some way displaced started to roll around in my head. Many of us never have the experience of *knowing*; we are born into unknowing and unknowingly pass it down. The default state is plant-blindness and disconnect from our landscape.

Deep knowledge of the land is passed down through generations. I think of my dad who moved to the UK as a child, leaving a country ravaged by the Biafran War. I think of the plants he would have known in his homeland, and the new plants he encountered on arrival in this land. He always talks his childhood into life, describing climbing gigantic trees that I have never seen, and gathering chewing sticks I have never tasted, and sweet fruits that, had we not moved to South Africa, I would never have known. I think of my grandmother who tells me of the roads lined with gigantic mango trees, how as a child she would leave home without a morning meal and pick the fruits for breakfast on her way to school, eating the skin and all, licking the sweet, sticky juice from her hands, because the mangos were so soft and ripe. I know that same smell, taste and feeling from my childhood in Johannesburg, but I've never walked below a path lined with mango trees.

My father and grandmother hold a whole world of plant knowledge that I will never quite understand because it does not transfer to this landscape. By no fault of their own, by the circumstances they found themselves in when they arrived here, all this knowing about their native living world was suddenly rendered irrelevant and random. It takes time to relearn, to become part of a new place. Because they were starting their knowing again from scratch, they had less connection to this new place to pass down.

I know one of the things my dad says he valued in my English mum was how she really knew the plants of his new country. Although she grew up in an RAF family, attended many boarding schools and moved a great deal, she spent most of her childhood in Wiltshire; she knows the land that is her home. Her father had taught her and his mother had taught him. As children, she and her three siblings would spend countless days wandering wild, abandoned airfields, catching butterflies in nets. When my mum was a baby she would try to eat caterpillars in the cabbage patch.

Her dad passed on little nuggets of knowing about the countryside, and she remembered them and then layered her own little nuggets of knowing on top until, one day, the nuggets became irrelevant, but not because she had to move to a different continent. In Mum's case, the landscape itself had moved on, she grew up and went off to work in a city, and a knowledge of butterflies or wildflowers was no longer valued. Grandad says he left Wiltshire for Cornwall because, as industrial farming took hold between the fifties and seventies, he couldn't bear to see the hedges ripped out and wildflower meadows ploughed up.

My dad lost his nuggets when he was forced to leave his home country; Mum's lost relevance because her world was transformed.

Today many of us spend less and less time in the world outdoors and more time inside on screens. Natural England's annual report 'The People and Nature' found that only 16 per cent of people surveyed spent time in green or natural spaces daily. Meanwhile, digital advisory firm Datareportal estimates alarmingly that in the UK we spend around six hours each day on screens. Our attention is being constantly colonised. So-called archaic English words which describe our environment – like acorn, beech, bluebell, bramble and buttercup – have been taken out of the Oxford Junior English Dictionary to make way for words like attachment, block graph, blog, broadband and bullet point. There is less and less room for land-based nuggets of knowing passed generation to generation and so what's not valued erodes. The reasons are complex and many but the trend is clear: a vast gap has grown in how we physically, emotionally and spiritually connect to our wild home.

I rummaged about all summer here in the Devon hedgerows searching for plants and weeds whose names I'd only recently learnt and was not ready to say goodbye to. I refuse to let any more nuggets go missing. I may never know the mango-tree-lined roads my grandma knew, but I bloody well will know this Devon hedgerow with its nettles that scratch and welt my legs and these berryless brambles that rip my clothes to shreds.

In this context, perhaps my weed obsession makes more sense. It's not just about them and me, but the most ravenous hunger for truly knowing my home. These weeds are the backdrop to my existence here; they literally are my home. I've tethered myself to them by accepting that I am part of their interconnected world. It has crept up on me over the years, but now I really need them. I don't think this is a bad way to feel.

*

One of those weeds I searched for desperately is one that is not often missed: Japanese knotweed, 'Knotweed the Terrible'.

My obsession with finding a crop of knotweed became quite intense. One night I dreamt I was searching for it in the damp open woodlands near our cottage. I couldn't find it. My search went on for hours and I started to feel a sense of loss and panic. I woke up feeling edgy but couldn't quite recall the content of the dream.

Later that day, I went foraging in the same woods from my dream. I'd walked there weekly for the past couple of months and knotweed had been on my mind every time. I'd pick through my surroundings with my eyes, scanning intensely. That day I had spent twenty minutes slowly gathering bundles of wild garlic which only a month before had started to appear as tiny soft green swords, slicing up through the surface of the boggy earth. Now they were a thick lush carpet that could easily withstand my light dispersed foraging. As I was leaving, some fresh nettle tops caught my eye. I needed to get home but they called out to me that they'd go well with the wild garlic in a spring soup.

I paused to pinch off their young tops down to a single pair of large leaves, a harvesting method that encourages lots more fresh bushy growth, but with bare hands requires real precision. The herbalist Jo Dunbar says nettles are attention-seekers – if you don't give them your full attention, they nip you to remind you who you're dealing with! I tend to agree. The repetitive motion of quickly pinching off their tops also provides a perfect meditative pause: a state of flow and the ideal situation for the mind to expand.

I settled into the rhythm of carefully picking and dropping the nettle tops into my bag when, all of a sudden, standing tall out of the patch of nettles and nearly brushing my hand, Japanese knotweed appeared. I had found my old friend! My dream from the previous night came into sharp focus.

I looked up from my nettle and with my newly attentive loose mind, it was as if I was seeing the wood for the first time. All around me I was surrounded by little pink knotweed spikes poking up out of the mud, among the brittle woody stems of last year's growth which lay collapsed across the woodland floor. Knotweed plant clues had been all around me every time I walked here, but I had missed them all. It wasn't until nettles drew me deep into a moment that I finally, truly saw this place.

This is the sort of knowing that I dream of passing down and that I fantasise about others passing down to me. Decade upon decade of knowledge loosely woven down through the generations. How many more secrets are hiding in plain sight? I suppose that's wisdom really.

WILD GARLIC SALT

- 30 g wild garlic leaves and stalks, washed
- 250 g salt flakes

Around the same time the hens start to lay again, the wild garlic comes out, and by mid-April it has established dense fields of pungent emerald green.

Wild garlic is an indicator, along with bluebells and wood anemones, of an ancient woodland. In the UK it means that the woodland has been in existence since at least the 1600s. These days, that's not so common. Ancient woodlands are very special places, so enjoy and respect them. It is important not to pick wild garlic right when it first emerges. Wait until it has put on some growth and is well established, and always avoid over-harvesting.

This recipe preserves the sharp, fresh garlickiness of spring-time woodlands – it's good for you too. In terms of health benefits, wild garlic is even more potent than regular cultivated bulbs.

All measurements are approximate – the salt flakes should be fully coated in the green garlic paste but not so wet that they retain any moisture after drying.

- In a food processor, blitz the wild garlic into a paste with a pinch of salt.
- In a bowl, stir the paste into the remaining salt flakes until well combined. They will turn an emerald green.
- Using a spatula, spread the now-damp green flakes onto a large platter or tray lined with baking parchment. Loosely cover with a clean tea towel and set aside in a warm spot out of direct sunlight. Leave them to dry for a day (or perhaps two depending on the climate).
- Once they've dried and the salt has regained its crunch, jar them up and store in a cool dark place. The salt will gradually lose its pungency over time. So enjoy sooner rather than later.
- The tea towel will probably honk of garlic and need a wash!

ITADORI

In the UK, Japanese knotweed (*Fallopia japonica*) is considered an invasive 'weed'. The Wildlife and Countryside Act classes it as a controlled plant, making it illegal to cause or allow the plant to spread in the wild. Personally, I class this plant with such a terrible reputation as a wonderfully delicious edible that I've come to respect.

Fallopia japonica is native to Eastern Asia. In Japan, where it is known as itadori, the plant is widely foraged as a wild edible vegetable. I will now refer to it as itadori, which seems to better honour the delights of the plant rather than focus on its tough weediness. The young itadori stems are gathered in spring when they are up to 30 cm tall and before their leaves begin to unfurl. Grasp the stem at its base, then firmly snap it where it meets the ground. They make a satisfying hollow pop! The stems resemble bamboo shoots or asparagus and are soft to eat but become tough and fibrous as they mature. In Japan itadori is considered a seasonal delicacy and many recipes can be found for preserving the young shoots, including pickling them in brine and enjoying them as a salty, tart, savoury food rather than sweet, which is how I like them.

In my opinion, itadori is a far tastier version of its relative, rhubarb. They share the same wonderful texture but itadori is a great deal sweeter, while retaining that delicious fresh tang. It is also a useful springtime source of the antioxidant vitamins C and A. In Japan, Korea and China, traditionally itadori (literally translating as 'pain puller') is used in folk medicine to treat a host of ailments, including coughs, sore throats, gum problems and as an anti-inflammatory.

Itadori was first brought to the Kew Botanic Gardens in London in the 1850s as an ornamental garden plant, and quickly became a popular choice in parks and gardens, sold in nurseries until the 1990s. It is a towering plant, easily reaching an impressive 3–4 m height in just one summer. The stems have beautiful purple flecks, the leaves open to attractive heart shapes, and in autumn the plant produces cascading tassels of creamy white flowers. Itadori dies back to overwinter below ground, providing huge quantities of dead, woody, brown biomass (which, dare I say it, is great for building soil!). Due to its abundant, rapid growth and creeping networks of underground stems, known as rhizomes, it was also used functionally to help stabilise soil in banks, particularly along railway lines.

It wasn't long though before itadori's insatiable appetite for growth was revealed. Its creeping rhizomes spread rapidly and the plant's height suppresses any neighbours. In the UK, we only have female itadori, so any plants found here have either been planted, spread from another plant, or are the result of small portions of the plant having been transported somehow – one thumbnail-sized piece of itadori can produce a whole new plant.

A key to the plant's success in this country is that it has no natural predators. Horses, goats and cattle have all been known to enjoy munching on itadori, but most populations do not have a friendly herd of herbivores browsing close by to limit its spread. And since itadori is not native to the British Isles, and sadly the story of its reciprocal relationship with humans in Japan did not travel with it to Kew all those years ago, it is not widely known as a delicious edible and so is not harvested for human consumption. Thus it can roam unchecked.

Itadori is so incredibly tasty and easy to harvest that if this knowledge were more widespread, I do believe it would help to protect ecosystems from the plant's tendency towards unchecked growth, while also supplying us with an abundance of healthy food.

Instead, itadori is currently listed as one of the most invasive and destructive weeds in the UK. Much of its fearsome reputation is due to rumours that knotweed has the ability to burst through concrete and up through walls, making homes structurally unsound, and ultimately bringing them to the ground. In 2013, a Daily Telegraph headline declared: 'Japanese knotweed: the tarmac-smashing thug invading our gardens.' Sometimes lenders will not offer a mortgage on a house whose garden harbours 'Knotweed the Terrible'. The reality is far more mundane: a 2018 study by Leeds University confirmed that, in terms of infrastructure damage, itadori is fairly harmless and causes far less damage than many trees and climbers with clean reputations.

The real threat is itadori's potential for turning biodiverse, native landscapes into knotweed monocultures.

Typically to kill itadori, it is sprayed with a chemical called glyphosate, the active ingredient in the herbicide 'Round Up'. Glyphosate is incredibly toxic, a dangerous carcinogen for humans and other animals, it kills pollinators and the life in our soils, and devastates our waterways too – a tragedy as itadori loves waterside settings. If the plant is in plain sight, it will likely have been sprayed and so is best avoided. This makes gathering itadori a risky business in the UK.

Perhaps my love for this misunderstood plant comes from my belief that the trouble with itadori lies in a lack of plant knowledge.

Itadori came to this new and unfamiliar land for its beauty and function, but the story of its connection with us humans was left behind and so it spread. Now we have made up a new story in which itadori is no longer considered a delicate springtime delight, but as evil knotweed, an invader and destroyer of homes.

In a culture that places more value on profit from the sale of poisons that promise to eradicate weeds, we miss out on knowledge of how to manage them in a way that is good for both us and the land. When our interconnections are understood and our stories and actions are allowed to grow up out of them, we can change the world around us.

Consistent and total harvest of itadori eventually weakens the plant, and can help to manage its spread, protect landscapes and eliminate the supposed need for toxic chemicals. In the not-so-distant past, it was common for whole communities to turn out in force to gather a seasonal crop. Bilberries are tasty little berries, most closely resembling miniature blueberries, which grow wild on acidic moorland soils across the British Isles and come ripe between late July and early August. Whole days were put aside for people to go out and collect the wild bounty. In Ireland, the last Sunday in July is known as Fraughan Sunday, which literally translates to bilberry Sunday; in the south-west of England it's known as 'whort' or 'hurt' day, short for their local name, whortleberry.

I wonder what would happen to itadori if we all committed to harvesting it with as much organised gusto.

ITADORI AND APPLE COMPOTE

- 15–20 fresh young itadori stems
- 2 apples or pale honey, to sweeten

Optional: cinnamon, ginger, raisins, lemon verbena or meadow-sweet leaves

Itadori cooked down tastes like a sweeter, less sharp rhubarb, and with the same texture. It makes a very good (perhaps better!?) wild alternative and needs considerably less sugar. We often make a large jar and keep it in the fridge to have with granola or on toast in the mornings, or as a pudding in the evenings.

Gather the young itadori stems in mid to late spring. The stems that are good to gather should be practically leafless. Do NOT disturb the rhizomes – this encourages spreading. Place the stems in a bag, taking care not to drop any on your way home. The smallest stray fragment can grow fast and furious. Do not dispose of any trimmings or any other parts of the plant in the general rubbish bin, in green waste, a worm bin or on the compost heap – not even a sliver!

Instead, offcuts should be burnt, cooked, fermented into liquid plant feeds or fully pre-digested in a bokashi bin before you combine it in your compost heap or with your local compost collection.

Remember, as a controlled plant, it is an offence to spread Japanese knotweed in the countryside. If you decide to give this recipe a try, make sure you eat every last bit of the itadori you have harvested!

- Wash and remove any leaves from the itadori stems. I tend to chop off the tip too (out of habit and instinct rather than necessity).
- Chop the stems into roughly 5 cm pieces and the apples into small chunks. If you omit the apples, pale honey adds a lovely sweetness to stewed itadori.
- Place the itadori and apples in a pan with a splash of water and place on a low heat. Gently simmer until they stew down to a soft warm mush.
- Optional: depending on your taste, add extra flavourings. I recommend trying it simple and plain the first time!
- Remove from the heat.
- Serve the compote immediately or leave to cool and store in the fridge.

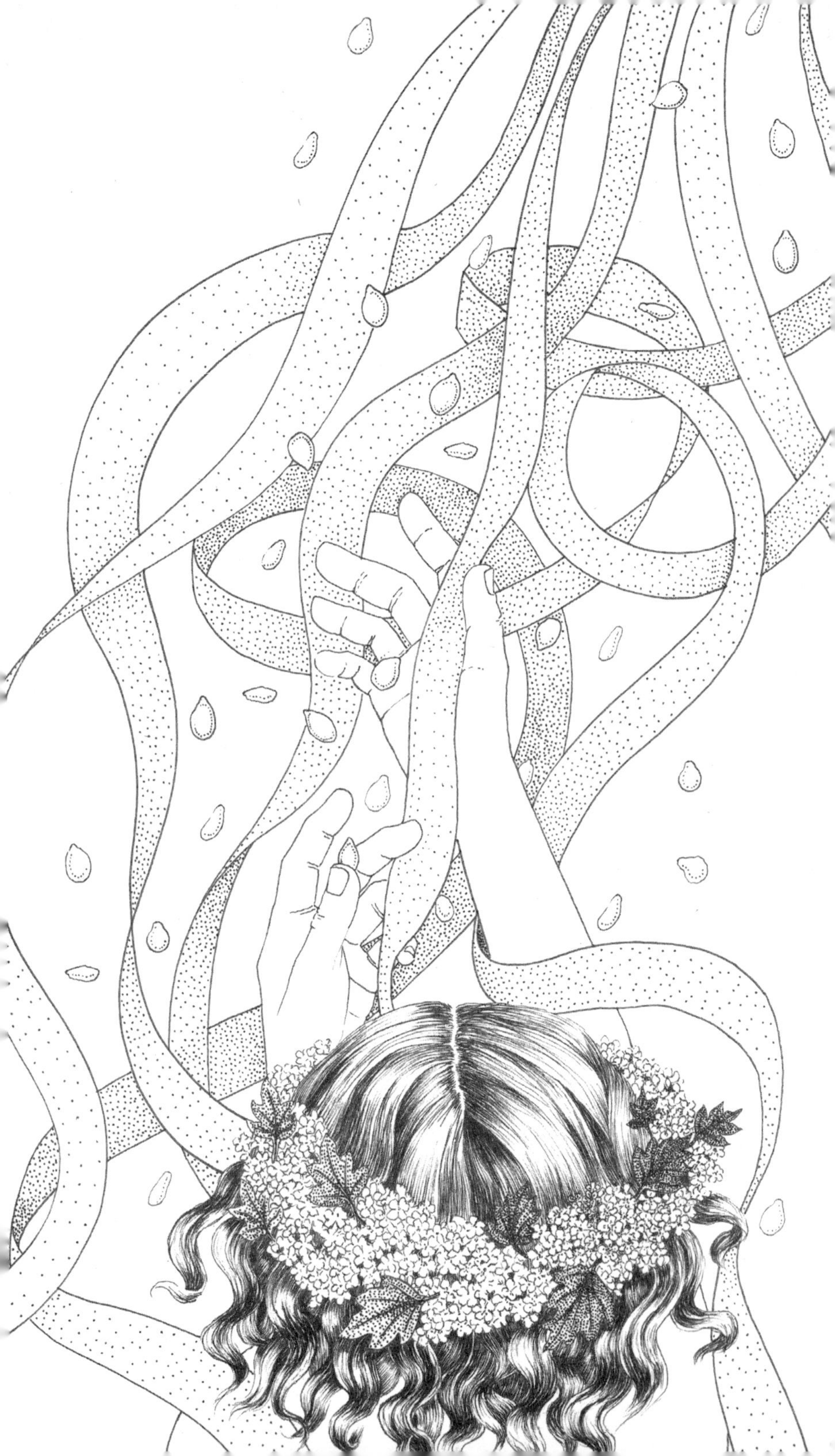

May

MAY DAY

Falling between the spring equinox and summer solstice, May Day is celebrated on 1 May. It marks the shift to late spring and the start of summer. Spurred on by ever-lengthening warmer days, rapid growth pelts full steam ahead. May Day – or Beltane, as *The Wheel of the Year* calls it – is a celebration of this abundance and intensity. It is the cult of excess. I love this festival of wild blossoms, ribbons, dancing, sun, sensuality, fire and fertility.

May Day is a festival of the people. It is thought to have its roots in the hedonistic Roman festival Floralia, a celebration of the goddess of fertility and flowers, which spanned several days from the end of April to the start of May. Floralia was a festival of revelry. When the Romans colonised parts of Britain, it is thought that they brought this celebration with them.

Others speculate that the celebration of May Day predates the Roman Empire, originating in the even older Celtic festival called Beltane. Like Floralia, Beltane was closely linked with the people's deep relationship with the land and the wider wild landscape. Historically, it celebrated the start of summer, when livestock were taken to pasture. In *The Wheel of the Year*, Beltane directly opposes Samhain; if Samhain is slugs and snails and puppy dogs' tails, Beltane is sugar and spice and all things nice.

To some, the word Beltane means 'bright fire'; to others it refers to the Celtic sun god Belenus. As people welcomed the heat of summer's sun, Beltane included the ritualistic and symbolic lighting of a sacred, communal fire. Revellers would dance around and jump over the fire, driving their livestock around it before delivering them to their summer pastures. Bones often made up the bulk of these fires, burning into thick billowy smoke, and bringing us the word 'bonfire'. The smoke and heat was thought to be cleansing in preparation for the ascent into summer, then once the fire died out, people would scatter its ashes on the fields as a purifying offering and blessing. (Just like the Celts, I regularly put ash on my compost heap, though only wood ash. A sprinkling of ash on the soil is useful as an organic soil amendment – it has a gentle liming effect and provides a source of potassium, calcium and other trace nutrients.) As with many ancient festivals, Beltane speaks to circularity. We can see it quite literally in the bones of the livestock, which fed on the field the previous summer, being returned as life-giving ashes.

The transition into May and its promise of summer is tangible. We all feel it. The signs of change are everywhere. Plant life is rowdy and green, blossoms burst open, birds sing and seeds seem to germinate overnight. Sometimes the rain is mild rather than cold. Warmer weather coaxes us out bare skinned and a certain sweaty sexiness that winter lacks. Longer days mean I forget the time, stay in the garden too long and have dinner past my bedtime.

The wheel of the year has turned, the world has shifted gear. We are now in an outward phase of high energy, production and creation. It's a time for action. To harness all that growth energy, I plant seeds and try to get any summer cropping plants into the ground before the window between Beltane and summer solstice closes.

*

I am fascinated by the significance of this May festival through history, as it illustrates how our relationship with the land is political and coloured by the values of the times.

When Christianity first came to medieval Britain, at a popular level and in its very early form, in practice it was much like the paganism that had come before it. The new faith appropriated many pagan festivals, and simply used their main themes and motifs to carry different messages from the Bible. Celebration of the rebirth of life at spring equinox morphed into Christian Easter, commemorating the Resurrection. Winter solstice feasts transformed into Christmas, celebrating the birth of Christ.

May Day, however, was an exception to this rule. It continued as a convivial, largely secular festival with various weird and wonderful rituals, particularly enjoyed by the labouring peasantry who could take a pause from work to welcome in 'The May'. The festival had, and still has, many connections with eroticism, flirting, fertility and the incredible power of women and the land to bring forth new life.

In some parts of the country young people would head into the woods on the eve of May Day, returning the next morning laden with flowers and greenery to decorate homes, towns and villages. Traditionally the hawthorn, or May Tree, freshly covered in its fluffy white or pale pink blossom, was and still is a favourite. (I like to bring cuttings into our home throughout May.) In a nod to the pagan veneration of trees, revellers danced about May poles. A May Queen and sometimes a King were picked from the gathered crowd to be crowned and festooned with garlands of flowers. Folkloric tales tell of the Maiden Goddess or May Queen 'blossoming'. She falls in love with the May or Oak King (who presides over summertime); they make love and the May Queen becomes pregnant. All around us in May, we see parallels to this tale in nature, as insects fertilise the blossoms, which soon ripen into fruits.

As the late medieval period tipped into the Early Modern period in Europe, feudalism gave way to capitalism. Throughout the 1500s there was a shift towards centralised power both in the church and government. This applied to how the land was run too. Feudal peasants had previously subsisted on common land owned by the king, aristocracy or the Church; the wealthy shared the earth's bounty with the people. Most agricultural work was a collective and cooperative endeavour, as the community grew and processed food, fuel fibre and materials together. However, in Britain by the beginning of the 1600s, through a series of Acts of Parliament called the Enclosures, landowners turned the peasants out from the common land so that they could begin to make money from it themselves. Vast numbers of country people were removed from the plots they had farmed and lost their access to and connection with place. Those displaced were forced into towns and cities to find a new livelihood. It was these former peasants who ultimately powered the industrial revolution.

During the Second English Civil War the country endured further social upheaval as, under Oliver Cromwell, the ultra-pious puritans began to push for religious reform. By 1644, May Day was outlawed as ungodly, unruly, libidinous and sinfully idle. Philip Stubbes, a particularly staunch puritan, complained with outrage in his book of social criticisms *The Anatomy of Abuses* that, on May Day, of all the women who might head into the woods to welcome in the May, only a third would return home as virgins.

Meanwhile, as more and more former peasants left the land, cities grew to house this new labouring class and urban industry began to expand. The radical shift from a largely agricultural economy to one driven by manufacture was financed by the transatlantic slave trade, which was given royal assent in 1663, less than twenty years after Oliver Cromwell's Act of Parliament had banned May Day in England for interrupting orderly and pious labour.

In its celebration of abundance, complexity, sexuality, interconnection, circularity and community, the spirit of May Day seems to fly directly in the face of the industrialisation of humanity that is necessary for modern capitalism to function. To my mind, all that came before – the Enclosures, the banning of May Day and widespread repression of indigenous culture that connected land and people on British soil – was a rehearsal for global colonisation. Erasure of a people's tradition and culture is the perfect recipe for cultivating the disconnection and sense of detachment that is necessary for the global pattern of abuse and exploitation of one another, land and life on earth, in the name of profit.

In 1660, when the puritans fell and 'The Merry Monarch' King

Charles II came to the throne, he welcomed back May Day. But by then the celebration had lost its radically unruly nature and the festival's popularity declined. It seems no surprise to me that the festival did not return to the people in its former glory. People change when they are deprived of their culture; and without its people, a culture can change too, losing its meaning, becoming empty and small.

As I desperately reach for the cosmology of my Nigerian ancestors, which my people knew so well even as recently as eighty years ago, when my grandmother was born, I recognise this myself. During British rule, much of the traditional Igbo pantheistic belief system and the stories of Odinala floundered in the face of the pressure placed on people to convert to Christianity. To me it is now a mystery to relearn. Having neglected it for too long, I am acutely aware that the more time passes, the smaller and emptier the culture I eventually unearth might seem. It's sort of like plunging your hands below a potato plant to root around for its tubers, only to pull them up and find you have no idea what to do with them. Or worse yet, to find them old and shrivelled, all nourishment faded and gone.

May Day tradition enjoyed another revival of sorts in Victorian Britain. Stifled by growing industrialisation, urbanisation and an authoritarian culture, by the mid-1800s, there was an atmosphere of nostalgia amongst many Victorians. People yearned for connection to the land and their pastoral history. However, times had changed and wild Bacchanalian revelry was muted. The festival was quickly taken up by the church as a fundraising opportunity; people sang the national anthem instead of folk songs; and now the crowning of the May Queen became a symbol of the monarch instead of a pagan goddess of fertility. This May Day was merely a sanitised reminiscence, entirely missing the point of its origins. Sometimes it's best to dream up new ways of finding connection rather than attempting to breathe life back into tradition.

However, in 1890 May Day did come to enjoy a more vigorous grassroots revival, this time as a spirited day of the people, associated with socialism and workers' rights. The majority of the working class now laboured in factories, and with the advent of artificial lighting the working day had broken free from the limitations of daylight. It was not uncommon for people to work for twelve–fourteen hours (or more!) at a time. May Day was declared the 'International Workers Day' to honour the Haymarket Martyrs, the eight workers executed for alleged involvement in a peaceful protest calling for an eight-hour working day in the US. May Day was called on once again by the people, *for* the people.

Today, for me, 1 May is an opportunity to commemorate the power of life and our right to the freedom to revel and share in Earth's abundance. It gives me the chance to take note of the quiet endings of early spring and prepare to welcome the liveliness of summer. All around us the land seems to rebel and break free from the austerity of winter, and I think, perhaps, we are inspired by this victory.

CLEAVERS WATER

Galium aparine (commonly known as cleavers or sticky willy) flushes with growth in spring and early autumn. If you spot a hawthorn, or May Hedge, you will likely find cleavers lurking below.

Some people say they like cleavers chopped into salads, but I don't believe them – I'm not sure how anyone could enjoy eating those raspy leaves. Nevertheless, this abundant plant does have its uses and benefits. In herbal medicine, cleavers is traditionally called on to support gentle detoxification of the body. It is a diuretic, promoting urination, and a cooling, soothing tonic. I gather and consume cleavers regularly in the spring, autumn and when I feel run down, sluggish or bloated.

As a home remedy, the plant is most potent when consumed fresh and raw. To get round the texture problem, I like to whizz it up into smoothies and juices to enjoy its watery fresh cucumber flavour. I also sometimes blitz it into salad dressings.

This recipe is for a cold infusion for a tasty but subtle drink. If I have even the slightest hint of the beginnings of a UTI, I prepare a large jug of this as my first port of call. It is especially refreshing on a warm spring day.

- Rinse a good handful or two of freshly gathered cleavers in cold water.
- Place in a clean receptacle: cup, jug, bottle, jar, bowl – anything will do.
- Cover with cold tap or filtered water.
- Leave in the fridge to infuse overnight.
- The next day the greenery will have imparted its flavours and goodness. Fish out or strain the cleavers if you like (I leave them in), and the cleavers water is ready to drink.
- For a stronger infusion, after infusing overnight, remove the first bundle of cleavers and add a fresh one to the water before drinking.

THE MAGICAL WHIMSY OF IT ALL

During the period around – and certainly after – May Day, time seems to speed up. All about me I see a self-willed type of growth that can't be controlled. Each day a new flower is blooming and plants seem to double in size overnight; seeds are germinating and asking for constant care. The pesky slimy folk are out too causing trouble. We have so much daylight, more and more warmth, more beauty, seeming infinite growth.

It's a busy time. I *do* love high summer, the sweltering intensity of it, but it is not the soft tickles of late spring. I know that by the time we reach the other side of the summer solstice, I can start to find it all overwhelming, oversaturated, the hot, bright light just a bit too much. So I savour these days while we still have a balance of daylight and darkness and while plants are young, soft, lush, delicious to eat, and wonderful to look at.

Sitting at the table in front of the greenhouse in early evening, the spring sun softly warms my edges. I've been working in the garden all day and am now eating a huge dinner which is also my lunch. I'm alone, apart from the chickens and the garden. I chew my meal. Tender steamed sprouting broccoli tossed in sharp lemon. Boiled potatoes, bashed up, fluffy and stirred through with hazelnut and wild garlic pesto I made a few weeks ago when spring was only just carpeting the ground. A cool and crisp fennel leaf, spring onion and coriander salad. And an omelette made from our hens' eggs, with a handful of chopped, fragrantly bitter wild marjoram, which grows by the little footbridge to our front door and tickles my ankles when I walk by. I'm regularly cutting the plant back now to delay the arrival of its lovely lilac flowers and encourage more leafy growth. I keep a vase full of the prunings in the kitchen, pretty and useful.

All my dinner is made with fresh, seasonal, local ingredients, grown without the use of chemicals, and most tended to and gathered by my own hands. I feel equal parts grateful, empowered and satisfied. My body feels good when I use it, content with the labour it contributed in producing this food, and my mind and soul feel enriched by the experience of tending the plants and hens who are now tending to me. Of course, my belly is filling up too. I chew and I watch the sun as it dips low in the west.

A few more minutes and it will have slipped behind the great big tree in the distance which blocks the late evening light. I observe my surroundings through my multi-layered, time-lapse gardener's vision: simultaneously, I see the garden as it is now, as it looked back in January, in our first summer here, at exactly this time last year, in two months' time... and many more iterations of the garden past and future. I look at a patch in front of me, and I see it as it was a couple of weeks ago, bare and freshly sprinkled with seed. I see it now, with its tufts of green getting ready to flower, and I also see its future glory, California poppies and calendula, every shade of orange and flecks of white chamomile. I also see that patch as it was when we first arrived here – a tangle of wild things.

To my right, some gentle rustling and cooing in the greenery catches my attention. It's coming from one of the remaining islands of wild in the garden. When we moved here, I was so enchanted by this little strip that it convinced me I should just let it do as it liked. I decided that I'd keep the brambles and bindweed at bay and otherwise leave it to its own devices.

Usually the chickens live under the apple trees, but while the bluebells bring a cloudless summer sky to the ground, the flock has been limited to the rest of the garden and advanced, with their scratching, into this wild stretch. Tunnels have now appeared in the once untouched tangle of plants where the birds have made their way through the dense periwinkle, raspberries, baby dog rose, wild marjoram, primroses and fennel fronds. Now the chickens are weaving a network of paths around the great big myrtle shrub in the middle.

I sit there watching these plants quiver as the birds move about under their green, leafy ceiling, and I worry that they don't think about the garden as I do – they never worry. They don't care that this area was meant to remain untouched. They mill around in there willy-nilly and now the wild island is going bald in places. My gardener's vision begins to picture the scene in layers again. I see the strip full of evening primrose standing tall that first summer; I see last year's jungle of fennel, and I try to envision it later in this third summer too... But the worry clouds my vision, I can only see it scruffy and bare, ruined by the flock's disturbance.

I worry that I have done too much to this garden, that not much of it looks the way it did when we first came here and that it's not wild enough anymore. I worry that by tending this space to try and feed us, I'm starving other creatures who can't pop to the supermarket for bread if needs be. Sometimes all this worry seems silly.

Other times my worrying feels right; we are facing a climate crisis after all, a loss of wild spaces and the ensuing biodiversity collapse. A dose of worry seems a fitting response to the potential demise of life on Earth as we know it. At least my worry spurs action, ensuring that I continue to steward this garden with care and help to build a world in which it is just a small part of a wider, healthy, life-filled landscape. A world in which my little garden really is just that, little, insignificant – something to love but nothing to worry about.

Now I'm sitting in front of the greenhouse with my food and my worry, gazing at this quivering, cooing, balding wild strip of garden. My eyes trace the tendrils of the now quite ragged periwinkle, pausing on its pale purple star-like flowers, when a bumblebee briefly visits them but decides not to hang around. And then I see it: the *whole bed* is *full* of periwinkle. Left untouched, over these two years the patch has almost been taken over by this one plant. My eyes, I realise, find no rosettes of biennial evening primrose leaves and the fennel is looking a bit swamped. Those worrisome pockets of bare earth begin to look inviting. Little open glades, allowing light to reach the soil to trigger germination, the right sort of size to pop herbs and wild annual flowers into. Perhaps the chickens haven't ruinously interfered after all; perhaps this wilderness is long overdue some healthy disturbance. Were it not for the chickens, the periwinkle left to romp may well have shaded everything else out by the end of the summer. This small flock of chickens, though not adding to biodiversity themselves (they are not native, and in Britain about 116 million chickens are farmed for meat and 29 million for eggs at any one time), are helping to encourage it.

The chickens haven't worriedly sat on their hands, scared they might ruin this space. They have marched right into the spot most in need of change, showing me where to add new native life. I start to envision this patch in late summer, once the chickens are safely back below the apple trees. I see the bald patches filled with the annual wildflowers I started from seed and which are now ready and waiting for their permanent homes; fresh perennial herbs greening up the bare soil.

I recall walking through the garden that first January when we came to view the house. How the whole area had been scalped, as though an army of chickens had been quickly herded through it. The following summer the ground was bursting with wildflowers. I chew some more and wonder if our chickens have the right idea. These little scratched up patches do look temptingly like a 'fine tilth', the seed sower's obsession.

I can let them simply do the job of making room, then follow their path, filling up the gaps, slowly adding more herbs and edible perennials and native plants to the wild spaces outside the annual beds. After all, from death new life grows. In the garden the chickens and I can be the disturbance which drives opportunities for dynamic, healthy change; we can be the keystone species. Our own garden-scale form of rewilding.

Winter's stories of thoughtful light touch and stillness can so easily invite worried inaction, but tentative idleness can lead to stagnation. Healthy people and landscapes require interaction and some disturbance to make way for new growth and life. Sometimes the ground needs clearing, the soil needs digging, the fruit needs harvesting and the flowers need picking. In the process of taking food from this garden the chickens have created fertile destruction. They've shown me that we don't have to retreat and tread lightly. We are of the earth and the earth's ecosystems, and as well as giving to them, we can and must take. We *can* make a greater positive impact on this earth than we do negative, but that requires energy and engagement, not only stillness... Taking along with giving.

The cord that runs between us and the land has been worn thin under the strain of our modern culture. Reknotting it requires a tradition of exchange of the kind that was censored, abolished and enclosed all those years ago.

*

The lessons of autumn and winter have taught me plenty, most importantly that in the cycle of life, energy must and will go around and around.

In my search for a different world-view, rooted in the realities of living on Earth, I have built strong foundations and a sturdy structure with the solid stillness of winter, but now it's springtime's turn. Life on this Earth delights in the rosy goodness of spring and summer, and I now challenge myself to dance with beauty, action and healthy excess, too. I am beginning to grasp the necessity of pure joy in living.

As a woman, there is something confusing in this. For so much of my life I have pushed back against the idea that any of my value lies in my beauty or softness. I've hardened myself, focused instead on the sensible, the factual, the cerebral to become a strong, distinguished woman who is not distracted by the transitory loveliness that life can offer. As a Brown woman, I have often found that I absolutely needed to be strong and hard, not because I was rebelling against the feminine stereotype, but to keep my heart safe from a world that was often uncomfortable. Perhaps that's why I found such a sense of safety in the garden soil and the compost heap, a mighty environment of intense transformation and sometimes painful destruction, all governed by that powerful Earth deity Ala. It is a world you need to be strong to stomach, so I walked straight in. It suited me.

I filled my mind with facts about soil care and decay. But I was so moved by this beautifully dark underworld and its cycle of reciprocity that I forgot about the spring above. I overlooked the fact that all this giving grows the softest, most delicate, most wonderfully pretty and yet transient power that bursts up out of it in spring. Sweet fruits for taking. The bits of me that had hardened cringed at the whimsical magic of it all.

But as I and the garden grow, I am reminded of the words of bell hooks in *Sisters of the Yam*: there is a need for 'Growing food to sustain life and flowers to please the soul.' It is OK to pick these flowers; it encourages the plant to give *more*, so long as the plant is not harvested to death. There is strength too in the wild, whimsical magic of late spring abundance. It feeds our bellies and our souls.

DIRECT SOWING

I wiggle my fingers into the dark, moist layer of compost blanketing the soil. Just a few months ago winter had frozen it to a firm, sparkling silver grey. Now on this warm day at the end of May, the sun has rested his hot hands on the soil surface for long enough that the ground has softened and warmed.

Those flat smooth squash seeds are still loose in my jacket pocket. Each is just a little smaller than my thumbnail, rounded on one side and pointed on the other. My hand is in there with them, tracing their shapes and jangling them about like coins. I vaguely recall the feeling of fiddling with the pennies in my pocket on my way to school. That money would get me a small box of raisins at break. If I look after these seeds now in my pocket, they will get me five great romping squash plants with big yellow goblet flowers and hopefully a collection of sweet squashes to enjoy through autumn and winter. Each squash that grows will yield possibly hundreds more seeds, each seed containing a store of nutrients, carefully packed away for its dormant period and germination next year, when it could grow into a strong plant all on its own.

These squash seeds will get me a great deal more than those pennies did back then, but they ask a lot more of me too. I only get all this future bounty if I give my care and time. There's something thrilling in the promise of these seeds – even though they require my contribution. They are a gamble. I have sympathy for Jack and his beans.

Sifting through bits of paper and unidentifiable pocket dust, I search all the squash seeds out in the corners, collect them up into my palm and pull out a fistful of future. They look like pearlescent, cartoon droplets of spilt milk, paused in time, which is funny because they sort of are paused in time. Seeds are alive, but dormant; they respire on a cellular level. Once the conditions are right, the seed begins its germination process and respiration increases, making its built-in energy store available for that initial thrust of growth.

I have cleared the bed of the weeds that had begun to crop up between the garlic plants, which I won't harvest until June's solstice. Squashes and garlic will be bed-mates for a while, useful for saving space and building diverse soil life. When I planted out the garlic last autumn, I mulched deep with homemade compost, so this bed won't get another dressing until these squash plants have swelled their great big, sweet fruits.

Kneeling, with my right hand I part the warmed earth, shuffle one seed out of my left palm and into the ground. It falls flat, glowing against the dark soil. Before pinching the earth closed over the little seed, I reposition it, propping it up on its side so that water can't pool on its surface and cause it to rot. I repeat the process until all the seeds are tucked away.

For me, leaving these seeds to be raised by the soil, sun and rain always takes a leap of faith. Part of me can never quite believe they will survive, let alone rise up tall and strong.

Mothering seedlings takes time and resources, compost, water, pots, feed, so giving these seeds to the warmed ground to be raised wild by the garden means less work for me and stronger, happier plants in the long run. When I compare the pot-raised plants with the ones that start their lives outside in the beds, the soil dwellers always seem healthier, more capable of dealing with challenging weather and pests. Best of all, they don't suffer from that window of awkward vulnerability while they recover from the shock of being finally transplanted to their permanent homes.

Unaided by human hands, most plants are sedentary – once rooted, they can't get up and walk about the way we can. But over many millions of years, they have become incredibly wise, building up strong communities of support which help them to succeed.

When a seed is placed in the soil, it starts its growth by sending out its radicle (the botanical name for the first juvenile root) which helps to anchor the seedling. Since the plant can't move, it works to cultivate a surrounding environment in which it can thrive. The radicle draws up nutrition and begins to pump exudates out into the earth, a cocktail of molecules which entices what the plant needs from the soil to it. Through this process, the seedling recruits its rhizosphere (see page 172). I think of this little underground world like a sort of garden tended by the plant roots.

As the seedling pushes its leaves into the air, they meet a world of microbes, and an above-ground family of plant-friendly microbes develops too. This process is essential for the plant's ability to withstand and respond to a potentially hostile environment which it cannot flee.

Obviously, a seedling raised in a pot on my windowsill or in the greenhouse doesn't have quite the same access to all these local microbes, particularly the soil-borne ones. Any relationships the plant does build while living in the pot are likely to be disrupted once I finally introduce it to its permanent home, and with it a vast new collection of microbes both above and below ground. I often wonder if part of the reason direct sown seedlings are more resilient is because they are able to cultivate their 'gardens' of plant-friendly microbes right from the start.

I unfold myself from my crouched position in the future squash patch. My knees click and my eyes adjust to take in the whole garden. Back in March, when the earth was just waking up, I hoed the bed back alongside the annual veg and sprinkled the tiny seed of California poppies and chamomile straight onto the soil. I then covered the bare ground with spikey prunings from the thorny pyracantha to keep any chickens, cats or birds from scratching up the seeds. Now the poppies have risen and I watch them grow daily. Once the apples have stopped with their pale pink, these poppies will start with their dazzling orange. I will gather their flowers and dry them to use as a soporific anti-anxiety herb to add to teas.

HOW TO DIRECT SOW

Plant with the best weather conditions in mind – sowing during a warm, wet spell is a good idea, as watering won't really be necessary. The elements can tend to the seeds, giving them all they need.

Depending on your patch of ground, its intended final uses and the seedlings making it their home, you can follow two different approaches. Firstly, you can clear the chosen spot of any plants and weeds which might out-compete the seedlings, removing roots and all before sowing. Or you can simply throw handfuls of seeds about amongst what is already growing and see what comes up. This latter is a bit of an experiment, more of a 'rewilding' approach to gardening.

For the former, more controlled sowing, follow the no-dig method (see page 43). Alternatively, simply cover the weeded bed with compost. If you go with the card method, you may need to break through it with a spade so you can sow your seeds directly into the soil.

When I sow larger seeds like courgette, squash or even garlic cloves in a veg bed that is a bit weedy, I tend to card, compost and then slice slits into the cardboard and plant the seeds through the slit and into the soil.

If I'm sowing smaller seeds which like a less rich soil, as with this year's California poppy and chamomile seeds, for example, I tend to just weed the area and don't bother to add card or a compost mulch. I simply scatter the seeds directly onto the bare soil surface, agitate them in roughly with my fingers so they are exposed to sunlight but also remain moist and in contact with the earth. In dry, hot weather, once the seeds are in the soil, I give them a good watering.

It is also possible to sow seeds earlier than nature intended. This can be done in the spring in a greenhouse, a cold frame, under cloches or plastic bottles with their bottoms cut out, even a pane of glass, plastic sheeting or bubble wrap will do as insulators. With any one of these placed over the earth, the soil will warm up sooner than it would uncovered.

Once the ground is warm and I have deposited the seeds safely in the soil, I tend to keep the protection on until the seedling has grown a little. With bubble wrap, a sheet of plastic or glass pane, promptly remove it as soon as you see any signs of the seedlings rising. I only ever sow hardy crops directly using this method because after they germinate and sprout, the seedlings are able to tolerate the cooler conditions.

BIODIVERSITY

At twilight in spring, the garden catches my gaze and holds it for a very long while. In contrast with the lingering muted tones of the winter, all is verdant, the colours and textures unbelievable. It seems impossible that both worlds coexist on the same Earth. I stare, eyes wide open, flooded with sensation. It's hard to pull myself away.

MAY

This is my favourite hour in the garden, when the sun has slipped down low and the sky turns a muted watery blue. An old Devon word for this time of day is 'dimpsey'. Everything is intensely soft, the lush greenery, red valerian, bluebells, sharp yellow kale flowers and baby blue forget-me-nots seem to gently glow. The apple trees, fluffy with pale pink blossoms, sigh and I sigh back. Some years the spring rains send their petals twirling to the ground, beautifully bedraggled. But this year the showers are gentle and the blossoms linger for two whole weeks, after which I've forgotten winter ever existed.

The garden trees come into bloom in the following order: first, in early spring, weeks before the apple trees, is the viburnum by the shed, whose smell is heaven (even more so in the evenings), drawing me out of sedentary winter and back into the garden, nose first. Second comes the crab apple by the small, old stone wall, followed by Little Apple Tree, closest to our house. Fourth is the Great Big Grandma Apple tree who leans over, growing sideways, her thick trunk standing up out of the ground and then bending and growing parallel with the soil. Grandma Apple provides the perfect perch for Mervin to sit on, stretch his neck up and crow. Fifth and last, standing in the middle of them all, comes the Diddiest Apple Tree.

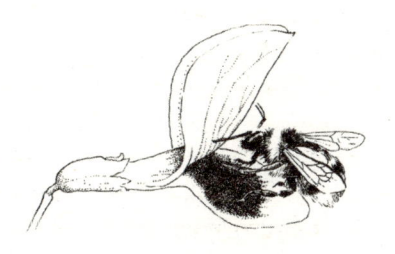

Some evenings, when the sun has set behind the valley but the sky is still dusky blue, I settle in the garden and just watch and listen. The birds chatter, the chickens coo to one another, bumblebees busily bury themselves in the autumn-sown broad bean flowers, searching out their sweet nectar. Various insects visit the apple trees and the many weeds in flower now, too, particularly the alkanet and dandelions. I sit still, stupefied by the loveliness of it all. So much life just getting on with living as the day slowly fades.

I think some would say I am 'simply' pleased, but what I'm witnessing is not simple at all. Visible in the dimpsey light is an incredibly complex web of life. I try to trace the millions of interconnections that play out before my eyes, but I can't, there are too many. I start to follow one, hold on to it for a while and then lose it.

I look at the apple blossom and the insects that visit it. The insects will feed the birds whose songs I hear; they will also pollinate the flowers, which will turn to fruit and which will feed me, more birds and many more insects too.

Some of the apples will fall to the ground. Some will be left there and lazily rot into the earth to nourish the soil food-web, contribute to the soil's organic matter content, improve aeration and increase its ability to hold water and nutrients. The trees will like this. The soil food-web, supported by the decaying organic matter, will deliver nutrients, minerals and even information to the trees. The trees will appreciate this and, in exchange, will provide the soil biology with as much as 40 per cent of the sugars they produce through photosynthesis.

Some of those soft rotting apples will be pecked at by the chickens, as yet more life receives the gift of sustenance. These exchanges feel generous. The trees give so much and receive so much in return – in this garden it seems there is plenty to go round.

In turn, the chickens will give their own gifts to the garden. As they scratch about, they fertilise the soil with their poo and when I clear out their coop, I'll add their manure to the compost heap or brew it into liquid plant feed. The compost in turn will feed the veggie patches, including the one beside the trees where the broad beans grow. And, of course, the hens will also give me eggs, which I might eat with some fried broad bean tops.

A bumblebee shuffles down from the apple blossoms to the bean flowers. The chickens peck at baby snails sheltering amongst them and in the process knock down some of the slender plants. Any that don't bounce back, I will chop at their base and add them to the compost heap, leaving their roots to break down into the soil to provide a source of nitrogen.

*

Broad beans (*Vicia faba*) – along with other bean varieties, like peas, chickpeas and lentils – belong to the legume family. Legume plants tend to form symbiotic relationships with nitrogen-fixing bacteria in the soil. The bacteria invade the plant's root hairs, forming nodules; you can often see these little nubbins on the roots of legumes if you pull them up. Once the bacteria is safely in a root nodule, the collaboration begins. The plant passes sugars (produced through photosynthesis) to the bacteria, and in exchange the bacteria uses the vital sugars to transform nitrogen in the atmosphere from its stable and *un*useful form, into one which is usable by plants. The air we breathe is made up of about 78 per cent nitrogen and the soil is about 25 per cent air, so there is a plentiful supply of atmospheric nitrogen down there. Thanks to this partnership, leguminous plants can tolerate lower levels of available nitrogen in the soil, as long as their bacterial teammates are present to convert it for them.

Once legume flowers are fertilised, the plant focuses all its resources into forming healthy beans and pods. Now the legume plant converts nitrogen to protein in the plant's seeds, and once this process of setting seed begins, the plant can contribute less available nitrogen to the soil. I grow broad beans as an annual vegetable rather than a soil conditioner, so Toby and I end up eating most of the atmospheric nitrogen the plant harvests via the protein-rich beans.

But before the broad beans set pods, they store nitrogen in their plant bodies. When the plant drops leaves, the roots die back, or when the plant is toppled by the chickens and then chopped down by me, the nitrogen harvested from the atmosphere can be deposited in the soil. Legumes therefore can contribute to the availability of usable nitrogen in the soil, and so other plants benefit from this exchange too. The other soil microbiology and fungi distribute the nitrogen by forming further reciprocal relationships with plants, again in exchange for sugars. I like to imagine that some of the nitrogen harvested by these broad beans and returned to the soil by the chickens and me might be passed via the soil web to the apple trees blooming nearby.

To really build up healthy nitrogen content in the soil, however, the most effective method is to grow several leguminous perennials whose main function in the garden is to supply nitrogen. These plants can also be beautiful, provide cover and forage for wildlife, and some may also yield a harvest. Each year the perennial will drop their leaves and their fine roots will naturally die back to offer an above- and below-ground supply of nitrogen. We can support this by pruning green growth from the plant and using it as mulch, either simply leaving it to rot down on the soil surface, or covering it with a layer of cardboard and compost; I find the latter most effective as it seems to encourage the greenery to break down more quickly and reduces habitat opportunities for our slimy friends. Or you can add the cuttings to the compost heap.

You can also grow a leguminous, annual green manure by planting cover crops like clovers, lupin, vetch or winter tares. They offer a very welcome source of nectar and pollen for insects, but the challenge is to get the timing just right. You need to chop down the plants in the small window at the end of flowering and before the plant begins to set seed – a process called 'chop and drop'. Legume cover crops are very effective builders of soil fertility, paving the way for other plants.

As I sit and watch, I trace all these connections, all this giving and receiving, taking and offering, attempting to follow and savour all the many layers of interactions. The world feels busy on this spring evening, far busier than in winter.

I learnt about the food web in my usually stark science lessons at school – most of those classes felt so dead, when really, science is all about the miracles of life. But when our science teacher, with a kind, soft face and freckles, who liked to wear colourful high heels and dresses in the summer, told us about this web of life, her eyes grew bright. She drew out a food chain with a squeaky black marker on the white board, and as I watched her swirl a circle of exchange, I felt her excitement too. I was curious about the many circles, the names and arrows connecting them to further circles, lines wiggling around the board, transforming a food chain into a web, and I loved copying the diagrams into my workbook. Those were the parts of science class I found easy to remember because they felt tangible yet vast. All this life linked up and interconnected. I don't think the word 'interconnected' was ever actually used, but I got the gist. Life was bound together by the arrows on my paper.

It was exciting, but not quite as exciting as smoking weed in the park – that gave me giggles until my belly ached and tears streamed down my face and I experienced a seemingly total transformation of my trusty sensory perception... or the giddy high of standing next to a boy I fancied so much my brain felt like it was melting. So, all those food webs I'd spun hung out somewhere in my head until I was ready for them.

Now, on these gentle spring evenings, those swirls of exchange come crowding back into my mind. In this garden, the chain is too complicated for me to follow entirely. I love that, and I hope I never can, because if that moment comes, it's my warning that the garden's biodiversity is dying. The mind-boggling networks I glimpse in the garden are a part of a functioning, complex ecosystem. Greater diversity brings with it complexity, and this complexity offers resilience.

To help understand this rule, we can look through the simple lens of me growing my own food. In my garden, I grow a couple of varieties of annual kale, chard and spinach, I also have giant perennial kale, and I allow nettles to grow, too. Together these plants give me an ample supply of leafy cooking greens. I am not dependent on any one plant. If the kale plants are knocked back by aphids, I turn to the chard; if leaf miners munch through the chard, I gather from the giant perennial kale. If hungry cabbage white caterpillars turn the leaves of my giant perennial kale into delicate lace, I harvest from the spinach. And if the spinach has perished in a drought, I can still harvest from the reliable patch of nettles happily growing in the shade of the apple trees. In the face of challenges, diversity creates resilience and, since the garden is alive, challenges do come. This is true of all webs of interaction or systems.

According to systems theory, to understand the complexity of the world we must shift our focus away from isolated objects or individuals. It requires instead an appreciation of the whole, and thus an exploration of the various interactions between beings, objects or landscapes. This approach jives with the idea that 'the whole is greater than the sum of its parts'.

When we focus too heavily on individual factors or players, we can miss out on vital connections. This way of understanding the world may have an impact on all areas of our lives. I can vividly recall the period in my life when I began to really understand that all life on Earth is connected. That Earth and its life gave me my body, sustains me and one day will take my body back again. As the Igbo saying goes: 'Ala *nwe mmadu*' – 'Ala owns the people'.

That shift in my perspective has had a lasting impact on me. In the past, I've found it hard to open up to people, connect, make friends, or even to be open with the people I love and trust. When my perspective shifted, that changed too. When we feel closed to the world, for whatever reason, it can become a self-fulfilling prophecy. That certainly was the case in my experience. (In the UK, 88 per cent of 18–24-year-olds report that they experience loneliness.) Isolation breeds isolation. Isolation brings with it weakness, weakness brings fear, and fear's best friend is isolation.

Learning that needing others is OK, quite safe and, really, just the normal state of things, continues to be one of my life's big lessons. What those science classes didn't show me, but what I now suspect made my teacher's eyes twinkle, is that I too am part of those webs of life. I am just a tiny part of a vast muddle, barely an individual at all. I find something cosy, comforting, yet awe-inspiring in understanding that I need the moths as much as the bats do; I need clean water as much as the frogs do. And I need my fellow humans, too. In a world obsessed with the individual, this is a radical and, in some ways, scary truth to accept. But it is one that has helped me to relate more easily with *all* life – humans and more. That change has shown me that real, resilient power lies in the complex connections between us all, and not in brittle, centralised power structures, however they may present themselves.

*

As I watch life unfold in my own green space, I see how this multi-layered food web operates on giving and receiving, and how that leads to health for all the participants. When we grow and tend a garden wisely, the garden tends us. My job really is just to assist the garden in doing what it already knows – generating sustaining complexity.

We urgently need to change the way food is produced, for our own health and that of the earth's. By growing food well, we can not only put the brakes on climate change, but actually work to restore, reverse and improve, regenerating landscapes, and in the process ourselves.

'As we work to heal the earth, the earth heals us,' writes Robin Wall Kimmerer in her brilliant book *Braiding Sweetgrass*, which I recommend reading and then rereading. Kimmerer's perception is by no means novel. For the longest time, people in communities around the world have understood themselves as Earth gardeners – part of a wider living world – responsible for tending ecosystems with care. In such cultures, folklore, rituals and deities remind of the truth that we humans are interdependent with the whole. It is only when we disconnect ourselves from other life that we can ignore this unavoidable fact.

Real strength lies in being part of an ecosystem which cares for us as we care for it. These ecosystems might take many forms: family, friendships, neighbours, animal companions, a garden. Gardens patiently teach us the practical reality of interdependence. They receive as much care as we are willing to give, and in return offer us sweet summer fruits, blossoms that glow in spring twilight, a place we feel we can safely belong; I feed the garden soil, and the garden soil feeds me.

'Connection is health,' writes Wendel Berry in *The Unsettling of America*, 'and what our society does its best to disguise from us is how ordinary, how commonly attainable, health is. We lose our health – and create profitable diseases and dependencies – by failing to see the direct connections between living and eating, eating and working, working and loving. In the garden, for instance, one works with the body to feed the body. The work, if it's knowledgeable, makes for excellent food. And it makes one hungry. The work thus makes eating both nourishing and joyful, not consumptive, and keeps the eater from getting fat and weak. This health, wholeness, is a source of delight.'

Connection makes us and our gardens healthy and strong. It makes our social and political movements healthy and strong, too. No wonder imperialist Britain utilised the strategy of 'divide and conquer' to dominate and subdue the people of their colonies. No wonder the modern concept of race was invented and institutionalised to prevent uprisings born out of collaboration between the working class white and enslaved Black people in the late 1600s. No wonder the export of extractive capitalism globally necessitates a split between fellow humans and the ecosystems we are asked to exploit. When we feel the truth of our interdependence, how can we exploit one another? When I consider the humans across the oceans as my own siblings, how can I eat the food grown on their land when its cultivation has poisoned their waters, eroded their soils and led those siblings to starvation? I can't. It's only possible if I remain disconnected, oblivious, be that in my heart or mind, through my own informed choosing, or through the input of a culture that encourages me to see myself as only *I alone*.

The dominant culture has an obsession with speed and efficiency – fast food, fast information, fast news, fast travel, fast learning, fast fashion, fast anything, really – at the cost of connection, complexity, depth and quality. And so we are left with mile-wide but shallow relationships and levels of knowledge, when what we truly need is deep understanding: knowledge and relationships of infinite depth and breadth.

Exploitation goes hand in hand with this sense of shallow disconnect. Engaging in a deep, meaningful relationship with a living space shatters that deadening detachment. There is nothing more humbling yet empowering than the knowledge that we are connected, that we belong to the earth. It provides life that gives and gives and gives. All we have to do is accept its gifts and give back to it in return.

'Let's bring Eden back to Earth.' I often go into the garden muttering these words to myself in my head, sometimes out loud. We know how. For various political, economic, cultural and possibly spiritual reasons, we just aren't quite doing it yet.

CULTIVATING BIODIVERSITY – A HOW TO, OF SORTS...

Eighty-seven per cent of UK citizens have access to a garden, and those gardens cover a vast area. They offer a patchwork quilt of opportunity for grassroots action, both in cultivating human connection with land and life and as a safe haven for wildlife too.

I should start by clarifying that there is no single recipe for cultivating biodiversity and health in the garden. There are too many ingredients and variables to ever create a set of standardised, step-by-step guidelines. Though handy, general guides tend towards homogenisation and simplification, in direct opposition to the beautiful, localised variety required for true biodiversity.

However, I can suggest a number of practical things we can all do in our gardens, which enough trustworthy land lovers have recommended that I consider them in the category of 'general wisdom'. Bear in mind, though, that this wisdom might not apply to your particular plot of land and the life that engages with it. Working with a growing space requires what it says on the tin: working *with*. Working effectively to regenerate the land and complex living ecosystems requires a deep understanding of how local circumstances dance with blanket rules or guidelines. It's a dance whose steps I am still learning. Guidance helps, but never let general advice override what your garden may be trying to tell you or you risk standardising biodiversity... a strange oxymoron.

- Create and allow as many niches for diverse life as possible. Often the most opportunities for life are at the margins, the points at which two different features overlap. For example, the shallows and edges of a pond, or the perimeter of a woodland area. The greater variety of boundaries the better.
- Go organic in the garden and, if you can, in everyday life too. Chemical herbicides, pesticides and fertilisers have a detrimental impact on the health of the ecosystem, which includes us. Growing organically helps to create a space that is safe for the creatures who visit it.

- Grow lots of different common native plants and wildflowers.
- All life needs water. Create a pond. It doesn't have to be huge and it doesn't even have to be dug into the ground (see page 48). Even a shallow tray of water with pebbles or gravel offers a welcome watering stop for insects such as bees.
- Take a lenient approach to native weeds, like nettles, dandelions, brambles, docks, ragwort. These plants reliably support so much life, since they usually grow vigorously, whatever the conditions.
- Create piles of logs, bricks or rocks. These provide homes and forage for all sorts of creatures, from toads and hedgehogs to slow-worms and woodlice.
- Plant hedges and shrubs with berries for birds. Elder and rowan trees and the guelder-rose shrub will feed us, the birds and pollinators.
- Make and use compost.
- Ensure wildlife can move between your garden and the next by creating access points in any barriers... or, if you get on with your neighbours, take down the fence altogether!
- If you have a lawn, mow less often. Lawns can offer important habitat and nectar. The charity Plantlife recommends leaving some patches completely uncut and others mown monthly or quarterly to create a diverse habitat and opportunities for different grasses, flowers and the creatures that depend on them. Participating in 'No-Mow May' alone can allow plants to provide up to ten times more nectar to support pollinators.
- Grow some of your own food and support local agroecological growers who support healthy ecosystems.
- Support policy and groups pushing for biodiversity-friendly legislation.

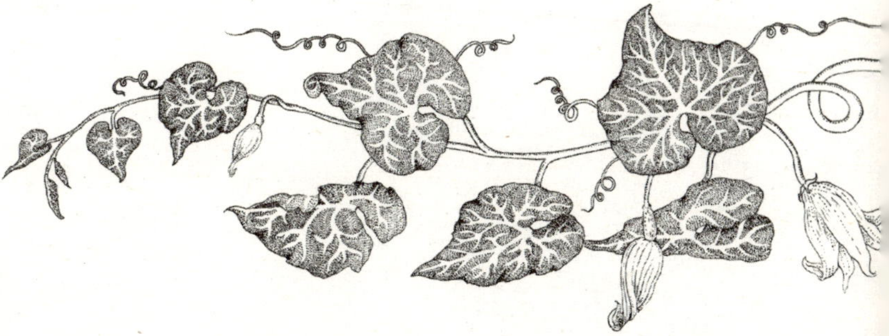

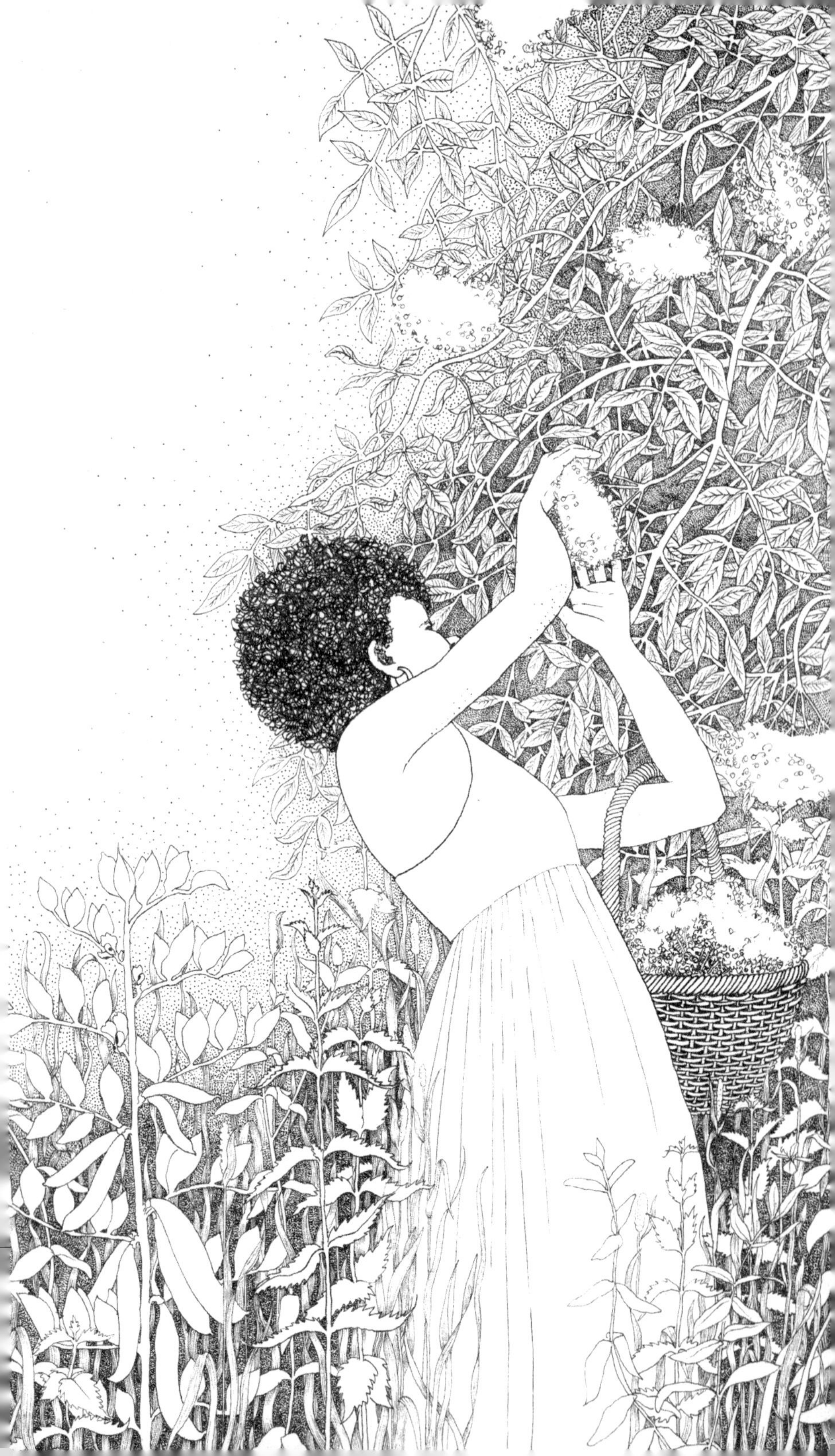

Summer

June

GUT HEALTH AND SOIL HEALTH

The last few weeks have been so hot and dry that despite the cool, damp day we're having, the earth is warm to my touch. I sink my hands into the soil, attempting to follow the sturdy taproot of a green alkanet (*Pentaglottis sempervirens*), down deep into the depths, hoping to pull it up in one go. I have to carefully manage these plants. They have pretty, star-shaped, delicate blue to pale lilac-pink flowers, and leaves that are soft and velvety when young but scratchy when old. They are charming but if left to their own devices, they tend to dominate large patches.

My loose, dark garden soil would be classified as 'friable loam'. When moist, it resembles breadcrumbs; when dry it turns to dust, like cocoa powder mixed with granulated sugar. This kind of soil lets my hand go exploring wherever I like and so it's easy to follow down the alkanet taproot. In the community garden, in contrast, the soil is a brown, orange clay – slick, heavy and dense when wet, firm and hard when dry. It is much less inviting to an explorative hand, and I have to slide a smooth, sharp trowel in instead. Being friable means that the soil easily crumbles in the hand, like breadcrumbs. As a loamy soil it is made up of a mixture of mineral-rich materials all with varying particle sizes, with sand particles being the biggest, and silt and clay the smallest. Loamy soils possess an optimal mixture of all three materials and so some of their more challenging properties are balanced out. The garden loam is rich in precious organic matter too, so it is not prone to compaction and warms quickly in the spring, retaining its warmth right through until late autumn. It therefore provides a cosy bed for baby spring plants to get started and stay warm in mild autumns. It also holds moisture, but does not become waterlogged, making it a comfortable environment for plants to overwinter. In contrast, the small particle sizes of the clay soil on the community plot make it prone to both waterlogging and compaction, but it does hold huge fertility. Clay soil rarely lacks nutrients. It takes its sweet time to warm in the spring but it is also in less of a hurry to cool off again come autumn.

By handling these soils it's possible to decipher clues to tell us which plants they are most skilled at growing and when. My friable loam can happily grow Mediterranean herbs and support chard throughout the winter. The community plot's clay will also grow herbs but perhaps not quite so well, and if chard is left to overwinter in the lower parts of the garden it will rot due to waterlogging and cold – just like those sad broad beans!

For many years, modern horticulture saw soil as merely a medium for growing, an inert substance made up of minerals, water, organic matter and air. We forgot that soil is in fact a vast and complex network of interconnected life. Today the warm and moist earth is full of all that life getting on, being busy. Later, as the soil cools with the seasons, many mobile organisms will delve deep out of frost's reach and microbial activity will slow. With fewer hours of weakened sunlight, and occasional lack of access to water in deep cold frosts, plants reduce or even halt photosynthesis and so have less sugars available to pass to their friends below.

I feel a deep snapping thunk through the ground as the alkanet taproot suddenly releases its grip. It comes flying up with a shower of loam. It smells good, of geosmin – from the Greek *geo*: earth; and *osme*: odour – that wonderful moist earthy scent emitted by soil. I bring a handful to my face and breathe deep. It's not as heady as the rich doughy humus I dig my hands into on the woodland floor, but it's got a pretty good whiff, nonetheless. The life in the soil is what gives it this moist aroma, the billions of microorganisms that call it home, in particular the group of bacteria called actinomycetes. I take another long deep breath. Never in my wildest dreams would my younger self have imagined me squatting in a damp garden, taking drags on a handful of soil and loving it, yet here I am.

Humans are incredibly sensitive to the smell of soil, which can generate a sense of calm, peace and general well-being. It can even activate cells which reduce inflammation in the brain. In *The Well-Gardened Mind*, the psychiatrist and psychotherapist Sue Stuart-Smith describes these cells as our 'brain's resident gardeners'. The calming effect is partly thanks to the pleasing smell of geosmin, but also to a harmless bacteria called *Mycobacterium vaccae*. This bacteria is commonly found in the earth and especially in soils that are rich in organic matter, like those enriched with compost. It stimulates the release and metabolism of serotonin (also known as the 'happy hormone'), one of the hormones responsible for lasting feelings of contentment and ease; it helps to regulate our sleep and our sex drive, as well as influencing memory and learning. *Mycobacterium vaccae* is easily inhaled and ingested while working in the garden and it can act much like an antidepressant. So, when people say they feel great after a day in the garden with their hands in the soil, scientifically speaking, they may well do. Tending the earth and feeding the soil is good for our minds.

Having been so actively embedded in the living world for most of human existence, our brains respond positively to many of the experiences of safely engaging with it. Smelling living soil, tending and harvesting plants, looking out over green vistas, the sound of a stream, walking in a woodland – all of these experiences have been shown to increase serotonin levels. Exploring our interconnection with the living world, be that through gardening, ambling, swimming or foraging, can offer psychological protection.

Sitting here with the uprooted alkanet, I take in another long huff of geosmin. I imagine the hundreds of thousands of generations of my ancestors before me inhaling this smell of life. They lived closely with the soil. It's only really been in the last 500 years or so that so many of us have begun living in sprawling, packed, urbanised areas with reduced access to patches of earth. And since we now mostly buy our food from a clean fridge in a supermarket, plastic-wrapped and with no sight or scent of soil, our connection to this smell is further diminished.

But the human brain basically still functions in the same way it did back then, so when we sniff the sweet, nutty scent of warm wet earth, we respond. I do wonder about the many other stimuli in the wider world, including plants, insects, birds, moss, rivers and streams, to which we have evolved sensitivity but which so many of us rarely encounter nowadays; how much of life we don't experience by separating ourselves from it all. I throw the mighty muddy alkanet root into my compost bucket where it hits the bottom with a resounding thud. When I first came here, I pulled up a green alkanet with a taproot as wide as my forearm. The outside of their roots are dark, while internally they are a vibrant orange. The only other roots I pull up anywhere near so girthy are parsnips and carrots, but a carrot released from the soil is more likely to get a quick wipe and go straight into my mouth than the bucket.

Eating food directly from the earth is fun, empowering, grounding. Its loveliness comes from its honest simplicity. It's also good for us. Along with the benefits of serotonin-stimulating actinomycetes and *Mycobacterium vaccae*, having our hands in the ground and interacting up close and personal with a garden, eating its bounty fresh from the earth is also beneficial for our gut health. In our highly sterilised lives, it can be hard to find a good dose of healthy microbes – gardening, foraging or eating soil-fresh plants can help with that. This intimate contact inoculates us with a vast array of beneficial bacteria, enhancing the diversity of our microbiome. You don't have to actually eat the earth, though. Just interacting with it regularly is enough.

Science now shows that regular access to a diversity of friendly microbes is integral to our well-being. A healthy gut microbiome affects skin and heart health, sleep quality and our digestion. It is also vital to a fully functioning immune system – our gut houses about 70 per cent of the cells that make up our immune system – as well as maintaining our mental health, as 90 per cent of all our serotonin is produced in the gut. Much as the soil microbiome supports plants, our own microbiomes support us. They too pass us nutrients extracted from the organic matter we eat and help us to break down fibrous plants.

It's funny, not only does the soil do us good, but the mysterious world of microbes inside us is strangely similar to the soil's. I think of the Igbo tale of the Earth Goddess, Ala, who gives us our bodies from her very self, and who then, when our time is up, embraces us, taking us back again. From that world-view, it's no surprise we humans are so soil-like. How perfectly poetic that in tending the earth we quite literally tend ourselves too, growing healthy gardens both inside ourselves and out.

ELDERFLOWER

Arms held high in the air for too long, my hands start to feel bloodless and cold. I have been stretching up to gather blooms from an elder tree. I let them flop beside me and plop myself down on the soft earth, cushioned by a layer of decaying leaves and bracken. I'm sitting in a small copse of elder, hazel and baby oak trees – I suppose you'd call it a 'spinney'. I remember that word from a story tape I listened to as a child, a collection of creepy folk-tales, the most terrifying of which opened with the line: 'Walking late through spooky spinney gives me wobbly knees!'

On this still, high-summer day, the spinney gives me anything but wobbly knees. But swaddled among the dense foliage, it does feel like a spot from a fairy tale, full of wild secrets, enchanted. I love it here. The sun trickles between the leaves, which glow green as though lit from within. I look up, head tilted back, and they rustle. There's birdsong and fluttering in the branches of the trees, and insects dust the air, little specks, floating, twitching, swooping. It's not always common to see and feel so much life about outside. My mum has taken me to many secret meadows, discovered on her long rambling walks, that she says would have buzzed and fluttered with life when she was a child. Now they are still and silent, a pretty picture rather than a living landscape. It's comforting to know that despite being one of Earth's most nature-depleted countries, in pockets life persists, if given half a chance. From where I'm sitting, I can hear water too, but I have no clue where it's coming from because the foliage is so dense. There is no path into the spinney, instead I scramble over a gate then wade my way through dense nettles and bracken that grows taller than me before the thicket becomes too overgrown.

A witch might live here and may set me a challenge – to find the mysterious stream and fetch water for her cauldron, perhaps. In reward, she might ask me to choose between a sack of gold or an unassuming plum stone. I should choose the plum stone, because I'd later discover that it grows into a magical tree, forever in flower and fruit, while the sack of gold would have turned to a bag of mud on my arrival home. A fairy tale ending, telling of the pitfalls of greed, the riches to be found in the seemingly unassuming and of the regenerating abundance in life. I start willing a witch to appear.

I look up at the elder. These trees have been special to me since I was a teenager. When we were about fourteen, a friend and I went gathering elderflower. I remember trying to explain the difference between elderflowers and cow parsley to her. I didn't really know how to communicate it, I'd never thought about it, I just knew. Back at my mum's, we made buckets of elderflower cordial which we bottled to sell at the village car show. Later that summer, I used that money, along with birthday money and the pennies I had earned working in a tearoom, to go to my first music festival.

Elder trees present a dichotomy. Their notoriously gnarled, twisted bark looks as old as time, yet year on year lush greenery springs from their dry twiggy fingers followed by the most flirtatious of flowers. Folklore tells us that a woman, Frau Holle, lives inside the trunk of these trees. Frau Holle, sometimes depicted as a hag, other times a fertile young maiden, can both curse or protect, and offers gifts, but only to those who treat her well. For many years, people refused to chop down elders, afraid they would provoke her wrath. Frau Holle's tree is at once ancient, firm, unyielding while also new, soft, luscious and sweet; a symbol of how the softest abundance grows up from the wise and sturdy. Structure facilitating flow. Death creating life. This is a lesson the garden has taught me many times over, and is a story this elder tells so well.

Powerful, magical women often seem to offer us this duality of creation and destruction. We see it too in the Scottish myth of Cailleach, a crone goddess associated with storms, wildness and winter. Just like Ala, it is believed that Cailleach's body literally is the landscape. While presiding over abundance, Ala is seen to hold us accountable for wrongdoings. All three, Ala, Frau Holle and Cailleach, are perceived as complex, gentle and fierce, capable of giving life while also bringing about devastation and destruction.

The elderflowers are what first brought me to this magical spinney; they beckoned me in like a bee, seducing with a promise of fruits, whispering of the sticky sweet future to come. There is something whimsical yet so powerful about the flowers' ability to draw us in; we humans are besotted with them. Toby enjoys our garden, but I wouldn't go so far as to say he has a *passion* for it. But one day, visiting another garden, as we walked through a passageway of hollyhocks that towered over him, their trumpet blooms in all shades, pink, white, creamy and inky purple, nearly black, wide-eyed he turned to me and exclaimed, 'We HAVE to have these flowers in our garden.'

I think we can learn a lot from flowers. In our movements to safeguard life on Earth, metaphorically speaking, we need flowers. Their beckoning beauty can inspire the way we transform our culture. People need to see the beauties and benefits this transformation could bring – from community-owned renewable energy; eco villages; suitably insulated homes to reduce energy use and costs; food models like Community Supported Agriculture; high-quality, nature-based solutions to sewage management to restore the health and beauty of our rivers; and affordable, accessible public transport. I believe we need to be reminded of the better future we could bring about if only we act *now*, if we press for widespread, effective legislation and embrace the resulting necessary changes to our way of life here in the 'WEIRD' (Western, Educated, Industrialised, Rich and Democratic) countries. Politicians have shown and told us they need to feel certain there is a public mandate in order to legislate in the face of corporate pressure. We all need to sign up for this change – loudly – and draw enough others in too. Grassroots work can help generate that. As we see in the garden, flowers – or promises of the fruits to come – draw people in. Simply, solutions can galvanise and connect us.

*

For now, there are many elders all around, but once there were many elm trees too, and now they're nearly all gone. Looking up at Frau Holle's tree, I decide to plant an elder in our garden later this autumn. There are several varieties and cultivars of varying height, types and colour leaves, fruit and flowers. I like the common variety found here in the spinney and hedgerows; and the cultivar 'Black Lace', with delicate, deep purple to black leaves and red wine-stained flowers. In general, 'Black Lace' has a punkish look about it – nothing like the fluffy white and glowing green above my head. I'm not sure which to choose, but I harvest so often from these trees in the wild, it somehow feels right to nurture one in exchange.

I stand up and continue to gather the fragrant white umbels. I make sure to leave plenty of elderflower behind, not only for the other creatures of the spinney, but also so the blooms can develop into plump, dark berries, which will feed more life still, and which I will use to make syrup to ward off winter colds.

ELDERFLOWER VINEGAR

- 5–7 generous sprigs of elderflower blossom, gently rinsed to remove dirt and insects
- 500 ml cider vinegar

Recipe

Elderflower is best gathered in the late morning on a warm, sunny, still day. This allows any moisture from the night before to dissipate, and a few hours spent soaking up the summer sun seems to make the blooms more fragrant.

More and more I try to cook with local ingredients that require less industrial processing before they get to me. I also try to cut down on the amount of sugar I use in foraged recipes, for my health but also as a challenge. Near everything is tasty as a cordial or candy, that's too easy!

These days, instead of making cordial, I use the elderflowers to flavour my homemade apple cider vinegar (see recipe on page 54). When I gather the apples from the garden to make the vinegar in late summer and early autumn, I often look forward to the following summer and picking the elderflowers which eventually will flavour the golden liquid.

These quantities are approximate. Before you make a large batch, it's worth filling a couple of jam jars with vinegar and experimenting with the number of elderflower sprigs and the timings, to test the strength and get to know your preferred taste, really making this recipe your own.

I find if I want a more intense flavour, it's better to use more flowers rather than leaving smaller numbers to infuse for longer.

- In a large crock or glass jar, submerge the elderflower in the vinegar, weighing it down if needs be. Leave to infuse for a couple of days – it's worth keeping an eye on the brew and tasting as you go. I like to remove the flowers before they turn a brownish colour because at that point, the flavour loses the fresh, soft floral tones and the vinegar becomes a bit darker.
- Use the flavoured vinegar in dressings, sauces, or add to water with honey to make a sweet, sharp soft drink.

NOTE:
You can also use elderflowers to make a tasty 'oxymel' syrup (see recipe, page 296).

SUMMER SOLSTICE

Summer solstice: the longest day and shortest night. With the moon only up for seven-and-a-half hours, we have sixteen-and-a-half hours of sunlight.

The busyness of spring is cooling off and my garden and I are settling into a steady rhythm. Long summer days stretch out ahead, punctuated only by brief, warm nights. Although each day seems to go on forever, in the garden the hours whirl past at speed. Life explodes up out of itself. There's so much to taste, smell, watch and touch. I can spend a whole morning sitting in the grass gazing at hoverflies going about their business; an afternoon gathering up herbs, flowers and the first flush of annual veg, cooking it, eating it in the sun; later, a cold plunge in the river to wash away a sweaty day outside.

To me, this is a vital, bewitching season. In times gone by, around midsummer, people would often report sightings of magical faerie processions. This first taste of summer, the heady muddle of days all souped together, and the long, light, hazy dusks, certainly feels like a good time to encounter the mischievous faeries of older traditional folklore.

These midsummer creatures were not the sweet, sanitised fairies of Disneyland. These were the wild faeries, or 'fae', powerful ethereal creatures who were alternately madly helpful and deadly cruel, offering humans either extravagant gifts or certain death. These faeries might play malevolent tricks, enchant and enslave humans, kidnap infants, and often waged war on small creatures just for the fun of it. First-hand accounts and tales of 'faerie rades' described hearing their mesmerising music and song as they drew near, followed by magnificent, dancing processions of fae folk dressed in their finest raiment, proud in their dazzling, eternally youthful beauty. It was said that some who saw a faerie raid were caught up in their spell, never to be seen again, while others danced with them for what they thought was just a little while, only to be released from their charm decades later.

Today, summer solstice is referred to by some neo-pagans as

JUNE

Lithe or Litha, a term which is commonly believed to have been the Anglo-Saxon word for solstice. It was, in fact, a word meaning 'pleasant or navigable conditions', used by the same Venerable Bede to refer to the months of both June and July. With summer's balmy weather, it's easy to see why. Many of today's solstice day traditions are undeniably steeped in pagan folklore – the veneration of trees and floral crowns, the plunges into lakes and leaps over bonfires, and the magical good luck spells. But, in fact, there's little evidence to suggest that the actual day of summer solstice was widely celebrated in pre-Christian Northern Europe. Perhaps because, without the help of an astronomer or calendar, it is difficult to pinpoint when *exactly* it falls.

Much like my Igbo ancestors, pre-Christian Europeans saw time as inextricably linked with events: time was *what happened*. So, if an event could not be felt, experienced tangibly, it simply didn't exist. Thus, date dependant events like the summer solstice were not typically marked. However, our ancestors *could* experience a prolonged period of brightness, hedges peppered with blooms that filled the night air with perfume, gentle warmth, luscious growth and an abundant grain harvest later in the summer. It's easy to imagine the festivities and superstitions marking this general period, our first taste of summer proper.

Oak trees in their full foliage are strongly associated with the solstice, along with the Oak King who presides over this light part of the year. The mighty oaks support more wildlife than any other native tree, providing food, shelter and breeding ground to around 2,300 species. A true symbol of powerful life-giving abundance. But despite the Oak King's potency, his reign must end at summer solstice, and the Holly King returns. From this longest day onward, as we start the march back into the darker half of the year, slowly, very slowly, the days will begin to shorten once more.

A WILDER WAY

MIDSUMMER TEA

(Recipe)

🌿 A good handful of fresh edible flowers, or a palm-full of dried flowers

I love to sip on this fragrant floral infusion in the late afternoon sun. Forage in your garden or the wild for edible flowers – honeysuckle, dog rose, linden blossoms, meadowsweet, yarrow, chamomile or elderflower. You can use them separately or experiment with a mixture of flowers. Alternatively, look in your local apothecary, herbal dispensary or health food shop for dried flowers.

— Add the fresh or dried blooms to a small saucepan and cover with water.
— Place a lid on the pan and bring to the boil.
— Once boiling, take the brew off the heat and leave aside to steep for 10–15 mins.
— Once the brew has cooled slightly, if preferred, add a spoonful of local, raw honey to sweeten.

NOTE:
Elderflowers are a brilliant herbal remedy for hayfever, and they pair well with chamomile and yarrow in this tea. Raw, local honey can help with hayfever, too.

THE GARLIC COMES BACK UP

This week we took up the softneck garlic at the community garden, and I pulled up the first bulb in my garden too. The plant's slender, once-green foliage had slowly turned to a crisp brown, peppered with the telltale splodges of the parasitic fungi called 'garlic rust'; a reliable hint that the bulbs below were ready for harvesting.

Garlic rust doesn't bother the plants to begin with, but as time goes on it coats their foliage, reducing their ability to photosynthesise and weakening them. As a result, the garlic bulbs do not have enough energy to continue swelling – they have reached their maximum size for the year.

The elephant garlic (*Allium ampeloprasum*) however has dodged the rusty parasite; its leaves still stand tall and are likely to remain so right into August, like green spires rising out from the young, establishing courgette plants nestled below. When we do finally come to lifting the giant elephant bulbs, we must do so carefully, without disturbing the courgettes who will take over the bed when the garlic is removed.

We squat along the length of the beds, our hands in the earth gathering back up what we put down a few months ago. The cloves that went in about the size of thumbnails have now swollen into bulbs, some as large as the palm of my hand.

The dry soil has a weak grasp on the bulbs, and with a soft tug they obligingly pop out. Piles of garlic mount up beside us, rustling each time we cast more crisp plants on top. When we start to gather up the piles in our arms, the foliage is scratchy against my skin, below my feet the soil is dry, up above the sun is hot and bright. I squint as I move towards the wheelbarrow and deposit my bundle there with the others. The passage of time, with the help of rain, soil and sun, has transformed our little bag of garlic cloves into barrows full of pungent treasure.

I love the rhythm of growing garlic; I think back to the days we filled these beds, bundled up in layers, our noses dripping in the cold descent into winter. Now, at the height of summer, my skin drips sweat in the heat.

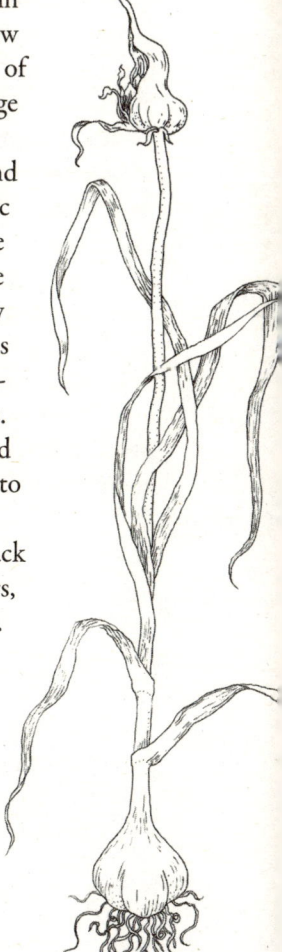

We wheel the barrow up to our cabin and spread the garlic out across three large trestle tables where it will rest to further cure and dry. The leaves will continue to crisp as any goodness left in the foliage is drawn down and into the bulbs. The leaf sheaths will dry out to a paper casing, sealing and protecting the sweet, sticky cloves inside. This ensures our garlic will keep. We separate out the biggest bulbs, putting them aside to break apart and resow again when autumn comes back around. The rest we will eat!

THE GLORIES OF GARLIC

Owing to its many benefits, garlic has become a bit of a solve-all superhero in my home, both as food and medicine. I reach for garlic to support healing from lurgies and infections, as well as to promote long-term health. Garlic is anti-inflammatory, can support the cardiovascular system *and* has potent antiviral and antibacterial properties. A great deal of its many beneficial qualities are down to an amino acid called allicin, which also contributes to the plant's eye-wateringly pungent sulphur-like scent. Allicin is part of garlic's defence mechanism, and is created when two different compounds in the plant's cells come into contact through damage to its tissue. So, when using garlic for its healing properties, crushed is best. Heating and cooking garlic can reduce the quantity of allicin in it, so it's best to eat it raw (for example crushed in a dip like hummus or in salad dressing), or to crush it and then stir it into warm food right before serving. Also, it's best to leave it aside for ten minutes before consuming to allow the chemical reaction that creates allicin to fully unfold.

JUNE

HONEY-INFUSED GARLIC

On my way home from the community garden is a little stall on the side of the road which in summer offers bunches of flowers, jars of liquid-gold honey and an honesty box. The honey, which comes from bees kept by the homeowner opposite the stall, usually arrives on the stand a few weeks after we harvest the garlic.

I love this recipe for fermented garlic honey as it only requires two ingredients. The sharp earthiness of garlic mixes so well with the sweet headiness of honey. When I pour it over the stiff, pale little cloves of garlic, it feels like I'm wrapping them in the warm arms of the sun they so missed through winter.

This sweet, garlicky ferment makes an incredibly versatile ingredient. And, of course, our guts benefit from the microbes produced by the fermentation too. If possible, use raw honey for this recipe as the live yeasts will help to kick-start the process.

— Peel enough cloves of garlic to half fill a clean glass jar.
— Pour the raw honey over the garlic until it is fully submerged – some cloves may float up and that's OK.
— Loosely secure the jar lid and leave in a dark place at room temperature for up to a week. The liquid provided by the garlic cloves will be enough to coax the honey into fermenting.
— Every few days, tighten the lid and shake the jar to agitate the ingredients, then loosen the lid again slightly to allow the ferment to breathe. As the fermentation takes place the honey will become more liquid and the garlic will change colour from white to a faint yellow or grey-brown tone.
— There is the option to add a modest splash of cider vinegar if you are nervous of the ferment not working.
— Taste test along the way, you may find you like it best earlier or later on! If you want to pause the ferment, just pop it in the fridge. After about a week, the ferment will be ready. It will keep in a cupboard for about a year.

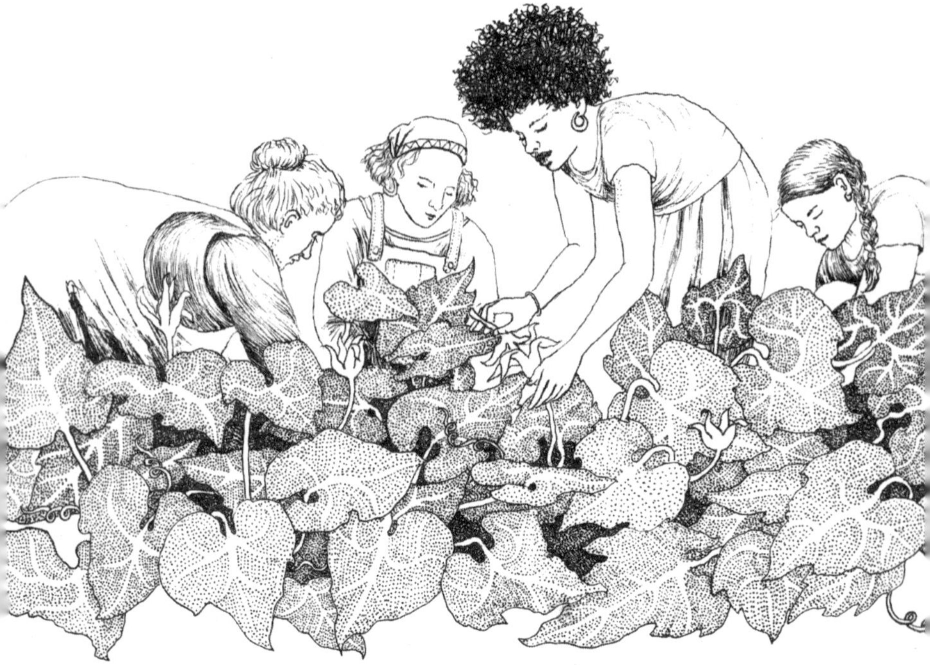

July

THE PLANTS WILL GROW THEMSELVES

Today it is hot and close. My sister Rosie is staying; she has come here with a sore heart and today she is restless. It's 6 p.m., still bright: we have hours of sunshine ahead of us. We go out into the garden together, fetch tools and begin the long overdue task of clearing the broad bean patch. The seeds settled into the soil eight months ago, and now the plants have become raggedy and tired, weighed down by their swollen pods, the leaves that remain beginning to yellow. Their time is up. We rip, snap and pull the pods from their fibrous stems, dumping handfuls into our baskets. Once each plant is stripped, we chop it at the base, cut it into pieces and leave them where they fall to protect the earth from the hot sunshine before they rot away. We talk a little while we work, but not much – we don't really need to share words when we're sharing this time and space.

We start off stooped, bent double at the edges of the bed. As we advance through the patch we squat amongst the plants, engulfed in green. I go inside to fetch iced tea. Coming back out I see my sister's head, wrapped in a silky lilac scarf that glows in the sun, offset by the lush of the garden's green, bobbing amongst the beans. I stand

and watch for a long while, storing the vision for the days when she's far away once more.

In that moment, the wild jumble of colour, texture and sound that makes up the garden in mid- to late summer seems the right place for a sore heart to be. The garden feels like an extension of me, holding her, giving her something to do that's also nothing at all, a task to help her heal. Its gifts feel like my gifts – we are caring for her together. This isn't manicured perfection, a place that looks back at you and says, 'do better', 'do more', 'get yourself together', 'be orderly like me'. Here death lives with life, chaos and order coincide; a place where wildness meets us humans and together, we gently dance. This garden says life is beautifully messy, not clinical and controlled. Broken hearts are as welcome as full ones here, and endings metamorphose into new life.

As dimpsey falls, we lug our harvest inside. That evening, we sit with Toby and Freddy Dog and shell beans. Its rhythmic work. Holding the pod in my left hand, with my right I snap one end, where it once hung from its stem. In one brisk motion, I whip this tip down along the length of the pod. It is attached to a fibrous thread, and as I pull down, I tug the thread free. Discarding the tip and its now dangling thread, I fluidly take the pod in my right hand, and as I press my left thumb firmly down along the length of the now vulnerable seam, it pops open and satisfyingly unzips. Five plump beans lie nestled in the velvet soft, fluffy white purse of the pod's insides.

Pod after pod lands in the compost bucket, beans plop into a gigantic bowl. We weigh them: 5 kg. Into a great big ziplock bag they go to be stored in the freezer. Three fresh portions kept aside for tomorrow's lunch. We are all three satisfied with our work. Rosie goes to bed, no longer restless. For now, the garden and its work have soothed her. Meg's broad beans have shown us the way once again.

*

I was recently asked what the difference is between my wild garden and an overgrown one, which I thought was a very good question.

To be honest, I don't know that, officially, there *is* any difference. Lots of people, I'm sure, would just think my garden is overgrown. Even to me, it frequently tips into the unruly and I find myself guiding things back to the edge of order. To others, it wouldn't seem nearly wild enough – it's subjective, I suppose. Perhaps, essentially, the difference lies in the act of my tending the space, how I both follow the garden's lead and coax it into this particular functional aesthetic of muddled beauty. I think I work more as a garden assistant than a gardener; I see myself as just one of this garden's many helpful inhabitants rather than an overlord.

In the first year in this garden, I largely let everything grow so I could see what came up through the seasons. I only removed the sorts of weeds that I know can turn a piece of land into a monoculture. I wrestled brambles, dug some out completely and cut others right back; I yanked up bundles of bindweed and dug out nettle, dock and green alkanet where they threatened to swamp. This contest between me and some of the more enthusiastic plants is ongoing. No doubt it will continue for some years more, until they loosen their grasp on the space and I can trust them not to bully the other plants.

The rest of the management is really just encouraging what's already here and making pockets for new arrivals. I might spot an emerging biennial evening primrose and tend to it so it has room to push through and flower the following year. I chop the patch of nettles below the apple trees regularly for material for the compost heap, the kitchen and to keep the patch in check, but also because I think fresh nettle growth is pretty and my continual chopping keeps them producing lush new foliage. I might weed a patch in late winter and leave it bare rather than mulching, because I know that that way I'll get scarlet field poppies coming through the following summer (they love bare, disturbed ground).

The winter we installed the greenhouse, inside in its warmth and on the disturbed ground a sea of poppy seedlings germinated. With nothing better to put in their place, I let them be. Allowing these fast growing annual 'pioneer' plants (see page 87) to do their job and carpet the ground, they quickly grew tall and bloomed on my birthday in May, earlier than those outside. The little glass house burned red. I left the door and all the windows open for insects to bustle in and out of the display. Then, in June, I chopped them all down, buried them in homemade compost and planted the tomatoes in the now eerily empty greenhouse. I ended up with a slightly delayed harvest, but it was a small price to pay.

Sometimes a plant takes over a bit, so I'll chop it back hard, clear the space it was taking up and then sow something new. This year I cut back a pink Japanese anemone (*anemone × hybrida*) which I thought was getting a bit greedy, filling the opening with calendula, California poppies and chamomile.

The 'wild' strip previously laid bare by the scratching of the chickens, is now blooming and wonderful with nodding heads of wild white yarrow, white pincushion flowers (*Scabiosa caucasica*), bobbing blue cornflowers (*Centaurea cyanus*) and wild carrot (*Daucus carota*), which I planted in the empty pockets our flock had left behind. I love that this patch was a collaborative effort, not entirely intentional and very much a result of life in this garden just living.

JULY

I grow by the philosophy of 'right plant, right place', which speaks to the common sense guidance that plants ought to be planted and grown in suitable environments – given the right environment, they will thrive. The concept was recently pioneered in the UK by the renowned gardener Beth Chatto, but has been and is still very much practised globally by folks who can't afford to and don't have an interest in attempting to bend the landscape to their will, trying to make it grow plants it doesn't know how. But first, in order to put the right plant in the right place, I need to know what this place *is*. I've had to learn this garden and the landscape around it well. I note the garden's free draining soil, its aspect, how water and wind flow through it and which plants already call it, and the wild places around us, their home, and pay heed.

I've planted a carpet of wild garlic, which loves the damp and only half-thrives in the well-draining soil, in the shade below the apple trees. The trees also provide the perfect dappled shade for the herb valerian (the root is used for calming and as a sedative), foxgloves, sweet cicely (an edible plant with delicious liquorice flavoured green seeds that reduce the tartness of rhubarb), and towering angelica (a big beauty which tastes like celery). Meanwhile, the lavender sunbathes in full sun against the hot stone wall, which radiates heat throughout the night when that great star has gone to bed.

When I first began gardening, I didn't understand 'right plant, right place' because I didn't understand the needs of plants or the qualities a specific plot can offer. When I did, it was like I had been given a key to a secret room full of surprise and delight. Through this new lens, the world around me was transformed, every view was to be analysed. What were the plants saying to me? Which way was the dominant wind bending them? Where on the hill was wettest? Which flat plane turned into a bog in winter?

In London, before I had this vision, beside our canal boat was a strip of heavy clay earth below a row of gigantic ancient willow trees. Beneath them I planted Mediterranean herbs and tomatoes. Miserable in the home I had given them, the plants failed. I was sad. Only later did I realise that putting those plants there was sending them to their death. Herbs and tomatoes need sun and good drainage. I had condemned them to a spot where they drowned and were starved of light.

Growing according to the 'right plant, right place', the garden becomes a playground between myself and the plants. On a personal level, this is a joyful experience. But it has also taught me so much about the wisdom of life and systems which have been going about their business for many millions of years. So, of course, they know what's good for them far better than I ever possibly could. I watch and learn and try to follow nature's lead.

It is a fairly low-maintenance technique of gardening as I'm not striving for anything too managed. Given the right conditions the plants tend to grow themselves so, other than seed, it requires few external resources. I continue to grow and make my own compost here in the garden, gather rainwater, brew my own plant feeds, and largely trust the space to manage pests and diseases because the plants are healthy and diverse. This approach allows room for experimentation and teaches true sustainability well. The garden looks wild because it is quite wild, and has been an invitation for me to think and live more wildly alongside it.

So, to return to that original question, perhaps the difference between this garden and an overgrown one is that here there are the telltale signs of *human collaboration* with wildness. I give this garden my love and it gives its own garden-love back to me and any other humans who may need it. In this garden, all are welcome. It's the sort of space that can tend and mend a sore heart.

GARDEN ICED TEA

- Bunch of garden (or foraged) herb(s) of choice – rinsed
- 4 Earl Grey tea bags or 4 tbsp loose black tea
- Sugar, honey or maple syrup, to sweeten
- Juice of 1 lemon

You can make this uplifting tea with just one type of herb – I like to use lemon balm, mint, lemon verbena, sage, thyme, chamomile, meadowsweet and linden flowers – or experiment by combining two or more complementary flavours.

- Pour 500 ml of boiling water over the tea bags or loose-leaf tea and steep for 5–10 minutes.
- Fish out the tea bags or strain the tea and add the bundle of herbs. Steep for a further 5–10 minutes.
- Remove the herb bundle.
- Add 500 ml cold water along with the lemon juice.
- Sweeten to taste.
- Add ice or chill in the fridge before drinking.

MARRIED TO MY GARDEN

I'm on a soggy footpath running down through a field. At the bottom stands an old gate, left open for so many years brambles have engulfed it and saplings have sprouted in its swing path. This gate belongs to a boundary that runs along a usually trickling stream, which now, with the heavy summer rains, has turned into a great big muddy bog. Freddy dog has happily bounded across it, but one of my welly boots has a leak and I don't want to get a wet foot. I gingerly tread on the fingers of the brambles that trace the surface of the bog's edge, hoping they will stop my foot from sinking into the mud. 'Please help me, don't hinder,' I mutter to the bramble bush as I get close to the squelching edge, attempting to use her spiked arms as supports while I skirt the bog. She promptly pricks at me, hard, and I get a bootful of mud as I pull back in alarm. With a bloody thumb and one soggy sock I turn to look for an alternative route.

From this path I used to be able to walk through three meadows, passing through ancient gaps in the overgrown hedgerows that separated them. I'm certain the passages were ancient because of the old oak trees that framed them. I naively let myself believe that this was it – I could get to know this place and it would remain the same, dependable, unchanged. I'd be able to create a reliable map in my mind which would be useful for years to come, the beginnings of a family heirloom I may be able to pass on to my children. But even in the short time I've lived here the land has changed. Many of the creatures I'd once shared this space with are now gone, too.

I now realise I had been harbouring a romantic idea of an empty countryside, one that I could wander about infinitely and which, in my lifetime, would remain more or less the same. Like in the book *Cider with Rosie*, or in Mum and Dad's descriptions of their roaming childhoods. Now I know better. This land represents people's interests, invisible until they make themselves known with a fence here and a hacked back hedgerow there. Someone has put up barbed wire fences along this path, sitting snugly against the hedges, so nothing bigger than a rabbit can pass through the gaps anymore. Barbed wire has cut through other paths too. I can return to a track or tree just one week after a first visit to find I can no longer access it or that it no longer exists. Part of me becomes nervous of looking away, as if the changes are happening sneakily behind my back... They aren't, but I can't help feeling that way.

It's a curious thing to try to embed oneself in a place that keeps shifting. Like committing to a marriage in which your spouse is constantly renegotiating the agreed terms of love, repeatedly and very suddenly changing themselves. It's hard to keep up, and each change brings grief with it. When a hedge is cut down on the edge of a field that I love, I arrive at a landscape I no longer know. Only a week might have gone by since I was last there, but everything looks different, feels different, sounds different. Along with the sorrow and anger that no one asked me if I minded, or told me to prepare myself, that I didn't even get to say goodbye, there is a sense of disempowerment that is often swiftly followed by flat disengagement. It is not easy to build a relationship without trust. And it's not easy to commit to a place that doesn't feel committed to you.

I felt this keenly living in London, a place that, by the might of invisible hands, forever ticks over. The rubbish is taken away, streets are cleaned, houses go up or come down, parks are turned into roads, canal paths into train warehouses, planters turn up on street corners and disused buildings morph into parks. Everything is in flux and I became accustomed to the infantilising feeling of being entirely out of control. The terms of the contract were that I would disengage so that all this development and change could simply happen around and to me. I was footloose and placeless, floating in one of the busiest cities in the world. I didn't feel embedded, connected or committed to a community or a place. Then, as I travelled more and more with work, I found myself drifting *between* some of the busiest cities in the world.

When I first began to grow food in pots while living on our canal boat, I didn't realise I was putting down roots, too. These plants were within my sphere of influence, lives I could care for, relationships I could commit to. Tending those plants was a bit like homemaking, only they cared for me in turn – they responded happily to my attention. This wasn't just buying an ornament or a nice rug; this was engaging with other living beings. At first, a growing sense of connection emerged, centred mostly on our floating home, but as the potted plants began to spill out onto the boat deck and then the roof, the sense of connection grew. I now felt allied with the insects that visited the flowers, the birds I heard while watering and sometimes the people on the towpath who smiled as they passed by.

As my awareness of and connection to the living world around me developed so, too, did a faithful love. I became curious about how human and planetary well-being were interwoven. I could see how my loving care for this little potted garden was not only grounding me but making me more *well*. So, I began to search for frameworks for growing plants and food that aimed to nurture this connection, and fell in love with an approach called 'permaculture'.

Permaculture design offers an ethos and structure for conceiving and tending gardens, buildings, communities, schools – anything really. It offers a set of twelve principles which can help to guide ethical and sustainable design, with three foundational tenets – Earth Care, People Care and Fair Share – underpinning everything we create. Along with permaculture's emphasis on resilient, diverse and local connections, these three beliefs opened my eyes to the potential of gardens to facilitate connection within an ecosystem – between people, and between plants and soil life – and to become sites for relearning what it can mean to be a responsible and contributing member of a community. I took keener interest in the community gardens, parks, heaths and green or neglected liminal spaces all around me. I started to recognise and feel *my* place in a previously invisible network of spaces that cultivated connection, or spaces that had the potential to: a world of gardeners, plant lovers, people lovers, place lovers, plants, insects, birds revealed itself to me.

There have been times in my life when I have been desperate to get away. To travel to the ends of the earth in search of connection to magic, meaning, perhaps myself? In my early twenties there were points when I would travel weekly for work, and leisure would mean going away, too. I found myself hanging onto home by a thin thread. I was so caught up in it all that I wasn't looking after the home in *myself*; in my body, mind and spirit. I was disconnected from my environmental home as well. But as my sense of connection grew, my desire and willingness to travel waned. Cultivating a sense of place in the world was developing responsibility in me too, a desire to do well by the lives I was engaging with. I went away for a week one summer, leaving the first significant food crop I'd ever grown – a gigantic squash plant, in a pot on the boat deck – with strict instructions for our floating neighbour to water and love it up daily. She texted me pictures to reassure me that the plant was doing well without me. But I didn't want to miss out; I wanted to be there to tend and care. I wanted to do my best, to fulfil *my* side of the bargain. Going away made it harder for me to do that. It meant missing out on the inevitable change that these plants and living spaces moved through.

The value of a place, I now realised, was in the interconnected relationships between lives that resided there. I wanted to stay in the spot I had fostered all these connections in. I wanted to feel and to be committed.

Now, years later in this garden, I see that life is change. Trees crash down in winter storms; blossoms bloom early one year and late the next; one year the garden is humming with hoverflies, the next butterflies silently swoop about the place. I watch as my garden grows and changes and I help it along. It does the same for me. It is harder and harder to pull myself away from this little patch that I am now so much of and that is so much of me. I want to tend and observe plants growing up out of seeds sown in the dark cold of winter and the warmth of spring. I want to see when the apples will bloom the next year, and after I chopped it back, how big the myrtle shrub will regrow.

I am finding different parts of me while tending this garden. Strong parts that can lift heavy logs; soft parts that sob when the chickens scratch up a seedling patch; silly parts that dance in the rain; and parts of me that know the feeling of safety and home. This garden is my mother, my child and my lover. It feeds me, calls out to me. We love and disappoint each other, and we quarrel, and it teaches me old lessons I would not otherwise have known. The garden and I get inside one another. The more time I give to this garden the more time I want to give. In truth, I have started to feel almost married to this garden: to the plants, the soil, the chickens and the young male blackbird who sings at the top of the holly tree. In summer, I find it hard to pull myself away.

Modern culture can persuade us that purpose and wonder lie elsewhere. That they aren't *within* us. That we must travel far and abroad in search of them. But I'm no longer sure that's true. Travelling the world can be life-changing and is magical. But it's not the only magic. What if, sometimes, the inspiration we seek is actually right here inside us, just waiting to be found? What if I could find or create whatever vision I was hunting *right here*? What if I didn't have to dash about? What if I could settle in? And what if the true magic was in my ability to find connection, peace, joy and wonder in the very mundane and to commit to it? I have found so much more of myself and so much more meaning in committedly connecting to one place than I ever did darting up, down and around this planet. When I first began to wonder at this, it felt radical.

The world has never been so quickly and easily accessible, so much so it feels as though the planet has shrunk. As geographer Edward Relph argues in *Place and Placelessness*, we members of a minority population on this planet who lead a global existence, as I did back then, are living through a period of 'space, time compression'. We are now members of a 'global village'. We can see what's happening on the other side of the earth in real time, and with the right amount of cash and paperwork we can get there in just a handful of hours, should we fancy.

Many of us now experience wide-ranging but shallow, diluted and abstracted relationships with place. Yet, until very recently our very survival was dependent on our ability to foster and maintain intimate relationships with the life, people and places around us. Our bodies respond positively to that intimate connection and when it is lacking our health can suffer. Similarly, I feel this in my *self*, my soul, my me-ness, *mmuo* – my psyche, I suppose. I feel keenly the empty floating that accompanies a lack of anchoring in a place, and I feel the grounded safety and empowerment that come with a sense of being placed.

I think about the enclosures, the severing of the bonds of community and land through greed, and the subsequent tide of the industrial revolution. I think about the further displacement of peoples as the colonisation of empires reached its fingers around the earth and beckoned globalisation. About the arrival of post-war modernism and humanity's dogged attempts to move forward to escape a past that held so much suffering and shame; to become efficient and so successful through industrialisation and uniformity. I think about how the false promise of wealth and comfort draws many more away from a connected life and world-view, and towards a disconnected one. How today's rising middle class – schooled in a culture of quick consumption, individual fulfilment and the promise of 'freedom' – has never been more able to escape the dullness of a life given to a desk by indulging in the joys of travelling a very living world, on a screen or in an aeroplane.

I feel sorrow for the people then and the people now, people who have gradually lost a sense and a love of place – perhaps even pride in it. It seems clear to me that people without a place are the most vulnerable to exploitation.

For me, relationships are what makes our experience of a place powerful. There's a difference between the summer compost turned by me and my sweat and the stuff bought in from elsewhere. One speaks of an alchemy that I have witnessed and engaged in. The other is just a bag of decay. Caring for a garden has the magic of a small yet expansive sense of belonging; an understanding that I am part of this place, and that it and I are part of the big wide world. Feeling married to a place asks for a caring, committed respect from us – something the earth's ecosystems could do with right now.

Freddy and I arrive home from our muddy trek, me wet-footed, and of us both hungry. Today the garden offers me yet another courgette. If I go away, even for a weekend, I have to be mindful to harvest all that are ready or risk them turning into marrows before my return.

SMASHED COURGETTES WITH GARLIC

- 2 courgettes
- 4 cloves of garlic
- 3 tspb olive oil (approx.) – be generous, this dish is best dripping in olive oil
- Salt and pepper

Optional: Lemon juice, fresh mint

This is a quick, simple and tasty recipe to help get through the constant stream of courgettes (any that have turned to marrows are welcome too!) that seem to be a typical feature of many garden marriages. This is Toby's recipe really; an integral part of our marriage pact is that I grow the courgettes and he cooks them.

1. Start by crushing your courgettes. Do this by giving them a good bash on a chopping board with a rolling pin; they should break open. Bigger courgettes may first need to be chopped in half, lengthways. Keep whacking them till they are in rough pieces but still loosely held together. If using marrows, you may want to peel and chop them in half, then scoop out the seedy insides.
2. Warm the olive oil in a large frying pan and add the courgettes.
3. Crush or slice the garlic and add it to the pan. Season well.
4. Continue to cook gently for 20 minutes over a medium heat, until the vegetables begin to caramelise, agitating only occasionally to prevent them from sticking. Add a drop more olive oil as necessary.
5. Once the courgettes are soft through and nicely browned on the outside, remove from the heat.
6. Serve with a good squeeze of lemon juice and a pinch of chopped mint leaves. You may want to mop up the sweet garlicky olive oil with bread.

COMPANION PLANTING

I'm at the community garden, scrabbling around in our squash patch. Coarse leaves the size of dinner plates graze my legs as I pick through the tumbling green plants, hunting for male squash flowers. Squash are monoecious, meaning that on one plant you'll find both the male and female flowers. In order for pollination to occur, someone or something has to move pollen from a male flower's anthers to a female flower's stigma. Today that someone is me and that something is a small paintbrush I brought with me just for this purpose.

I'm sweating but my feet are cool and moist as they step through the dense shadows cast by the broad leaves. As I go, I'm explaining to this year's cohort of community gardeners how to tell the difference between the male and female flowers, and why there aren't always enough insects about for reliable pollination. Distractedly, I launch forward to inspect a possible male flower and am gently struck in the face by a long floppy corn leaf, casually drooping down from its tall pole of a stem. I bat it out the way.

The flower *is* male. Everyone gathers around to watch as I twiddle my tiny paintbrush up against its anther to capture the fluffy yellow pollen. We then all manoeuvre back to the female flower at the opposite edge of the patch, weaving between the blocks of densely planted corn and trying not to crush the leaves and stems of the squashes below. We gather around the female flower and I gently brush the pollen against her stigma, then mark the flower by tying a piece of string loosely around the stem, so we will know if our pollination was successful. If it is, we decide we will eat this squash at our harvest meal and save some seed from this particular flower, too.

This patch was an experiment. Last year we planted our squash to ramble around wigwams of Greek Gigantes runner beans, grown for their buttery seeds which are great for drying and storing. Their pods were suspended high in the air above the plump squashes. Through summer, weeds were managed by the sprawling squash plants, soil moisture was conserved below their broad leaves and the beans provided some soil fertility. All the patch asked of us was some extra water and our admiring gaze. Come autumn, we collected up the dried Gigantes pods and brought in the squashes to cure. We then cleared the bed and sowed the ill-fated broad bean crop that floundered in January's frosts.

This year we fill another bed with squash, sweetcorn and sunflowers, chamomile and cornflowers planted at its edge. It looks beautiful. This trio has caught the imagination of everyone who has visited the community garden this summer. 'Are you growing the three sisters?' people ask when we show them this patch. 'Sort of,' we reply.

The three sisters – squash, corn and beans – are a Native American ensemble of plants grown together on Turtle Island for the longest time because they thrive in harmony. Squash sprawls across the earth, shading the soil from the sun, protecting it from heavy rain and conserving moisture. The corn – which must be planted together in blocks to aid wind pollination (I tend to space each plant 30 cm from its partners) – rises, tall and slim, providing support for the beans to twirl up. And the beans fix nitrogen into the soil, from which all three sisters benefit. The three plants occupy different niches in the space, none treading on the others' toes.

The notion of the three sisters captivated me partly because it seemed a good way of bringing some of the magic of forest gardens into the world of annual veg, maximising the landscape's ability to support many lives. Plants in the wild grow in gangs, but often the annual veg gardens I saw felt monotonous and a bit two-dimensional, lacking the woodland's dynamic, layered density. The three sisters, however, seemed to sing this song of complexity.

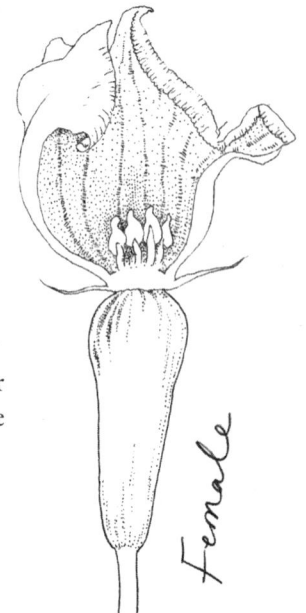

In the UK, I am yet to see or hear of a successful application of this trinity method. Nevertheless, for all of us at the community garden, the story of these three wise sisters sharing a space in a mutually beneficial relationship has bewitched our minds and cast a spell on our hearts. So, we decided to grow two sisters together, and leave the third to grow in our daydreams. Someday, perhaps, we will try all three, and eventually we might get the timing just right and our beans and corn won't be pushed out by the squashes' spreading growth. Corn will shoot up fast enough to support the beans' climb and will help them rise before they are engulfed. This perfect timing will be followed by a hot dry summer, so that all three are able to mature and ripen in time for autumn's arrival. But for now, we welcome two of the sisters. Next year I'd like to replace the corn with beans to see if they work well together with the squash and giant sunflowers.

Recently my dad was travelling through a village in Nigeria near where our ancestors came from. People were growing food around their homes. He sent me a photo of one patch growing squash and corn. My heart pulled. It meant something to me that, unprompted, we had chosen to grow that same combination in our community plot. I hadn't been sure if it was a good idea, but the peasant farmers of this village clearly think it is, and I trust them. Somehow our little patch now feels tied to theirs. Two patches of two sisters. When I replied 'sort of' to questions about the inhabitants sharing this patch, I used to feel as though we weren't doing the indigenous wisdom justice. Now I have attached a new story to this pair. They are no longer missing their sister; they are a double act of their own.

The three sisters have gained fame and notoriety in the world of ecological food growing, perhaps because they tell such a compelling story of kinship, collaboration and familial support. But there are of course many other classic companion planting combinations – basil and tomatoes; carrots, onions and lettuce. In Nigeria, Abakaliki farmers grow egusi melon along with sorghum, cassava, coffee, cotton, maize and bananas. This disparate selection of crops (less accessible in our climate) is grown to confuse pests and protect the soil. In other parts of West Africa corn is grown along with peanuts, black-eyed beans, cassava and yam. No matter the combination and whether accompanied by magical stories or not, the teaching is the same; grow a range of plants that get along well and have positive interactions between them in close proximity. This is the basic principle of companion planting. By cultivating gardens full of relationships, we also receive a more varied harvest, and as we now know, a diverse, plant-rich diet is one of the keys to human health.

Just like humans, plants like to have friends, or brothers and sisters – generally, appropriately increased biodiversity equates to more resilience in ecosystems. We can bring that lesson from the land into our gardens. Companion planting can create the conditions for a range of mutually supportive relationships to unfold. For example, some plants offer their ability to attract pollinators which can increase overall fertilisation and so harvest. Others, like nettles and comfrey, aid soil fertility by quickly putting on nutrient-rich leafy growth, which will eventually die back and rot into the soil. Then there are plants which can offer natural pest management, either enticing predators like hoverflies or deterring or confusing pests with their scent. As we have seen with the three sisters, some plants are happy to provide shade or support for their companions too.

The former squash patch, which had also been home to the lost crop of broad beans, we have now turned into a polyculture, culture of many – a wide mix of plants jumbled together. In the style of many peasant farmers of Britain's past, we simply scattered a range of seed. Then all we had to do was water this polyculture regularly and allow the plants to grow up together. Now we have a tangle of clover, peas, phacelia, buckwheat, calendula, poppies, cornflowers and sunflowers, and we also planted out some baby chamomile and runner bean plants, started in pots. Their complexity is beautiful to look at and, again, different layers are beginning to emerge, with the clover acting as a ground cover, the various flowers swaying up high and the beans and peas trailing, crawling and climbing. It's interesting to watch this diverse community of companions evolve without intervention: we don't need to weed, bring in supports, thin out or prune enthusiastic plants.

Intercropping, when we nestle crops between one another, is another similar approach, but with more emphasis on increased yield from the space, such as in the bed opposite the squash patch. In May we planted our young courgette plants out between the garlic rows. In midsummer, by the time the courgettes put on any growth at all, we were pulling the garlic up.

I have experimented with all sorts of plant gatherings over the years, but, obviously, not all combinations live in such graceful harmony as the three sisters. When I first got excited about forest gardening, I tried to train a vine tomato up a tree. Of course, the tomato was miserable under the tree, starved of warmth and light, promptly got blight and died. The plants need to enjoy the particular environment created by their companions and to a degree require similar growing conditions. No one size fits all. The three sisters may suit some soils, climates and situations and not others; we can adapt and grow according to the space's needs and offerings.

I step out of the squash patch and rub my legs, brushing away the scratches. I hand the tiny paintbrush to someone else so they can have a go. I suppose we, the gardeners of this site, are companions too. Being many rather than one, we bring a complex variety of perspectives, practices and sensibilities. There is a resilience in our interdependence. I sit down and watch the rest of the group search for male flowers or float off to return to other tasks, weeding, sowing, harvesting, chatting, sharing.

COMPANION PLANTING TIPS

In the main, herbs make excellent companion plants. Many have strong scents, lots of flowers which attract pollinators and, of course, offer us a harvest. Native wildflowers do a great job too.

Below is a general list of plants, which I find both beautiful and useful and so often employ as companions. As annuals (with the exception of garlic) they don't pose a threat of establishing and competing with the main crop, but left to self-seed they help me fill any gaps that arise here and there in the veg patches and edimental parts of the garden. In many ways, I suppose, these plants make as good companions for me as for the other plants around them.

For more recommendations and useful guides, see Further Reading, page 323.

HERBS

- **BASIL** (*Ocimum basilicum*) has long been respected as a tomato companion. It is believed to bolster the growth of tomato plants while enhancing the flavour of the fruits, but many suspect this to be an old wives' tale (the best kind of tale in my opinion). Basil and tomato are a classic in the kitchen, perfectly illustrating the saying 'what goes together grows together'. Grouping these two makes for an easy salad harvest. The basil leaves act as a living mulch, and their strong aroma can confuse potential pests. If let to run to seed, its flowers will offer pollinator forage, while basil seed can be gathered and sown the following season.

- **BORAGE** (*Borago officinalis*) is a very skilful pollinator attractor. The flowers offer copious nectar for pollinators to forage. Borage also holds large quantities of nutrients and minerals in its leaves, drawn up from deep in the soil, making it a wonderful addition to homemade fermented plant teas. The young leaves and flowers have a fresh cucumber flavour and can be harvested as an edible crop for salads, or cocktails! Borage likes to grow vigorously, flopping about the place, so can be a bit of a tricky companion to smaller, less forceful crops.

- **CALENDULA** (*Calendula officinalis*) is known as an aphid trap, distracting the insects from the main crop. Calendula flowers are favoured by hoverflies who are beloved pollinators, and will breed in the presence of aphids. Their larvae feast on aphids or munch on decaying organic matter. Calendula flowers are edible (if very bitter!) and medicinal, a long-loved ingredient in healing balms.

– **CORIANDER** (*Coriandrum sativum*) is also known to confuse pests and repel aphids with its scent. It is delicious (leaf, root and seed), medicinal, easy to save seed from and flowers in umbels which again are fantastic for pollinators. With their small frilly leaves, they make a very courteous companion, not blocking out too much sun or taking up much room. It can benefit from being grown in some light shade too.

– **GARLIC** (*Allium sativum*). Its strong scent is considered off-putting to many insects, making it useful for organic pest management (you can even make a garlic foliar spray from it). The oils found in garlic battle fungal and bacterial infection in both plants and humans. Garlic's leaves – as well as its root and green flower stems – are tasty.

NATIVE WILDFLOWERS
(WHICH ARE ALSO EDIBLE)

– **YARROW**
– **CORNFLOWER**
– **FIELD POPPY**
– **FIELD SCABIOUS**
– **WILD CARROT**

FLOWERS

– **NASTURTIUM** (*Topaeolum minor*) will forever have a place in my heart with its soft round leaves which, along with its plentiful flowers, are not only edible but fiery and delicious! It will self-seed freely and grow itself. In summer, nasturtiums make a great living mulch, protecting the soil through the sunny months and dying back when the frost touches it in the winter. This plant is a great trap for aphids and cabbage whites, so can be grown as a sacrificial crop.

— **SUNFLOWERS** (*Helianthus annuus*) will attract pollinators, are magnificent and can act as shading and support for other crops.

SHARING TIME, LABOUR AND HARVESTS

'At no time has the liberation movement not been singing. At no time has the liberation movement not been dancing. Everywhere, culture becomes a very central and very important element in this act of rebellion, in this act of assertion that we are human.'
– Thabo Mbeki, former president of South Africa

It was never going to be enough for me just to garden. I find myself unwaveringly curious and questioning. I don't like being told what to do; I like going off-piste, my mind seeking patterns and connections, noting where there are none. I enjoy searching for ways I can contribute to societal solutions, improvements, ways to connect life with life and not with fruitless pain. If you had told the younger me that I would find so much freedom, peace and power in gardening, I would have laughed. I still laugh now. Something so simple yet so liberating and uniting has become a form of activism. I wonder why resistance runs so alive in me.

My parents moved with us to South Africa eight years after the great Nelson Mandela was elected the country's first president following the end of apartheid. This victory was born of many decades of civil struggle for freedom and four years of formal negotiation between the architects of apartheid, the Nationalist Party, and the resistance campaigners. Mr Mandela was imprisoned for twenty-seven of those years. The country was reeling after over one hundred years of oppressive imperial rule, institutionalised racism, segregation and repression. Its people had finally won freedom, but South Africa still burned with resistance.

I was just six; the politics were lost on me. All I knew was that I was observing around me a type of suffering I had never seen before. I remember asking my mum why so many people there lived in little boxes. I had not yet learnt the words 'ghetto', 'shanty town' or 'township', and I had no understanding of the racist policies, settler colonialism and imperialism that had birthed this society. I didn't need to to understand that something had gone very wrong.

I began to notice patterns. The people living in cramped boxes were Black; the people begging on the streets were Black; the people cleaning houses, labouring in gardens, building roads or offices; the people trekking home from work in the sweltering heat to their corrugated iron boxes, carrying litres of Coca Cola and bags of white bread they had bought at a stall on the side of the road – they were all Black. The people living in immaculate sprawling homes surrounded by abundant gardens were white; those working in clean, air-conditioned offices and driving home in cooled cars with bags full of food they had picked up in fridge-lined supermarkets, these people were white. Apartheid no longer existed officially, but all around me I could see it alive and well.

There were exceptions to the rule, of course, our mixed-race family was one of them. But we were an exception to the degree that people would frequently ask my mum if we, her brown children, were adopted. People didn't assume a white woman would have a relationship with a black man. I began to learn that in this country, Black and Brown people lived one way and White people lived in another. I also learned that these differences were never spoken about, not in a way I could understand anyway.

Once my family went on a trip to the Apartheid Museum. At the time I couldn't fully process what I was learning or what I saw, all I knew was that I was scared and my heart was breaking. My chest still tightens when I recall the exhibit of a mother and her baby, life-sized puppets in a dimly lit, corrugated iron 'shack' that we could wander into. She rocked her crying baby back and forth, while on a speaker played the popular lullaby 'Thula thul, thula twana'. This was how the majority of South Africa's indigenous population lived while the settlers extracted wealth from their country.

After that, my heart broke even harder each time we stopped at the traffic lights by our house and the little blind Black boy came begging, hands outstretched, dirt on his face and wearing rags. My heart broke when Naomi, the lady who looked after me and my siblings, wailed and cried when she was told her adult son and his wife had burned to death in a fire that swept through their township. My heart broke again when I picked up from adult conversation that in those conditions, deadly fires were all too common.

We had met Naomi shortly after we moved to South Africa. She sold sweets and bags of brightly coloured sugary popcorn on the side of the road. On our first day at our new school, Dad tried to walk us there, but when we arrived at the back gate to the grounds, it was locked. The walls were high, with barbed wire twisting their tops. What we didn't understand then but do know now is that only certain people walked anywhere and the city was designed to keep them out. We found ourselves as simply another Black family trying to hop a gate. Dad lifted us over and then jumped the gate himself, but its top was covered in sticky, tacky tar which stained our hands and clothes. Determined to walk us to and from school, Dad persevered. He asked the school if in future someone could open the gates for us and they agreed. I wonder now if for my dad, it was a knowing form of resistance.

We met Naomi on one of those walks. I remember her warm smiles and the unfamiliar sweet taste and soft texture of the multi-coloured popcorn we bought from her. Not long afterwards, Mum asked Naomi if she would come to help look after us. She had a husband and more children of her own, but in South Africa it was common for anyone who worked in the house to live there too, returning home for birthdays, holidays and festivals. Sometimes her youngest son, a teenager then, would come and stay with her in her modest quarters across the yard. He would play with us, bouncing us high on the trampoline, help his mum in the house and the gardener in the garden.

I would visit her some evenings, dashing out of the kitchen in my pyjamas, scuttling barefoot across the mopped courtyard where the dogs slept and over to her kitchen. I'd smell her cooking as I went, boiling chicken feet – I didn't like it. She'd sit on her chair eating, pulling off the chicken's claws and stripping the meat with her teeth, bemused by my curiosity. I'm not sure if she minded me bothering her. Retrospectively I wonder if she ever felt uncomfortable or even shy, so accustomed to being in our space but not with us in hers. She had just one room with a single bed, one wall was used as a kitchen; in the corner was her traditional broom made from a bundle of straw that required her to stoop while sweeping. Naomi seemed to love to sweep, but I can't remember ever seeing her use the long-handled brooms our Mum had. Bent over, she'd brush the dry floors with brisk flicking gestures, and then she'd throw water down and sweep them again wet. Her room was clean and tidy and smelt warm and comforting, like her. She didn't have decorations or plush bedding. It felt plain and basic. I liked it there but would dash out as fast as I'd dash in, scared to linger, unsure of the feeling of discomfort, perhaps shame, that would twist up from my tummy and into my chest.

I could see that I lived differently than other Black people here, but I didn't understand why. I realise now that what I was feeling was an awkward, childish awareness of the power imbalance between us. I – a little mixed-race child of British parents who lived comfortably back in England but who were comparatively wealthy here – had more power, more privilege in this world than this grown woman. My bed was bigger, my kitchen grander, I had more clothes, I went to a good – and so predominantly white – school and I could read and write. I trusted that one day I would grow up to have a job that would not require me to live apart from my family. I felt sorrow at the complex injustice of it all, but as a child I didn't really understand, so the sorrow would simply break my heart and the rest I'd try to avoid and wriggle out of. I see now that I also felt unsafe. I was just a child with no ability or experience; Naomi was experienced, strong, clever, kind, she looked after us, and yet by default, power was bestowed upon *me*. To my young mind, that was confusing and scary.

I could feel Naomi's gratitude and her pride that she worked in a progressive, liberal, mixed-race household. To this day, I hold her pride close, and while her gratitude still makes me squirm, I can now appreciate the difference our family made in her life. She grew up in South Africa under Apartheid. But here in front of her was a safe, affluent mixed-race family. Unburdened by the psychology of racial segregation, we walked to school with our Black father, and our family welcomed her into our home differently to many others. I wonder now if her gratitude discomforts me because I feel she did so much more for us than we ever did for her... and yet she didn't see it that way. I wonder how much of my restless resistance is for her – big, strong Naomi – who, even in my childlike way, I could see was vulnerable in a system that tried to make her weak, and how much is to comfort and reassure myself?

*

Initially, I came to gardening to heal and to grow. I wanted to tend my body, mind and soul while I tended the earth. I wanted something that resisted while it grew, something that would say 'no' and 'yes' all at once. I wanted to help shape a world in which people were respected and the power imbalance and exploitation I had experienced both in South Africa and working in the fashion industry were righted. I wanted to find care as resistance.

It's the humble power of our food that originally drew me to it. While I learnt the definition of words like 'radicle' – the first part of a seedling to emerge on germination; an embryonic plant root that anchors the seedling into the soil – I also learnt the politics of food growing. How those same power structures I had witnessed in other spheres also limit access to land, skills, time and all other resources required to grow good food, fresh whole foods (not drenched in carcinogenic chemicals). That for too many people, easy, affordable access to good food is also limited; how poor nutrition leads to negative health outcomes through generations. And that simply spending time outside, growing food ethically, may have a profoundly positive impact on our emotional and social well-being.

I learnt how food growing and food ways are often the backbone of a society, giving physical sustenance and pleasure, but also cultural nourishment, from providing community and connection to place, to a more spiritual relationship to what nourishes us. I understood how so often those powerful traditions are broken down by structures of oppression.

In 1983, aged 33, Thomas Sankara, the militant economic and social justice revolutionary and anti-imperialist, became president of Burkina Faso. At the time he came to power, it was becoming more evident that, following political independence, many newly liberated African countries were still far from gaining economic autonomy. Most states were dependent (and many still largely are to this day) on trade with their former colonisers and were struggling to add value to any products they could exchange. Many had also been left without any cohesive, functioning society or infrastructure and were besieged by internal turmoil. As these nations grappled with their various challenges, political mismanagement was rife.

Committed to freeing his young country from its French colonial past, Sankara said: 'Some people ask me, "But where is imperialism?" ... Just look into your plates when you eat. You see the imported corn, rice or millet. This is imperialism. No need to go further ... We must produce more, because the one who feeds you usually imposes his will upon you.'

Central to his policy for the future of Burkina Faso was revolutionary self-reliance as a means for liberation. Before any other societal reform was possible, his people needed to be able to feed themselves rather than accepting handouts in the form of food aid. Sankara understood that the power of a nation was in its soil, and so he instigated urgent land reform policies. To combat the desertification of the land which was compromising farming, and thus prevent famine, he had over 10 million trees planted.

I find that inspiring. I grew determined to learn not just how to grow healthy plants, but how we can grow healthy people and cultures too – how we can grow food as *resistance*.

The power of food is in its ability to nourish, not to destroy. It can bring people together with the promise of vitality rather than the threat of annihilation. It encourages recognition of common ground. Food sustains us on a practical level, but it also has the potential to bring beauty into our lives, as the saying and political slogan goes, 'Bread for all and roses too.' We need both to thrive.

Growing food invites us to do something very powerful indeed – to share. For me, one of the most radical things about gardening is that it lends itself so beautifully to community organising or movement building and shows us so plainly the joy, abundance and impact of working as a collective.

I've now stepped up as co-facilitator at our community veg garden, meaning in addition to the time spent helping to manage the space, I spend one day a week guiding our group of 10–15 people to organically grow veg, herbs and flowers together. That day feeds me in more ways than one. Our collective tends this piece of land that none of us owns, exploring models of growing and living that are better for people and the planet. We provide a free learning experience in agroecological food production, particularly aimed at those who may not typically feel welcome in rural working spaces. We're inspired by the Community Supported Agriculture (CSA) model, whereby customers pay an upfront fee and subscribe to a season of produce from a local farm. This gives the farmer some financial security and the customer a relationship with the origin of their food. But in our collective, rather than members paying for their veg, we give our time and grow it ourselves, sharing labour, strength, skills, knowledge, ideas, feelings and harvests. We also share any excess veg locally, growing extra to be distributed by a local food hub in veg boxes for disadvantaged people. The most unexpected part of working on this project has been seeing how our time spent together growing food has taken on new meaning.

I came into the project thinking that participants would turn up week after week mainly to gain access to good food. In fact, we mainly come to the garden for access to one another, for living relationships as well as the space. I now trust and depend on these people and this piece of earth. We have grown a network of sustenance. I didn't expect this. I had never bonded with adults, long-term, over a collective endeavour of care like this one before. It's different to gardening alone. Working as a team, our joint effort builds resilience into our food growing. I know that when life happens, the community garden is not dependent only on me. While my own garden has grown wild as I write, the community garden plods along, tended by many more hands than my own. Within this community, I am finding caring resistance.

CELERY SALT

- Leafy celery tops and thin inner stems (I don't use the thick juicy stems as they take too long to dry)
- Sea salt

One of the community gardeners brings in a bundle of extremely tough, fibrous and leafy celery. It has not turned out like the crisp, watery vegetable we are used to finding in the shops.

It has a very strong flavour and she's not sure what to do with it, so I volunteer to take some home. This celery salt is what I ended up making with her shared harvest. It's a great way of preserving the excellent celery flavour to enjoy when it is out of season during the winter months.

Don't worry if you don't have access to a dehydrator – you can still collect and dry celery leaves to make this flavoured salt.

- Chop the celery and spread it out on a dehydrator. Run on a low setting until the pieces are crisp. Alternatively, you can dry celery leaves on a baking sheet in the oven on a low heat, or (if you're not in any hurry) place them in a brown paper bag and seal. Hang it in a warm place to dry, giving it a shake daily until the leaves have fully dried.
- Whizz the dried celery pieces and leaves to a powder in a blender. Roughly measure the volume of dried celery – you need twice the amount of salt as celery.

- Add the salt and give it a quick blitz.
- Store out of direct sunlight in a clean, airtight jar.
- Add celery salt to soups and stews, eat it with boiled eggs or cucumber sandwiches, or use it to flavour Bloody Marys – virgin or otherwise.

LAND OF PLENTY

The garden is full of food. Every day it seems a courgette morphs into a gigantic marrow and the house is filled with the sweet tang of the tomatoes that Toby is stewing into a sauce. Some of the apples are becoming ripe too. It's hard now to envision the fate of this land of plenty just a couple of months hence. But I know that, inevitably, autumn and winter will come.

In the fatness of summer, I scheme for the thinness of winter. Knowing that clever planning *now* will keep the garden full and able to feed me and others, I dream of those hardcore plants that will stand firm even if covered in crystals of frost.

So I set to work sowing hardy seeds – the beginnings of a robust vegetable garden that will know the soft touch of summer, the cold grip of winter and the first tickles of spring. We gardeners often fuss over sowing seeds in spring, but I find sowing seeds in the throes of summer far more exciting. Now, when everything feels at its peak, I like their quiet potential. Many crops, like Florence fennel, actually fair better with a summer sowing; they are less susceptible to bolting as the season tips into autumn. Crops like Asian greens – pak choi, mizuna or mibuna – are also best sown in the summer. They prefer a cooler climate, so will happily grow through autumn and milder winters to flower the following spring, easily so if growing undercover. Sown in springtime however, they often run to seed in the growing summer heat.

Don't tell summer, but I have found that the busyness of this season, being outside through all the many hours of sunlight, baking myself in the heat, eventually makes me tired. And once autumn does finally arrive, most often I am more than ready. I know that soon enough I will be listening out for its soft footsteps in the form of falling leaves, and I know these plants, currently just seeds, will be ready too. When I retreat into the warmth of my home, they will brave the elements, guarding the garden and waiting to feed me.

Today I sit out in the sun, sowing seeds for winter.

SEEDS TO SOW IN SUMMER WHICH CAN BE GROWN OUTSIDE

See seed sowing calendar for guidance, page 158.

Recipe

LEMON VERBENA SYRUP

- 1 handful fresh lemon verbena leaves fresh from the garden – add a little extra for a more potent syrup or just for good luck!
- 2 cups granulated sugar
- 1 cup water

(This ratio can be scaled up or down as needed)

Nothing says high summer quite like the sharp, citrus sweet scent of lemon verbena filling the greenhouse. I don't think lemon verbena has the fame it deserves. A slightly tender perennial, it needs winter protection in most areas, but grows enthusiastically all summer, flush with its bright green, raspy, arrow-shaped leaves that are intoxicatingly scented when brushed past, even more so when crushed in the hand. If the plant is not harvested regularly, tiny whitish-lilac flowers will appear from July to August. I can gather several crops from one plant throughout summer; it just keeps growing back! Lemon verbena is also incredibly drought tolerant, handy for our increasingly unpredictable weather.

It is possible to find dried lemon verbena in most good herbal dispensaries, however it tends to be much less fragrant than the homegrown herb.

---

1. Combine all ingredients in a thick-bottomed pan. Gently heat until the mixture is piping hot, but not boiling. The lemony scent will intensify as the syrup warms.
2. Turn down the heat to low and leave the syrup to gently infuse for 30 minutes to one hour, adding a little more boiling water if necessary.
3. Remove from the heat, cover and set aside to infuse overnight.
4. The following day, strain the syrup through a sieve. Spoon as much of the syrup from the verbena leaves as possible, rinse and add to the compost heap or bukashi bin.
5. Transfer the syrup to a sterile jar and store in the fridge.
6. Use diluted in drinks, bakes, ice cream and ice lollies.

NOTE:
This syrup is reasonably shelf stable. I have known it to keep for over a year in the fridge.

LEMON VERBENA AND ELDERFLOWER NECTAR

- 25 ml lemon verbena syrup
- 25 ml elderflower cordial
- 150 ml sparkling water
- 1 tbsp lemon juice

Optional: 25 ml vodka, approx.

I have never come across lemon verbena syrup in the shops, so this recipe requires access to a homegrown plant and a syrup to be made, following the recipe above. You can use shop-bought elderflower cordial, but it's even nicer to make your own using foraged blossoms. This drink captures the floaty headiness of summer – to make a sweet summer cocktail, simply add a good slosh of vodka.

---

1. Combine the lemon verbena syrup, elderflower syrup, sparkling water and lemon juice and, if making a cocktail, vodka!
2. Serve over ice and garnish with dried edible flowers, if desired.

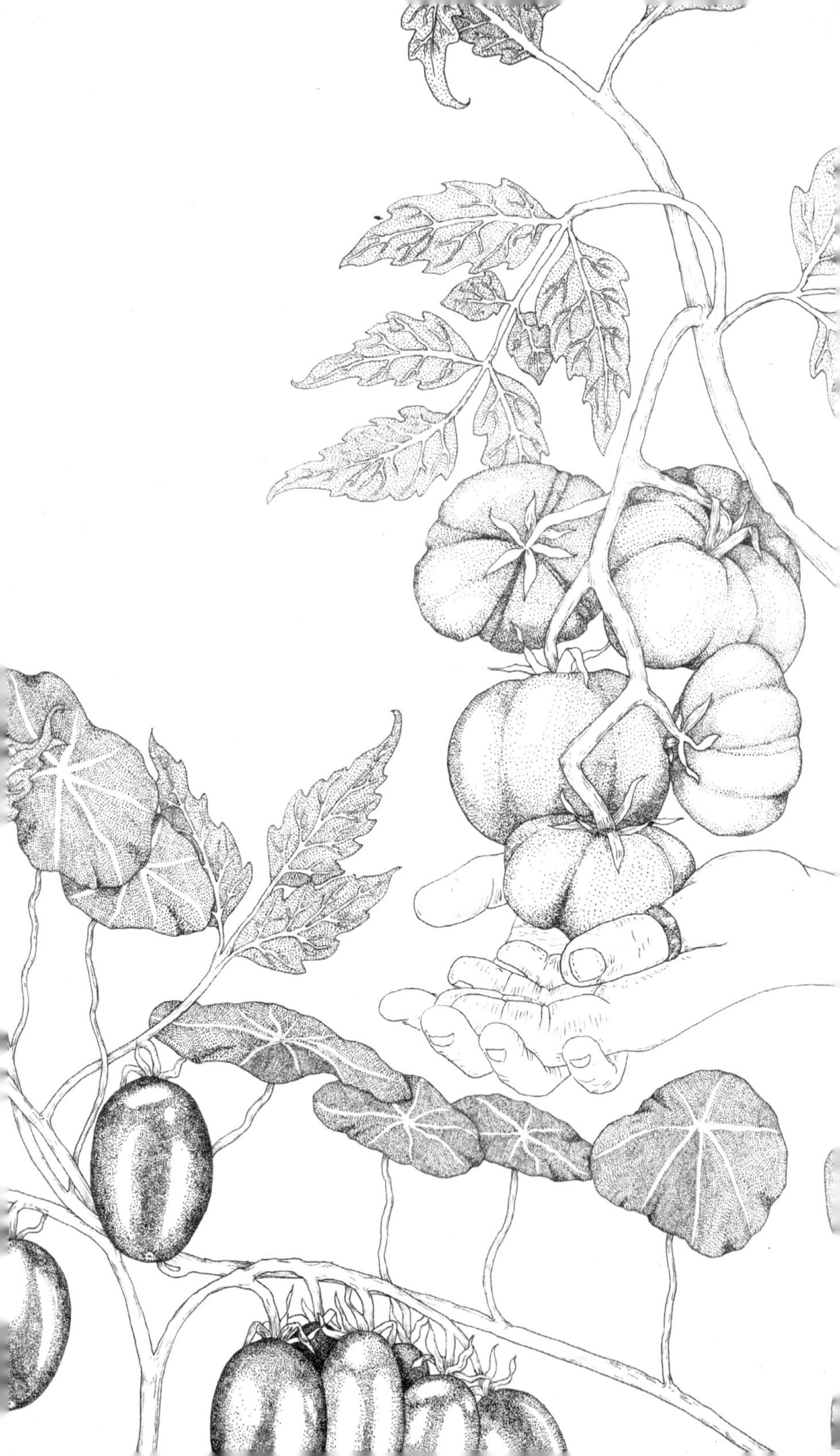

August

LIFTING POTATOES

It's the end of a still, warm and close day; up above, the sky is a dull grey. As I pull on my shoes to walk Freddy – we are heading to the north-sloping field where a communally managed orchard grows – it begins to rain. I toy with sealing myself inside wet weather trousers, coat and hood, but the thought feels suffocating and claustrophobic. I step out into the rain in my leggings and vest. It's not as bad as it looked from inside. As I walk, drops of water softly tickle my skin and I feel the atmosphere lifting. It's still warm and the cool water is fresh.

The orchard is looking shaggy when we arrive. The trees bend, turn and swoop, arching to the ground under the weight of their fruit, some of which have already turned rosy. I wade through the wet, hip-height grasses, reach up to twist and pull an apple from a low branch. It may be rosy on the outside but it's hard and tart on the inside. Not ready yet. I let it roll from my hand and pull myself back up onto the path.

I clamber over a stile at the edge of the woodland surrounding the orchard and arrive in a higher field with wide views reaching right out to Dartmoor. I find a dead baby rabbit with no eyeballs and stop a while, wondering if it's a sign, and if so, what it means and whether

I'd be able to decipher the code. I'm unsure. But before I walk on, growing at the base of the hedgerow beside us, I see the erect, firm, bright green stems of some lords and ladies, adorned with poisonous, plump, scarlet berries. I pluck one, hearing the click as I snap it from the ground and slide it between the bunny's front paws, then return to the hedge for a tassel of just-ripening haw berries, a blackberry bloom and berry. The haws I place on the rabbit's chest, where I imagine its now-stopped heart to lie, the bramble flower on its throat and the berry on its belly. I have celebrated the life of this little dead rabbit with no eyes.

*

Three days later, I am at the community plot; the sun is back and baking. I have brought a basket of warm, fragrant scones and a thick, pale green, garlicky dip made from the frozen broad beans Rosie and I harvested back in July. These are my contributions to our annual Lammas feast.

As my fellow gardeners arrive, the bench fills up with our individual efforts: a circular, twisted loaf of Lammas bread; salads full of edible flowers; a stew made entirely from the herbs and vegetables we have grown together here; fresh fruits; baked golden yellow courgettes grown in one of the gardener's own gardens; a large Tupperware of plain, gluten-free pasta; a great bowl of crisp, salty roasted potatoes rummaged from the soil a few metres away; watermelon and star anise shrub; and much more. Everyone has brought something.

As more people and dishes turn up, I roam about the garden, gathering flowers, stripping them of their lower leaves and chopping their stems to a sharp angle. I slide them into a black plastic bucket filled with rainwater and place the display at the centre of our table. Someone else arranges sprigs of rowan berries around it, to soften the grubby old bucket's edges. Bees, flies and hoverflies quickly find our floral centrepiece and we sit, devouring our lunch and chattering, while the winged insects hum and weave between us.

After lunch, we start to take up the rest of the potatoes. Many hands explore below the ground, searching through the dark for our treasure. I feel like an archaeologist sending my hands wandering underneath a potato plant. Feeling out their smooth, hard skin, I gently brush away the soil to reveal perfect little clutches of potatoes, glowing yellow, nestled against the dark black mulch. They look like a nest of Earth eggs, carefully excavated secrets of the soil.

Back in April, we buried the seed potatoes about a trowel's depth in freshly mulched beds. Since then, we have done nothing other than dump some wheelbarrows of compost and armfuls of hay onto the soil as their greenery began to emerge. We watched as lush foliage unfurled, followed by pretty, star-like flowers with pointed, orange anthers rising up from the delicate skirts of petals, brilliantly contrasting against the deep green leaves in lilacs, lavenders, deep purples and creamy whites.

The flowers nodded through early summer while, below ground, each individual seed potato sent out a network of roots and underground stems, called stolons. As the potato foliage photosynthesised, starches were produced which the plant then sent down to the ends of the underground stems. The stolons swelled to become tubers, or potatoes, grown by the plant to multiply and to store energy through the winter. Dumping those extra barrows of compost and bundles of hay around the plants excluded light, ensuring that plenty of young, pale white potatoes would form. Eventually, the potatoes detach from the plant as it dies back above ground. If left alone they would wait in the soil, ready to sprout up once conditions are right, as independent clones of the mother plant.

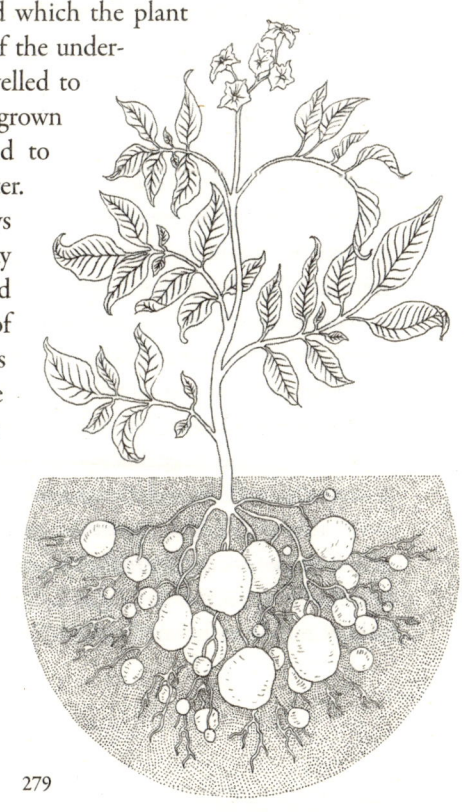

have grazed on significantly more diverse diets, with huge variations from place to place. As Dan Saladino states in *Eating to Extinction*: 'The human diet has undergone more change in the last 150 years than in the previous one million.'

Indigenous hunter-gatherer communities today are known to consume upwards of 800 different plants and animals, a diversity we now know to be crucial for human health. Our recommended five-a-day pales in comparison. Through breeding for efficient production and high yield, the once vast genetic diversity of those nine crop staples has shrunk. Our food systems *need* to change to embrace diversity and complexity in all its forms, for our health and the health of our planet.

At the community garden, by the end of the afternoon our hands are thoroughly grubby and we have unearthed several sacks of spuds from our three beds. We share them out to store and enjoy through the autumn and winter. Long ago, people high up in the Peruvian Andes on the other side of the world were doing this too. In truth, this hearty food is a gift from them. As I fill a sack with my share of our crop, I wonder if the indigenous people in the mountains had a potato god or goddess and, if so, whether they made spuddy offerings to them. I think they must have and, silently, I offer a special thanks up to this potato deity.

LAMMAS

Traditionally held on 1 August, Lammas is inspired by an ancient Celtic festival to celebrate the beginning of the harvest season. This critical moment in the year would decide the fate of the community for the year to come. As it still does for many today, for the Celts a bad harvest spelt disaster, and a good harvest was a cause for rejoicing. Either way, a day of festivities would allow the people to give thanks or pray for protection. In church on Lammas, which literally translates to 'loaf mass', the priest would bless the loaves made from the fresh grain harvest.

In Ireland, 1 August is now the Gaelic festival of Lughnasadh, named after Lugh, a young god of the harvest who battles an older god who selfishly hoards the grain harvest below the ground as his own treasure. On his victory, Lugh returns the harvest to the earth-bound mortals to share amongst themselves. It was believed to be bad luck or even dangerous to begin harvesting before a sacrifice was offered in thanks for Lugh's efforts.

In earlier times, Lammas celebrations would have coincided with the first harvest. According to the weather, that day would shift somewhat from year to year and place to place. The date only later became fixed to facilitate large group celebration. I like the idea of a festival so embedded in a locality that it changes year on year, literally growing out of the land with the crops.

At the community garden, we shared our Lammas, or Lughnasadh, feast on the day we took up our potatoes. A week later, I read that since the potato became the main storing crop in Ireland, Lughnasadh has marked *its* harvest, rather than that of grain. We had unknowingly repeated this custom, celebrating in a way that centred our very personal relationship with this place, rather than trying to fit into someone else's calendar.

I look at the sack of potatoes that's been living on our sitting room floor for the last few days and think how far these earthy treasures have travelled, through time and space, how they have been such a faithful companion to us humans for so long. I'm grateful.

BROAD BEAN DIP

(Serves 2–4)
- 200 g broad beans, fresh or frozen
- 2 cloves garlic
- Lemon juice, to taste
- Glug of olive oil

Optional: 1 tbsp yoghurt or avocado
- Handful fresh herbs, rinsed and roughly chopped – mint, parsley or coriander work well
- Salt and pepper, to taste

This is like a homegrown hummus. This dip is high in protein and fibre, a great way of getting some of garlic's health-giving allicin, and its vibrant colour makes it a beautiful addition to a summer spread.

1. Place podded beans in a pan of boiling water. Simmer on a medium heat until the beans are a vibrant green and tender. This should take 2-3 minutes if using fresh beans, and upwards of 5 minutes if cooking from frozen.
2. In the meantime, prepare a bowl of ice-cold water for your beans, using some ice cubes, if you have any.
3. When tender, remove the beans from the heat, drain and plunge them into the ice bath.
4. Use a knife or your fingers to remove the tough outer skin from the beans. (The skins can go on the compost.)
5. Place the beans, garlic, yoghurt (if using) and herbs in a blender and blitz to a smooth paste, or pound in a mortar and pestle.
6. Stir through the olive oil and lemon juice, and season to taste. If the paste is too thick, add a drop of water to loosen.
7. Enjoy!

TOMATOES

Back in June, I got a tattoo of a cherry tomato on my right forearm. There's just something about tomatoes. It's not just how they taste, but how they look. Smooth, plump, red, sometimes yellow, orange or purple skin... It is always a delight to find these perfect jewels amongst the plants' shaggy green foliage.

Cherry tomatoes were the second food crop I experimented with after my first gigantic squash on our boat deck. Squash plants are strong and easy to grow – seed them in a pot or veg patch and they're off. They need little more than rich soil and water on a dry day. But tomatoes are more complex characters. I love that you have to learn their quirks. You can be very hands-on with tomato plants, trimming here, tying up there, feeding and constantly harvesting. My first cherry tomato plants responded and even enjoyed my fussing, while the squash seemed to just brush me off, unbothered either way.

Before I began to grow them, I had only ever known tomatoes as round and red, in a packet, jar or tin, or on my plate. Before long, I discovered a vast, weird and wonderful colony of plants, full of diversity and unexpected characters. At first, I found the range of varieties bewildering, their different growing habits complicated. It was all a bit overwhelming.

In the UK, we grow tomatoes as annuals, but in warmer climates they can become short-lived perennials. Some plants grow to be bushy, slightly compact and give their fruit all at once – these are known as 'bush type' or 'determinate' tomatoes, as their eventual size is somewhat predetermined. Others sprawl to an undetermined size, flopping and spreading willy-nilly. Without the hand of a gardener to coax them into orderly trained vines, they can become wild beasts, rooting wherever their stems touch the soil, leaning on fences and walls, and scrambling over fellow plants. The plants fruit and flower gradually as they grow, giving a steady harvest – these are the 'indeterminate' or 'vine type' tomatoes.

First I had to choose which type of tomato I wanted to grow, determinate or indeterminate. I couldn't choose, so to begin with I grew both in containers on the boat roof. That first year, I grew a determinate variety called 'Tumbling Tom Red' and a very popular indeterminate variety called 'Gardener's Delight'. The Tumbling Tom Red became a satisfying little plant that grew up, out and over its pot. The pretty red gemlike fruits were sweet – made even sweeter by my underwatering which left them less juicy and more concentrated in flavour. But that summer was busy, full of work trips, and with the Tumbling Toms coming pretty much all at once, I missed out on most of them.

My Gardener's Delight grew less successfully that year. Equally underwatered, the plant attempted to go off on its usual indeterminate mission, but I wasn't aware of the special attention you can give indeterminate tomatoes, so with no support from me the plant didn't get far. Since I didn't know to remove side shoots and foliage, as the plant grew it became congested and succumbed to blight quite early in the year. Unaware of my shortfalls, I just thought that was normal tomato behaviour. The Gardener's Delight did give a more spread-out crop, which meant more of the tomatoes made it into my belly.

Tomatoes are tender, so I follow my general rule of thumb: if I'm cold outside, they're cold outside too. These days, I sow tomato seed in February or March, filling our living room windowsill with indeterminate varieties. In spring, once night temperatures are consistently forecast to be above 8°C, I plant them out into the sheltered greenhouse. When I slide their roots into the earth, I place the end of a length of string below each one and tie the other end up on the greenhouse roof. As the plants grow, I carefully twist them round the taut string, encouraging them to grow straight up. I don't like watery fruits, so to begin with I water them well, but ease off as the season goes on. I feed them with homemade fermented chicken-manure tea until the plants are about two feet tall, then I begin to remove lower leaves and any side shoots as they appear, to increase airflow and lessen the chances of blight setting in. Later, as fruits form, I continue to thin out foliage so the tomatoes can bask and ripen in the full light of the sun.

This year, I sowed seed saved from some magnificent heirloom varieties I'd grown here the year before. Big yellow orbs the size of my palm and sweet as sunlight called 'Moon Glow', a very popular variety in the USA; 'Tigerella', a variety that develops subtle yellow tiger stripes on its orangey-red skin; and 'Ukrainian Purple' (or sometimes called 'Purple Russian'), a variety that gives oval fruits with pointed ends in a dusty-red fading to purple, which grow too plump for their own good so split easily. I collected the mother plants of the Ukrainian Purple crop last year from an elderly lady in a nearby town who had grown too many. I wish I had asked her where she got the seeds and why she was growing this unusual variety.

Then, at the last minute, after I received an unexpected gift of the seeds in the post, I added an unnamed variety from the Greek island Santorini. I didn't know the sender, but she wrote that her friend from Greece had shared these Santorini seeds with her. We would both be growing them for the first time, she in London and me in Devon. Neither of us were sure how the plants would turn out; all she knew was that the fruits, being low in water content, were supposed to be ideal for sun drying (or dehydrating in my case). I worried they wouldn't be happy away from Santorini's baking sun but we exchanged photos of our plants as they grew large, and they seemed content enough! They had great big dark green leaves and small scarlet red fruits, which were quite flat, with lots of ridges and valleys in their flesh like a beefsteak tomato. She was right, these Greek tomatoes weren't very juicy, but they were sweet and very pretty.

On a curious whim I tapped 'Santorini tomato' into a search engine to see if anything similar came up. To my surprise, reams of results came back at me, all featuring the very same, funny, lumpy little tomato growing in my greenhouse! This famed tomato, it turned out, is believed to have been grown on Santorini since the 1800s, when a monk had first sown the seeds in a monastery. This variety thrives in the blazing sun, through the battering winds, dry climate and infertile limey soils of Santorini and other volcanic islands in the region, and is now a source of national pride. It is a key ingredient in many local dishes and once offered significant economic support to the people through the production of tomato paste.

I also learned that the Tomataki Santorini that I had grown in my greenhouse is a 'landrace' crop, placed under a 'Protected Designation of Origin' (PDO) since 2013 by the European Union. The term 'landrace' means the plant is genetically diverse and possesses significant genetic distinction from other tomatoes, which it has developed over many years of adapting to its particular environment and low input growing methods. Under a PDO status, in order to preserve the quality of the landrace, to be sold as genuine Tomataki Santorinis, the seed must be saved year on year, sown directly into the volcanic soil of the particular Greek island from which it originated. Devon is *not* one of those!

On closer inspection, my big, green Santorini plants – grown outside of their native home, in wetter, more fertile conditions – did not entirely resemble the hardy looking, low-growing Tomataki Santorini crops I saw online. Close to but not identical, out of respect for the landrace, I renamed my plants 'Devon's Giant Tomataki'. I will now be saving seeds from these plants, too.

My greenhouse has become home to quite an international tomato community. I value the histories of each of these plants, and I look after them like welcome travellers. Now these various tomato guests not only provide sustenance in the form of food but also in their stories. They tell of connection, to people and to far-off places. Now they are part of my story and I part of theirs. I wonder how long we will grow together. I think of all the crops that have been forgotten, lost with the decline of a gardening culture, or with the death of a person. All it takes is for one year's seed to be missed.

I move through the greenhouse, brushing past French marigold (*Tagetes petula*) flowers, basil, chilli plants and the tomato foliage, which is tacky with scent. I bend, reach, twist, pull and plop swollen tomatoes into my bowl. The smell of the plants is cloying, the greenhouse on a hot day is full of it. Seeds sown in March, plants tended for six months, all my caring is now being returned.

This harvest is bountiful and satisfying; warm sun-sweetened summer tomatoes, full of nutrients and fresher than fresh. We eat the fruits minutes after picking and as we suck sweet watery juice from our fingers and lick salty tangy oil from our lips, just like every other year, we swear never to buy supermarket tomatoes again and *never* to eat them out of season. This is the simple pleasure of eating ripe sunshine, captured in vegetable form.

None of my harvest goes to waste. I eat many, give many away – the chickens even get to taste any overripe ones. One year, Florette broke into the greenhouse with her chicks to feast on the low-hanging fruits!

Food grown and relished this way gives us so much more than calories. Growing tones our minds and bodies, breathes fresh air into our lungs, inoculates us with healthy bacteria and connects us to life. It teaches us gratitude for the food itself and for the time, skill and resources that are drawn on to bring it to our bellies. It shifts our relationship to food from an easily wasted commodity to precious sustenance, delivered to us by life.

DEVON-DRIED TOMATOES

Here in Devon, we don't have enough hot dry days to sun-dry the fruits, so instead I employ an electric dehydrator. I love transforming my tomato crop this way because it does not require vast quantities of sugar or salt; you can easily preserve lots of fruit which can be stored in a small space; and the dried tomatoes are incredibly versatile and maintain their pure strong flavour.

I store the colourful crunchy discs in glass jars with little bags of moisture-absorbing silica gel (saved from packets of seeds and jars of supplements). I munch on these crisp sweet goodies as a snack, crunch handfuls of them onto pasta dishes or on salads as a topping and throw them into sauces where they soften and impart their sweet tomato tang. You can also whizz them up in the blender with oil, garlic, pine nuts and parmesan to make a punchy dried-tomato pesto.

— Slice your tomatoes finely with a very sharp knife. Try to keep the slices intact without all the insides dripping out.
— Lay the slices out on your dehydrator trays and leave to dry on a medium-low setting until crispy and crunchy.
— Add the dried tomatoes to sterilised airtight jars, preferably along with a couple of anti-moisture silica gel bags. They can be stored for a good year or more.

ELDERBERRIES

Summer slips away. In late August she's always like this, sliding and ungraspable.

I am pregnant again. As I spend time indoors while this book and my baby take form, outside the garden becomes progressively formless. I set the ball rolling in spring and now I see all the energy I gave this garden back then blooming right here in front of me, an event of the past existing, transformed, in the now. I trust the seasons to grow the garden. I leave it to tumble, rapidly gaining momentum, picking up debris as it bounces and twirls. I feel myself becoming formless too. The garden and I now tell each other's stories as much as we tell our own. It is as if we're both giving our structure over to these new creations, their order growing out of our chaos. On the phone a fellow gardener tells me, 'I am the garden growing itself.' She's right. We are the Earth growing herself, the soil walking, plants talking.

As summer starts to feel old, turning faster into autumn, the garden is becoming more feral, a symptom of momentum and change – wildness seems to go hand and hand with motion. It feels very full, less… synchronised. 'Unruly' has become my word of choice for its demeanour. Fruit ripens while some flowers bloom and others begin to look tatty and tired. This is not the same satisfying, orderly march towards life that I observe in spring.

I return to the elder spinney, where everything seems the same but different. Like the garden and me, it too is giving in to a degree of formless chaos. Everything is still green, but now a darker, duller shade. The air feels hot and still. All around the plants look bigger, floppier, slightly jaded, like they've lived a little. Battered by the early drought and relentless summer rains, their leaves are ragged, less fresh, juicy and vital, paying the price for putting their energy into the creation of seeds, berries and fruits.

Again I'm reaching up into the elder branches, but this time I've come for the elderberries, and this time I've come with my baby in my belly. The creamy white flowers I left behind have metamorphosed into tiny, firm purple-black fruits, the stems holding them, once green, now tinged a soft purple-pink. The berries are very small, the size of a teeny pearl, or the deep black pupil of an eye on an overcast day. I pop a couple into my mouth. They don't taste very nice but I do it anyway out of habit, popping the flesh against the back of my teeth with my tongue, sucking out the meagre juice, extracting and spitting out the seed, and then chewing the skin left behind. I've done this since I was a child. The taste is strange, more a sensation than a flavour. I now know raw elderberries are toxic, the seeds containing a compound which can cause a build-up of cyanide in the body. Eating a few isn't a problem for most people but consuming a large volume of raw elderberries with their seeds is strongly *not* advised. When cooked, however, the seeds become harmless, so I'm filling a bag full of berries to make elderberry syrup, a dark sweet liquid to sip as a vitamin C-rich tonic through winter and double down on when coughs or colds take hold.

When I stepped into the spinney, a flurry of fat wood pigeons flapped up out of the trees. Along with many other birds, they come here for the elderberries too. They cling to the ends of long supple branches which sag and bounce under their weight and strip the fruits from their stems with their beaks. They've left plenty for me, though, and I leave plenty behind for them in return.

As the cool whispers of summer's end grow louder, all around other wild fruits will soon begin to appear. After the elderberries come rose hips and blackberries, haws and sloes. All are brimming with vitamins and antioxidants such as vitamin C and phytonutrients like the polyphenol anthocyanin (which is also responsible for the deep colour of the berries) and can help build up our immune systems in preparation for those darker, colder months when coughs, colds and flus creep about. Elderberries are particularly useful as an antiviral and immune-boosting tonic. If consumed regularly they can reduce our chances of falling ill in the first place, and if a virus does take hold, help ease the intensity and duration of flu-like symptoms.

Nature does seem to have an incredible habit of offering us what we need, right when we need it. Wild plant foods may often be healthier for us than shop-bought or even homegrown, because without a farmer or gardener to protect them from pests, disease and environmental challenges, to survive they must grow resilient, calling on their defence systems more regularly. As a result, they may have far richer stores of protective secondary metabolites (see page 172). These metabolites are good for us.

At germination, particularly high levels of these compounds help guard the vulnerable seedling in its early stages of life; the tender young leaves too, again to defend from early damage by predators or disease. At flowering, the plant produces secondary metabolites in their blooms, but in this case their role is to create vivid colours and scents to attract pollinators. The metabolites are also responsible for producing the diverse, vibrant colour palette of ripe fruits, signalling to us that they are ready to eat. These beneficial chemical compounds play a vital role in the plant's health and survival, and when we consume the fresh new nettle tops, wild garlic, foraged elderberries, blackberries and rose hips, for example, they can play a positive role in our health, too. Resilient plants grow resilient people.

I am lucky to be able to source wild, free goodness so close to my home. Much is made of the need to source locally and seasonally in a bid to reduce one's carbon footprint, in truth the issue is far more complex. Typically, about 80 per cent of our food's carbon footprint is attributable to land use and farm-stage emissions. In other words, we should prioritise purchasing agroecologically grown produce which usually has a greater impact than sourcing locally (although often the two go hand in hand). We must also consider what actually constitutes 'local'. To me, truly local food is that which is within reasonable cycling distance. Following that strict measure, many of us may have access to few, if any, local foods.

Although it may not reliably cut our carbon footprint, sourcing as locally and seasonally as possible *can* provide closer contact with the systems that feed us, increasing transparency of practice. It's also a means to invest in our local economy and enterprises that can be held accountable by their community, unlike large faceless corporations. Possibly most valuably, it helps us foster a dynamic relationship with what or whoever feeds us, which is healthy for all involved in so many ways. It also tastes good!

A wonderfully subtle property emerges from developing an observant relationship with the local wild plants we share our spaces with. This year I watched the elderberries ripening earlier than last, so I matched my own harvest to their schedule, not the calendar on my wall, gathering them at the moments when they are most rich in their valuable healing compounds. I bring an understanding of this synergy between plants and people back into my own garden. It's part of why I grow organically, why I welcome in some wild and why I watch the space so intently. In so doing I help the plants to grow to be resilient. These delicate interactions between plant and person remind me of our ancient interdependence. The plants were here, ready to feed and heal us long before we had the words or the science to understand the intimate relationship that was evolving between us.

ELDERBERRY SYRUP THREE WAYS

There is no one right way of making elderberry syrup; here I have shared three recipes that I find meet my various culinary and medicinal needs.

The given measures are intended as a rough guide. Experiment and adjust them to your preferences to create your own trusted recipe.

ELDERBERRY AND HONEY SYRUP

- 3 cups elderberries, fresh or frozen (if using dried elderberries, you can use less: 2.5 cups works fine for me)
- 3 cups water
- 1 cup raw, local, organic honey to sweeten (you may need more or less depending on how much you have reduced your mixture). Alternatively use fairtrade and organic molasses/muscovado sugar rather than white cane sugar. These will

give a deeper colour and flavour and contain some healthful nutrients such as iron

Optional: herbs. I add a thumb of ginger, 3 sticks of cinnamon and 5–7 cloves. You could alternatively try adding a few sprigs of fresh or dry rosemary, thyme, sage or chilli

NOTE:
You can use any sized cup or receptacle, but to keep quantities in the correct proportion, use the same one to measure each ingredient.

For this first standard syrup, I recommend using raw honey rather than sugar, as it offers its own excellent health-boosting properties, but note that to preserve the full health benefits of raw honey it's important not to heat it.

As it is not particularly shelf-stable on opening, this syrup must be kept in the fridge and is best consumed sooner rather than later. Since it is fairly quick and easy to make, it is possible to whip up a fresh batch whenever needed, either with dehydrated or frozen elderberries.

As a tasty tonic to ward off winter colds, I take a spoonful or small shot daily. If I'm feeling poorly or at risk of getting run down, I increase the dose to three times a day. The syrup is delicious in salad dressings, cocktails and cakes. I also add a spoonful to curries or stews that need a little dark, herby sweetness.

---

1. Place the berries and water in a pan and heat until just beginning to bubble. Turn down the heat and simmer gently, uncovered, for about 15 minutes. Crush the berries with a spoon or potato masher once they have softened slightly.
2. Once the berries are tender and juicy, add the herbs and continue to simmer on a low heat, uncovered, until the mixture halves in volume. This will take about 40 mins–1 hour. Be mindful not to let the decoction boil.

3. Pre-heat the oven to 160°C – ready to sterilise your storage containers.
4. Once the mixture is reduced to a syrup, remove the pan from the heat and leave to cool slightly.
5. Meanwhile, to sterilise your containers, wash them in warm soapy water, rinse thoroughly, and pop them, still wet, in the pre-heated oven for 10 minutes.
6. Strain the syrup through a sieve or piece of fabric into a clean container and set aside to cool to just above room temperature.
7. Mix the honey into the cooled syrup – you need 1 part honey to 2 parts elderberry and herb syrup reduction, so you may need to measure and adjust the quantity of honey accordingly.
8. Pour the syrup into sterilised containers and seal.
9. Stored in the fridge, the syrup should keep for 3 months.

SHELF-STABLE ELDERBERRY SYRUP

This recipe contains alcohol to make for a more shelf-stable syrup.

1. Follow the method above for Elderberry and Honey syrup.
2. Along with the honey, add into your syrup an equal quantity of vodka. Alternatively, some people like to use echinacea tincture in place of vodka to add more herbal properties.
3. Decant into sterilised containers as in previous recipe.
4. Stored in the cupboard, this syrup should keep for at least a year.

FERMENTED ELDERBERRY OXYMEL SYRUP

This recipe is made using equal parts of each ingredient, so you can scale the quantities up or down accordingly.

- 2 cups elderberries
- 2 cups honey
- 2 cups cider vinegar

Optional: herbs and spices to flavour. Cloves, cinnamon, ginger, bay leaf and rosemary all work well.

This is a recipe for elderberry 'oxymel', an ancient fermented folk medicine, requiring vinegar, honey and herbs. Being fermented, oxymels are excellent for the gut and have the added benefit of being more shelf-stable. It can be stored indefinitely so long as it doesn't grow mould. However, since the ferment is 'alive', the syrup's flavour profile can change over time.

---

1. Place the elderberries in a pan and add enough water to barely cover them.
2. Place on a medium heat, bring to the boil, then reduce heat to a simmer.
3. Mash the berries with a spoon or potato masher to extract as much of their juice as possible, then leave to simmer gently for 10 minutes, adding more water as needed to prevent sticking.
4. Take off the heat and leave to cool.
5. When the stewed berry mixture is cool enough to handle (you may want to use clean rubber gloves), pour it into a clean muslin or a tea towel, place over a clean bowl and wring the cloth to squeeze out every last drop.
6. Measure the volume of elderberry juice and measure out proportionate, equal quantities of cider vinegar and honey.
7. Once the elderberry juice has cooled to just above room

temperature add the vinegar and honey to the bowl and mix well to combine.
8. Optional extra: add any herbs as desired.
9. Decant into sterilised jars or bottles and seal.
10. Store the syrup mixture out of direct sunlight at a stable room temperature.
11. Shake the jar and open the lid daily to release any gas that may build up during fermentation.
12. After 4-6 weeks, strain off any added herbs and return to a sterilised jar.
13. Stored in a cupboard or the fridge (storing in the fridge will slow down or even halt any further fermentation), the oxymel should keep indefinitely.

NOTE:
Oxymel is a 'live' food and may continue to produce gases in the fermentation process. Please be mindful of this and ensure to burp your storage jar regularly.

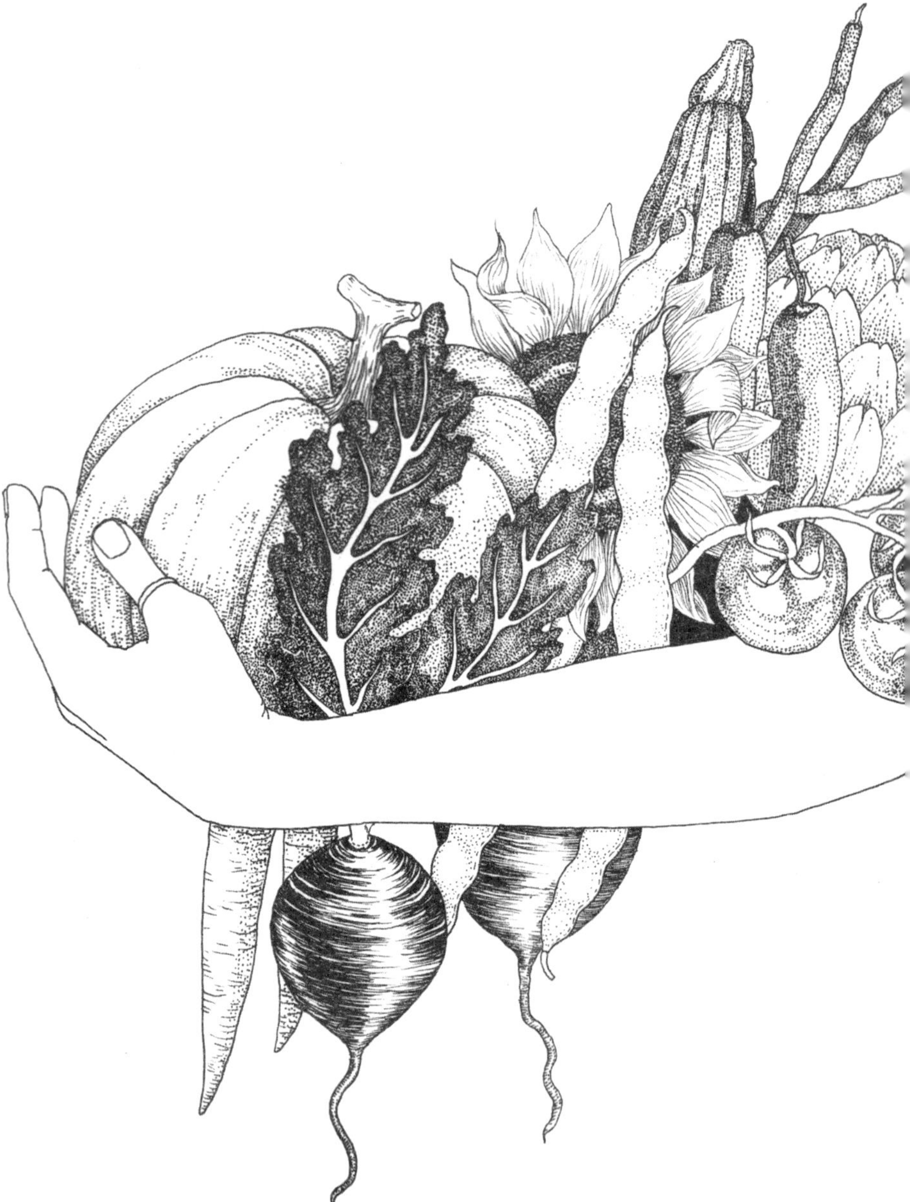

September

Early Autumn

ROOT OF THE WORD

Today I discovered that in English, not so long ago, the common noun for the period we now call autumn was simply 'harvest'. I spent the rest of the afternoon getting lost in dates, etymology and how language is changed by culture, how it tells us stories of our shifting relationship to the living world...

'Harvest' has roots in the Old English 'hærfest', which is of Germanic origin. In Dutch autumn is 'herst', in Norwegian 'høst' and in German 'Herbst'.

I personally prefer to think of 'harvest' as a verb, which points to a far more involved experience of the season. A verb we can *do*, we can be involved with it, it happens with us. A noun, on the other hand, is an object, something to point at and observe, maybe to touch and smell and hear. I much prefer the thought of doing autumn, my actions helping to make it what it is. These days I *do* autumn. I harvest, I store, I make warming meals, I clear garden beds, plant them up, dress them. I get muddy and cold and then I warm up again. I feel the soil chilling. I go home earlier as days get shorter. I *definitely* 'do' autumn.

But when I worked in fashion and lived in a city, I never did do much of autumn. I was travelling so much and shooting in brightly lit studios with no windows so often I didn't even really notice autumn at all.

In English, we first started using the word 'autumn' – from the Latin 'autumnus', and via the Old French of the Norman invaders – in the 1300s. But the word didn't gain much momentum until the 1500s, the age which, incidentally, saw the height of the Enclosures (see page 202) and a displaced population moving into towns and cities. Away from their traditional land-based activities, when people were no longer actually harvesting, perhaps it simply made less sense to use the word 'harvest' to refer to this time of year.

Our language is both shaped by experience and limits it. The way we talk about the world matters: 'give a man a hammer and everything's a nail'. Now that, in the UK, approximately 56.52 million people live in cities and we are facing a crisis of disconnection from the land, I wonder whether our language is limiting our perception and experience of our place in the world. Have we forgotten that we have the option to actively participate with land, both in terms of time and place?

Outside today the crisp leaves shiver in the cold wind. Winter is coming and we all feel it. Textures and colours mellow as life fades and decays. Everything around is 'autumning'. Harvest is nearly over.

If someone asks you what you're up to next September, you could tell them, 'I'm doing autumn' or 'I'm harvesting.'

CALENDULA HEALING BALM

- 500 ml jar full of calendula flowers
- 50 g ethically sourced beeswax (I've heard jojoba or candelilla wax are good vegan alternatives)
- 100 g mango or shea butter
- 30 g cocoa butter
- 150 ml almond oil
- *Optional: 2 tbsp avocado oil*

Calendula (*Calendula officinalis*) is a common ingredient in skincare. In ointments, it has anti-inflammatory properties, can relieve irritation and help heal wounds. Before summer's calendula start to slow their blooming, harvest the flowers to make a soothing balm for dry winter skin.

— Dry the calendula flowers in a dehydrator on a low setting. Alternatively, either spread them on a baking sheet and place in an oven on a low setting until crisp, or put them in a paper bag and hang this up somewhere dry and draughty. Shake the bag daily so the flowers dry evenly.
— Combine the dried calendulas and almond oil in a glass jar and leave it somewhere warm to infuse for 1–2 weeks (or longer, up to 8 weeks). Alternatively, to draw out the calendula's soothing properties more quickly, place the jar in a bain-marie and gently warm for 30 minutes to an hour.
— Pour the golden oil through a sieve into a clean jar. Rinse and discard the calendula flowers on the compost heap.
— Add all the butter solids to a bowl and gently warm in the bain-marie until melted.
— Add the calendula-infused oil into the melted butters.
— Decant the balm into clean dry storage jars.

TIPS
- *For a softer balm, add a little more almond or some avocado oil and mix to the consistency you like.*
- *You can use daisy-infused almond oil for extra potency. Daisies (gathered in early summer) are also excellent topical healers for bruises, sunburn and bites. The oil can then be used for a*

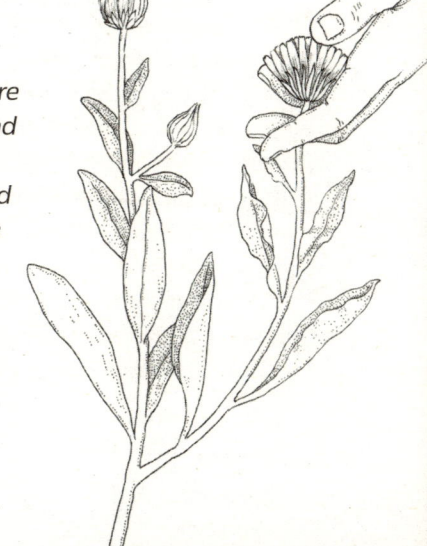

second extraction to increase the properties further.
- *I buy job lots of used mini jam jars online, clean them, remove labels and reuse them as perfect little balm jars that fit in a bag and make nice gifts.*
- *This recipe can be made substituting the calendula flowers for any dried herbs or flowers that are good for the skin; common daisies, also known as bruisewort (Bellis perennis), work well, as does chamomile.*

AUTUMN EQUINOX

September brings autumn's equinox. It is a gentle time; night and day stretch out together as equals.

The tomatoes continue to dole out treats; the apple trees' branches are peppered with blushing fruits; courgettes are still swelling by the day; and the squashes are growing plump amongst giant leaves. But behind all this bounty, the plants are already preparing for winter. The equinox has set into play a general dropping, drooping and withering. The tomatoes aren't putting on so much foliage; the leaves on the apple trees have a very slight yellow hue, and the courgettes greenery is dusted grey with powdery mildew. As the season progresses, life will begin to release and return to the ground, ready for the restoration that deep winter will bring.

With autumn equinox's arrival I start to prepare, too. It's time for me to gather in. The full moon nearest to the autumn equinox is known as the Harvest Moon. As the sun sets earlier and earlier, the light of the full moon allows farmers to work late into the night to bring in their crops. In my small garden, I don't have anywhere near enough crops to need to rely on the harvest moon, but I go out there in the moonlight anyway, more for the joy of it than anything else.

*

In the tropical east of Nigeria, throughout Igbo land people give thanks for the harvest of the *ji* (yam) crop. The yam plays a central role in Igbo culture, in which it is considered the first food given to the people by Chukwu and, as such, is the only food crop with a dedicated deity, known variously as Ahia Njoku, Njoku Ji or Ifejioku.

Ji (*Dioscorea rotundata*) is a tuberous root vegetable, much like a pale, deliciously plain sweet potato. After harvest, the yams are stored in barns which are guarded by shrines to Ahia Joku; some are kept for consumption through the year and some saved to return to the ground as seed.

The ji origin myth takes us back to the very beginnings of the Igbo people. According to this story, there was a great famine, so the people suffered and begged their king, Eze Nri, to guide them back to times of plenty. Eze Nri spent many sleepless nights searching for answers; eventually the gods told him that to end the famine he must kill his son Ahia Joku and his daughter Ada, taking care to chop their bodies into small pieces and then bury them in the earth. Desperate to restore well-being to his people, Eze Nri followed the gods' instructions. Six months later, plants grew from the earth where he had buried his children: his dead son had become yam, *ji*; his daughter the cocoyam. Ahia Joku thus became the spirit of the yam and Ada of the cocoyam. Ji went on to feed the Igbo people, bringing them out of their famine and becoming a staple food.

Dad recalls that, when he was a boy, in Igbo land the New Yam Festival celebrations (*Iriji* or *Iwaji*, meaning 'eating yam'), which take place at varying times between August and November, were much more important than Christmas. The entire month is given over to offering thanks to Ahia Joku, and to Chukwa and Ala, for the harvest. Dad describes endless feastings, the beloved ji prepared in every way imaginable. But before the great feasting begins, there are rituals of thanks – it is considered a taboo to consume the new harvest before proper gratitude is given. Someone, often a chief, older male in the family, or even a priest, who has taken the time to spiritually purify or cleanse themselves prior, offers a prayer. First, patterns are traced on the earth with ritual chalk and yellow powder. Kola nuts are broken, as they are at the beginning of any business, to evoke the spirits. There is more prayer, this time with the thanksgivers sipping drinks, which they also share with the spirits by pouring some on the soil. Finally, a chicken is sacrificed. Some of the yam is cooked in red palm oil to symbolise the blood of Ahia Joku. This cooked yam is then placed on the earth or at altars for the gods. Only then do the people eat. There are flamboyant celebrations with dance, music and masquerades sometimes lasting days.

In Igbo culture, Ji is a symbol of regeneration and fecundity. Its creation myth tells the universal story of renewal; a passage in the dark being followed by a period of light, and on and on. We see this cycle all around us, feel it in ourselves. But in our modern lives it can be easy to pass through that journey again and again, year in year out, completely mindlessly. The seasons turn, we wake and sleep, feel happy and sad, become sick and well again.

Since I have turned my gaze to the garden and given my hands to the soil, I am more mindful of this journey. It's harder to miss. By properly noticing it, marking it – in its grandeur at this time of year, and in its smallness when I get tired as I grow this child inside me – it becomes easier to navigate.

On Earth, one significant way we humans experience the planet is through the seasons. Moments throughout the year, such as the Ji harvest in Igbo tradition, give meaningful opportunities for us to experience life itself and through this, historically, to connect with some form of spirit, divinity or greater meaning. In many ways, at Iriji and so many other annual festivals, we not only offer thanks and prayers for good harvests to come, but we call on the gods to continue the turning of time itself.

In this spot between the abundance of life and the beginning of endings, I find myself often giving thanks for the turning of time. Somehow, gathering up and processing summer fruits' seeds seems like a good way to do this. After all, it would be rude not to accept the gifts of the gods... wouldn't it?

WE HARVEST THE WINTER SQUASH

At the community garden we gather in our squash crop to cure; some are larger than my head, some as small as my palm. We're going to have another feast, so I bring the biggest home for souping and harvest the other ingredients I need for the recipe too.

Winter squash is ready to harvest once its skin has hardened, so your fingernail cannot easily break through. The fruit should also sound hollow if you knock on it. A good way to ensure your fruits are ripe for harvesting is to wait until after the plant's foliage and stalks have crisped up and died back, but before the first frosts come.

When harvesting, chop the squash from the plant leaving a 'T' of stalk. This makes it less likely for rot to set in. If your squash haven't ripened before the first frosts, bring them in anyway.

To cure the squash, leave them somewhere warm and dry in the sunshine for a week or two. This allows the starches in the flesh to turn to sugars and the skin to harden further.

Then they are best stored in the home where temperatures remain consistently warm.

SQUASH SOUP

- 1 great big cured winter squash
- 4 sticks celery
- 2 onions
- 4 cloves garlic
- 4 sprigs of sage
- 2-3 cups of oat or hazelnut milk
- Olive oil
- Salt and pepper

This recipe is so simple, relying mainly on using a flavourful, sweet squash. From my experience, a homegrown, well cured winter squash, like the one I've brought home from our community garden, does that job best. Some excellent sweet varieties that are less common in the shops and so worth growing are: 'Red Kuri', 'Crown Prince' and 'Turks Turban'.

- Pre-heat the oven to 200°C or gas mark 6. Chop the squash in half with a very sharp large knife and scoop out the seeds with a spoon (if you like this squash plant, wash and dry them to sow next year). It is possible to toast some squash seeds to make delicious salty snacks. Generally, I find the seed from most tasty squash are not good for eating, but you can experiment.
- Again, using a very sharp knife, cut the squash into thick slices. If the skin is very tough, peel it, if it's not, leave it be – it adds a nice nuttiness to the soup.
- Place the squash slices on a baking try, toss in olive oil and season with salt. Place in the pre-heated oven and roast for 20 to 30 minutes.
- Finely slice the celery, onion and garlic, and add to a large saucepan along with a generous glug of olive oil, the sage, a pinch of salt and sprinkling of pepper. Slowly sweat the

vegetables on a medium heat – stirring occasionally and making sure they don't stick – until they are soft, sweet and have darkened and caramelised.
- Remove the squash from the oven. It should be soft, very sweet and only just starting to turn brown and a little caramelised on the edges.
- Add the roasted squash and stir. The squash may begin to fall apart, that's OK.
- Add the oat or hazelnut milk, season again to taste.
- Turn up the heat and bring the mixture to a boil, then reduce the heat and leave to simmer for 10 to 20 minutes or so, to allow the flavours to combine.
- Remove from the heat and fish out the sage. Mash or blend up your soup and add a dash of boiling water to thin if necessary.
- Check for seasoning. If your squash was not very sweet, you may want to add some sugar or maple syrup at this stage.
- Serve with a dash of cream or yoghurt, and lots of doughy bread.

BUMBLEBEES AT MICHAELMAS

According to one of my favourite half-Christian, half-folk traditions, on 29 September – aka Michaelmas, or the Feast of Michael and All Angels – after a vicious battle with Archangel Michael (God's right-hand man and leader of heaven's armies), Lucifer the Devil is thrown out of heaven and tumbles down into hell. Finding himself in a bramble bush, he promptly spits on the berries and curses the fruits. According to this tradition, therefore, you ought not to gather blackberries after Michaelmas for fear of eating ruined fruit or, worse yet, bumping into a moody prickled Lucifer.

Once, across the British Isles, Michaelmas Festival marked the end of the harvest season, and all sorts of pagan traditions were blended into the merriments and feasting in celebration. People made corn dolls from straw gathered from the final sheafs reaped from the fields. It was believed that the corn dolls would house the field spirits through the winter to come.

When I think back on what the onset of winter would have meant in the northern hemisphere – hard and cold with long dark nights – it makes sense. St Michael, the angelic hero, stood for bravery and the successful struggle against the dark or evil. I remember tales of him smiting down a great terrible dragon and the words to a song we sang in primary school pop into my head: 'St Michaele, heavenly hero, send thy, send thy strength and power, send thy, send thy strength and power, into our hearts, into our hearts.' As the daunting chills draw near, St Michael and his dark conquering sword might well come in handy.

I no longer have a particular interest in St Michael, but I am fascinated by the tales we tell which connect us to the turning of the year. As we move into winter season, it makes sense to me that we lean into a great power beyond ourselves. And it makes sense to care deeply enough for the fields that feed us to want to make dolls for them. I now also wonder about the birds who need to fatten up for winter and so depend on blackberries for food – perhaps we all ought actually to be very grateful to Lucifer for imposing this strict harvest cut-off date. Undoubtedly, if we scratch the surface, there is much good sense in some old traditions.

Today I went out into the garden to gather blackberries. I would have gone out foraging, but, much to my disappointment when we moved here, I've found South Devon doesn't seem to have a very tasty supply. I make a mental note to organise a blackberrying day with my mum in Wiltshire, where the few remaining hedges are often full of the tastiest berries.

I pick my way into the unruly border and stretch up, my fingers meeting with the bramble's thin thorny arms which reach out of the top of the old stone wall. Up here the fruits are ripe, sun warmed and juicy. I pluck, dodging the thorns that skewered poor Lucifer. The thornless varieties I planted last winter are not ready yet.

The chickens, eyeing me up from within the floral undergrowth, gingerly emerge and gather around, hopeful I'll throw them a treat. I try to give them one each, but chickens are utterly obsessed with their pecking order, so Mervin ends up wolfing four berries, Prim and Florette one each, and the young girls get none. I tried to share evenly but they simply wouldn't have it, so I tell them it's their own silly loss and get back to picking the berries for myself.

Depositing my bowl of berries on the garden table, I move on to check on the tomatoes in the greenhouse. They have slowed their growth and look a little tired but they continue to flower. Over the last three years, my greenhouse-grown plants have given fruits right up to the start of November. As I pass each plant, I tap it hello, sending delicate clouds of pollen into the air. This helps ensure as many flowers as possible are pollinated.

Tomatoes are self-fertile, which means that both the male and female reproductive organs are within each flower, so the flower can pollinate itself. The pollen simply needs to be released from the stamen and successfully land on that same flower's stigma. But they are fussy about who or what aids them in their reproduction. The wind rustling the plants can encourage pollen release, but the pollen grains of tomatoes are sticky and tricky to dislodge, and in any case there's little to no wind inside the greenhouse. Honey-bees and most other common pollinators won't pollinate tomatoes because they can't get at the pollen and the flowers don't produce nectar, however, tomatoes will welcome bumblebees as collaborators in a process called 'buzz pollination'. When the bumblebee alights on the flower, it loosens the pollen grains from the stamen by vibrating its body, legs and mouth parts. The bee then gathers up the protein-rich pollen grains, some of which inevitably get caught in the bumblebee fuzz and hitches a ride to the flower's stigma and that of the next bloom the bee visits.

Since the early 1990s, nearly all tomato crops in the UK have been buzz pollinated. Commercial growers purchase native bumblebee nests and place them in their greenhouses. The thought of hundreds of bumblebees happily humming around toasty tomato-filled greenhouses is joyful. But in a morbid turn of events, due to the threat of disease spreading to wild bumblebees, the nests must be destroyed at the end of the growing season.

On the one hand, I think it's pure genius to enlist the help of a creature so perfectly fit for and who actually wants to do the job of pollinating. On the other hand, the sheer scale of the endeavour, requiring transported bumblebees rather than the help of the local, naturally occurring population, and the ultimate destruction of the little helpers, leaves me uneasy. And all the more keen to grow my own.

As I tap the Marmande tomato plant at the end of the greenhouse 'hello', I hear a bumbling buzzing. Just above my head, a plump bumblebee is bouncing against the glass ceiling. I gently guide it out through the skylight and watch it drone off into the bright blue sky.

Basket full of tomatoes and blackberry bowl in hand, I head into the kitchen to make a Michaelmas lunch.

NEARLY RAW TOMATO SAUCE

- Freshly gathered tomatoes, roughly chopped
- Handful of freshly picked blackberries
- Garlic, finely chopped – to taste
- Olive oil for frying
- Salt and freshly ground black pepper

Optional: Balsamic vinegar, raw honey

Quick to prepare and just as quickly devoured, I like to serve this wonderfully fresh and fragrant sauce with nasturtiums (peppery), very finely sliced dandelion leaves (bitter) and chopped toasted hazelnuts. It's a delicious way to enjoy the fresh sweetness of just-picked fruits.

— Heat a glug of olive oil in a pan and lightly fry the garlic over a low heat. Once softened, add the tomatoes and very gently warm for five minutes, bashing them about a bit so they juice up.

— Add a pinch of salt, a generous grinding of black pepper, and a glug of balsamic vinegar.

— Add the blackberries and continue to gently warm the sauce for a further five minutes.

— Taste. Add a dash of cider vinegar for added tartness. For more sweetness, I like to add happy-bee honey.

— Remove from the heat – you want the tomatoes and blackberries to be warm and juicy, not overcooked.

— Enjoy the sauce immediately with rice, pasta or a crusty loaf to mop up the juices.

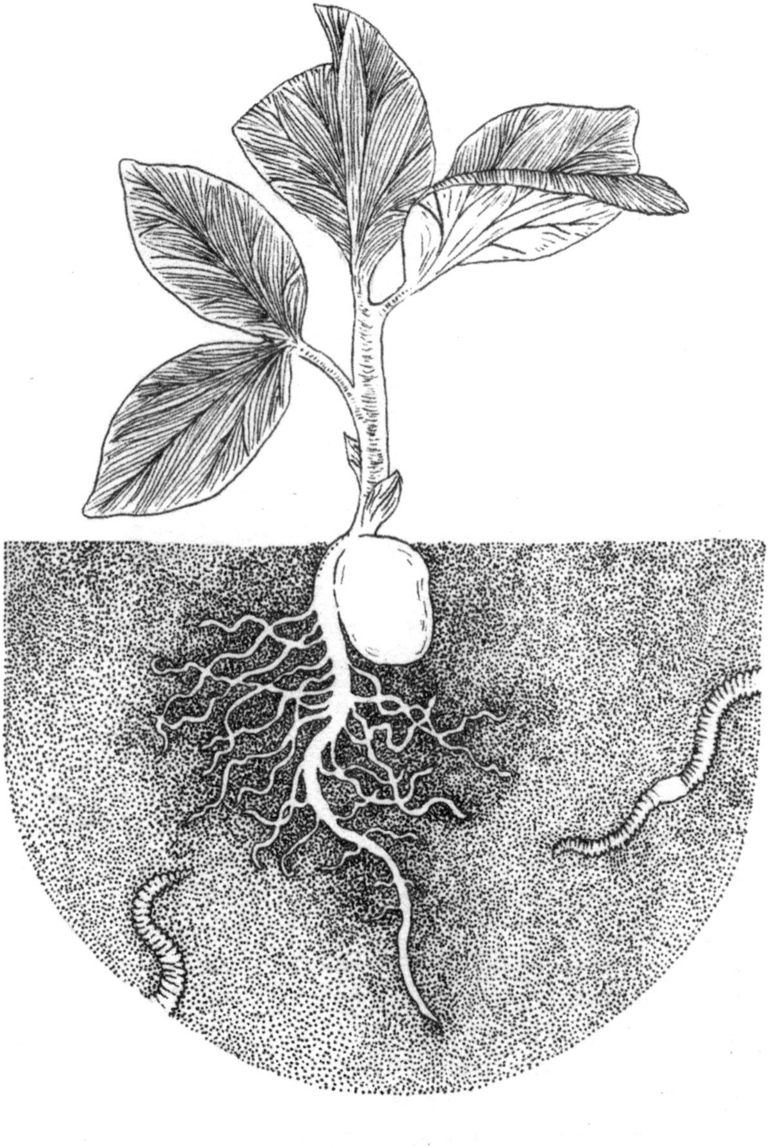

October

SAVING SEED

On the sideboard in the kitchen is a cream enamel dish covered with a tea towel. A couple of fruit flies hover around it. It's been sat there for days, quite possibly weeks. Inside are, or were, tomatoes. When I finally do pluck up the courage to peek under the tea towel, I know that what lies beneath will undoubtedly be unrecognisable. A little patch on the cloth has become damp where the fruits' juice must be breaking free of the skins. They don't smell, which is good, and really the main reason why I still haven't got around to dealing with them. Last night I dreamt of a bowl full of maggots, so today those tomatoes have got to go, before the flies make my dream a reality.

These were the last good tomatoes harvested this year, and hold the seeds for next year's crop, each from a variety I want to grow again and from a parent plant I admired. For two of the varieties, Moonglow and Ukraine Purple, this will be the second year I've saved their seeds. For my 'Devon's Giant Tomataki', the first.

Leaning against the kitchen table with a mug of tea in my hand, I contemplate the enamel dish. Today is the day. I whip off the tea towel to inspect the rotten mess underneath. The tomatoes' skins have split and their insides are oozing out. I can only *just* tell the three varieties apart.

I spoon out one lump of a tomato and slop it into a bowl... Now that it's out in the open, it does have a whiff after all. I slop in two more tomato lumps that look as though they were the same variety. Next, I fill the bowl with cold water and stir, sloshing all the skin and mushy pulp off the pale seeds. I drain the slop away, careful to keep the seeds in the bowl and top up with more water. I repeat this a few times until the seeds are clean. They spin around in the bowl of clear water. Then I pour them into a sieve and tip them out onto a dry tea towel, gently patting them dry. Finally, the seeds land on a little saucer, ready to spend a few days drying out.

Once these seeds are dry, I will slip them into little envelopes, scrawling their variety, the date, location and method of saving on the packet (probably illegibly).

I repeat the process, fishing out the other two varieties of tomatoes one by one and washing and drying their seeds. If I store them correctly, they will happily remain viable for five to six years.

For many thousands of years, and until fairly recently, anyone who grew plants understood almost innately how to save their seeds too. Usually, I follow a more traditional, less rotten method of saving my tomato seeds, which involves fermenting the tomatoes in water for a couple of days to one week, extracting the seeds, then washing, drying and storing. But somehow, I never got around to processing these tomatoes properly... and then I got curious about what would happen if I interfered less... and just let them rot in their own juices... much like they do when neglected on the vine, plopping to the greenhouse floor in a squishy splat. So, this is a bit of an experiment and I will have to check if the seeds are still viable. Sometime soon, I'll sow a pinch from each variety, I'll keep them warm and moist and see if they awaken. If they don't, I'll know that left to rot in the enamel dish, they were deprived of oxygen for too long.

I've saved tomato seed enough times now that the habit is ingrained in me. But I haven't entirely mastered this process with other crops I'm less familiar with, so I often stumble and need to remind myself of the exact steps.

To grow a plant, we start with a living material – cells which can replicate and grow. We need a cutting, some root or a seed.

Without this starting material, we can't grow a garden. Each year, people saved seeds from the plants that had thrived, following the age-old observation that 'like begets like'. Gradually, over many generations of plants and people, crops would adapt to the particularities of their locality and to the needs of their stewards, just like the landrace variety of the volcanic Greek island, Tomataki Santorini. Rather than holding an intimate connection to place, as landrace crops do, the heirloom or heritage varieties I grow in my greenhouse are intimately connected to people. These plants have been selected and bred for their special traits, perhaps their large size, vibrant colour or health-giving properties. Once a form of the plant is chosen and stabilised (so that offspring consistently present much like their parents), these 'heirloom' seeds are passed down from generation to generation, usually in a particular family or community, for fifty years or more.

These days, in some parts of the world – in particular in the WEIRD countries – the ability to simply save seed or even breed plants is a skill many of us have lost without even realising. This is partly due to a decline in populations engaging in gardening, for pleasure and for food production. But it's also largely due to the rise of staggeringly large multinationals who now breed, develop and sell seed globally, both to farmers and to gardeners.

More recently the emergence of 'patented seed' has made saving-seed criminal and dangerous for some farmers. Patented seed, strangely, 'belongs' to the company or person who 'invented' it. In the UK, intellectual property rights over seed are known as PBR, 'plant breeders rights'. A PBR can be secured for any new varieties, including genetically modified plants, and allow the breeder to charge royalties for use of the variety. If anyone is found reproducing that plant without their permission, for example saving seed to share and sow the following year or even allowing self-seeded volunteer plants to grow, the PBR-owner is entitled to sue for damages.

'Protected' seed is becoming more and more commonly used on farms around the world. If a farmer fills their fields with seed that is 'owned' and this seed mixes in with the next-door farmer's crop, and the next-door farmer then saves the seed from their crop, they would be at risk of prosecution as it could be contaminated with the genetics of the 'owned' seed. This locks farmers into purchasing commercially owned seed in perpetuity.

This is a significant and curious step away from the communal practice of seed stewardship that brought us heritage and landrace plants. Curious because by its very nature, seed and plant reproduction is wildly abundant. It shows us 'bounty' like nothing else – and bounties are for sharing, not *owning*. A single tomato fruit is able to bring forth many hundreds of babies; a single tomato plant many thousands. The seed of one tomato fruit, in the following year, could feed a hamlet. And the seed from just one plant, perhaps a village! Plants uncontrollably and generously proliferate through their seed, producing far more than enough for us all. There is a certain oddity in the idea that someone might want to stem this flow of abundance, to somehow claim and profit from the wisdom of plant reproduction, a miracle in which, no matter what paperwork might say, no one has property rights *really*. Stranger still is the thought that in co-creating a beautiful new variety with a plant, one would want to own it, or even believe that one *could* own another life, or rather many lives, since plants do what plants do – they multiply, wildly! Seed is so obviously for sharing. In fact, plants want and need us to share and to spread their seeds – their future selves, their babies – far and wide!

Over the last century, many varieties of vegetables in the UK have lost their stewards and so have vanished. In that time some estimate that we have lost as much as 90 per cent of our unique vegetable varieties. In the UK, by law only certain seed that has undergone extensive testing can be bought or sold, driving further variety losses. At the time of writing, two multinational firms control 40 per cent of the global seed market. These companies are producing seed designed for industrial food production requiring high inputs, from water to fertilisers and pesticides. These plants are bred for uniformity so that they are easy to process and satisfy the supermarkets. The traits valued by a small-scale or home grower, such as nutrient density, quirks and even beauty, are not necessarily favoured. Often the multinationals produce the seed globally

– North Africa and the Middle East are popular locations – using industrial, chemical agricultural methods and with poor human rights observations. This seed is then shipped across the planet and is not necessarily going to be adapted to the local growing conditions it ends up in.

In the span of merely a few hundred years, led by the paradigms of industrialisation, homogenisation and globalisation, we are losing the vibrant diversity cultivated over millennia between plants and people.

Seed sovereignty and the growing of under-utilised seed were both cited in the IPCC's Special Report on Climate Change and Land as ways to increase food system resilience and biodiversity in the face of climate change. Resilient and diverse community networks of seed-savers, vendors and sharers are the guardians of the genetic diversity stored in these humble plant germs. The intimate exchange – the plants feeding the people and, in return, the people tending the plants – is a powerful relationship built on care. In growing the descendants of particular plants year after year, the garden can again become a closed loop system full of profound connections.

Seeds root us to our past and reach into our future. They hold the wisdom of generations of people and plants, tell stories of weather, of disease, of care and neglect. Through epigenetics, plants pass the wisdom of their lived experience onto their progeny. Their seeds carry the microbiome of the parent plant on for future plants. Even the tiniest, dustiest seed holds a whole complex microbiome in its tissue. These microbes are inherited from the parent plant(s), gifted by the environment, or can be gathered from pollinators. The microbes support the seed through dormancy and then on germination they colonise the newly emerging root and aerial parts of the plant.

The seed's exterior is also caked in microbes, and when I handle these little velvety tomato seeds, we exchange microbes too. Emerging science is starting to show us that the homogenisation of the seed industry is also homogenising the microbiomes of seed, altering the microbes which are able to pass from parent plant to their offspring. Every aspect of plant life is being standardised – from the size of tomatoes to the height of wheat and the crunch of an apple. Right down to the microbes passed from one generation of crops to the next.

Saving and sharing seeds is practical, cheap and engaging. It's a radical act in the face of the nightmare of monoculture, and a pledge – or perhaps an act – of devotion to the abundant wildness of life, both past and future. There is magic in shepherding a plant through its full life cycle, starting as a seed and ending once again as a seed. Yet more circles. Looping into eternity.

HOW TO SAVE TOMATO SEEDS (PROPERLY AND WITHOUT ROTTING TOMATOES!)

- Choose your favourite plants, notice which are giving the best crop, which are free of pests and diseases, which have a growth habit most suited to your growing space. Pick a good-looking, ripe tomato from your chosen plant.
- Chop the tomato in half and scoop out the wet jelly insides that hold the seeds.
- Slop this into a jar of water and cover with a piece of fabric held in place with an elastic band or string. Label the jar with the variety and date.
- Leave the tomato water to ferment for roughly 5 days, maybe less in warm weather or more in cold. This process breaks down the outer coating of the seed which can inhibit germination. A fuzzy white skin may appear on the surface of the water, that's fine.
- After fermenting, pour the lot through a sieve and rinse the seeds several times until they are clean of any slime.
- Place the fabric you used as a lid on a plate and spread your seeds out on it; leave them to dry. I usually wait 3 days to a week just to be sure. If they are at all moist they won't keep and will rot.

— Bag up your seed in labelled envelopes; record the date, crop and any other information you'd like to add – I like to note where the crop came from and how many years I've been saving it, e.g. 7 October 2024, Tomato Moonglow, Devon garden greenhouse, year 3.
— Store somewhere dry with a stable, low temperature.

F1 PLANTS:

If you want to save seeds, avoid F1 varieties.

F1 seed is the result of breeding two seed lines to create progeny with certain traits, which can be really handy!

The benefit of F1 is that some lines have very useful traits like disease resistance. However, seed saved from F1 plants, or F1 plants that self-seed, will grow a daughter plant that doesn't bear semblance to the parent plants and will generally be very poor quality.

Open-pollinated heritage seed, however, produces plants which can be pollinated by a natural mechanism, such as self-pollination, insects, birds, the wind, or even a human with a paintbrush! Generally, their progeny will be like the parent plants, with some natural, healthy variation. This makes them great for seed saving.

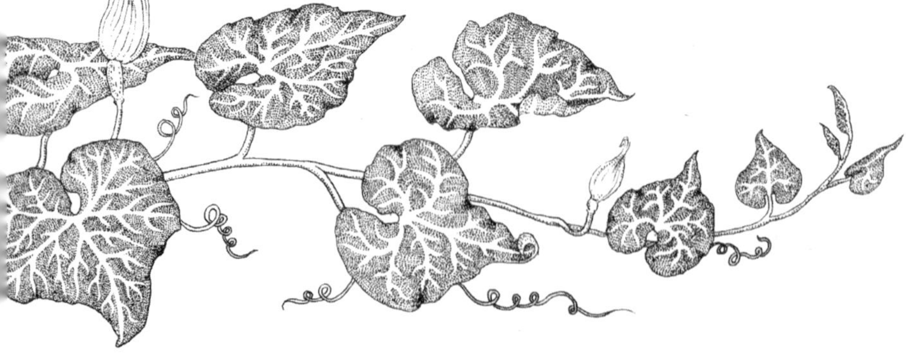

epilogue

ENDINGS AS BEGINNINGS

I'm sitting in the low boughs of the Great Grandma Apple tree. It's late in the day and the golden autumn light shines through her deep green leaves, some of which have been lightly brushed with rusty tones. Her branches swoop low under the weight of the rosy fruits she now carries. I reach out my arm to pluck an apple. It's not quite ripe, but the crisp tartness is pleasing. I'm sitting here because it turns out that growing a baby has my energy swooping low too. Tending the garden is not so easy now, and I'm tired. I'm relieved that as autumn progresses it will be going to sleep, taking its annual life-giving rest.

I didn't expect it so soon, but already pregnancy has started to change my perception of the world and my place in it. I grow the garden, but it grows me too, and this baby in my belly is much the same. The process of giving and caring is altering us both, binding us to one another.

This child is coming in the spring, and I find myself planning the garden for his arrival. I want it to be beautiful for him, safe, a place he can first begin learning about the world that has given him life and meet the people who will love him and help him to grow. I wish I could prepare the wider world for him too. But I can't. I yearn for the assurance that the Earth he grows up in will be one that hums and sighs with life, but I don't know, I can't be sure. All I can do is continue to care and to actively hope that one day, soon, there will be more of us tending the planet and one another as Earth's gardeners. I can only hope that my voice and the many, many others calling for a future of fruits and flowers beckon in enough positive change that we all, including my little boy, will know the beauty of many abundant autumn harvests and so many more endings as beginnings.

Further Reading

GARDENING

Companion Planting
Carrots Love Tomatoes and Roses Love Garlic, Louise Riotte
How to Grow More Vegetables, John Jeavons
Farming While Black, Leah Penniman
Gaia's Garden, Toby Hemenway

Seed Saving
Back Garden Seed Saving, Sue Stickland
Sacred Seed, edited by Global Peace Initiative of Women

Compost
The Humanure Handbook, Joseph Jenkins
Holy Shit: Managing Manure to Save Mankind, Gene Logsdon

Soil
Teaming With Microbes, Jeff Lowenfels and Wayne Lewis
For the Love of Soil, Nicole Masters

Ponds
Ponds, Pools and Puddles, Jeremy Biggs and Penny Williams

Forest Gardening
The Forager's Garden, Anna Locke
Eat What You Grow, Alys Fowler
Creating a Forest Garden, Martin Crawford

Permaculture
The Permaculture Way, Graham Bell
Milkwood Permaculture Living Handbook, Kirsten Bradley

General
The Regenerative Grower's Guide to Garden Amendments, Nigel Palmer
Hot Beds, Jack First
Grow Yourself Healthy, Beth Marshall
Biodynamic Gardening, Monty Waldin
Designing Regenerative Food Systems, Marina O'Connell
Growing Beans, Susan Young
Living With the Earth, Charles and Perrine Hervé-Gruyer

FARMING

Rooted, Sarah Langford
Miraculous Abundance, Charles and Perrine Hervé-Gruyer
Regenesis, George Monbiot
Wilding, Isabella Tree
A Small Farm Future, Chris Smaje
Soil, Matthew Evans
Sowing Seeds in the Desert and *The One Straw Revolution*, Masanobu Fukuoka

FORAGING

Spirit of the Hedgerow, Jo Dunbar
Edible Seashore, John Wright
Edible City, John Rensten
Hedgerow Medicine, Matthew Seal and Julie Bruton-Seal
Wild Food UK Foraging Pocket Guide, Marlow Renton and Eric Biggane
The Forager's Almanac by Danielle Gallacher

EATING AND DRINKING

Eat Right, Nick Barnard
The Noma Guide to Fermentation, Rene Redzepi and David Zilber
The Creative Kitchen, Stephanie Hafferty

Gaia's Kitchen, Julia Ponsonby
Forgotten Skills of Cooking, Darina Allen
Riverford companion books
How to Eat More Plants, Hugh Fearnley-Whittingstall
Wild Mocktails and Healthy Cocktails, Lottie Muir

HERBS

The Herbalist's Guide to Botanical Drinks, Michael Isted
Self-Sufficient Herbalism and The Working Herbal Dispensary, Lucy Jones
Yoga of the Herbs, David Frawley and Vasant Lad
A Modern Herbal, Alys Fowler

GENERAL

Small is Beautiful, E. F. Schumacher
Living on the Earth, Alicia Bay Laurel
Eating to Extinction, Dan Saladino
Entangled Life, Merlin Sheldrake
Rest is Resistance, Tricia Hersey
Saving Time, Jenny Odell
It's Not That Radical, Mikaela Loach
Losing Eden, Lucy Jones
The Well Gardened Mind, Sue Stuart Smith
Half of a Yellow Sun, Chimamanda Ngozi Adichie
Braiding Sweetgrass, Robin Wall Kimmerer
Who Owns England?, Guy Shrubsole
The Book of Trespass, Nick Hayes
Gardens of the British Working Class, Margaret Wiles
Animate Earth, Stephan Harding
Wintering, Katherine May
A Sand County Almanac, Aldo Leopold
This Changes Everything, Naomi Klein
Urban Jungle, Ben Wilson
Local is Our Future, Helena Norberg-Hodge
Pilgrim at Tinker Creek, Annie Dillard

THANKS AND DEDICATIONS

Dedicated to my sunny sunshine boy, who has shown me that even the smallest, seemingly incapable beings can make mountains move with the spell of love. Thank you for accompanying me in writing most of this book, either inside me or beside me!

Thank you also my darling lover, Toby, for all you do. To my family and friends past, present and future who inspired this book and supported me through making it a reality. To Meeja the cat who kept my lap warm as I wrote. Particularly to my Mumma, for her endless support and for being the best Grandma for my boy while I've worked.

Thanks to my agent and editor(s!) who made this book happen!

And with thanks to the gardens and garden folk who let me tell their stories.

ABOUT THE AUTHOR

Poppy Okotcha is an ecological gardener, forager and home cook, trained in regenerative growing practices. A regular garden writer for the Observer magazine, Poppy has been featured on *Gardeners' World*, co-hosted the *Great Garden Revolution* (Channel 4), and has been heard on both the RHS podcast and Kew Gardens' 'Unearthed' audio series. Poppy grows herbs and vegetables in her own garden and in an established local community garden.